The secrets behind my smile

JUNE DALLY-WATKINS

with *Louise Gee*

VIKING
an imprint of
PENGUIN BOOKS

To Mother

Viking

Published by the Penguin Group
Penguin Books Australia Ltd
250 Camberwell Road, Camberwell, Victoria 3124, Australia
Penguin Books Ltd
80 Strand, London WC2R 0RL, England
Penguin Putnam Inc.
375 Hudson Street, New York, New York 10014, USA
Penguin Books, a division of Pearson Canada
10 Alcorn Avenue, Toronto, Ontario, Canada M4V 3B2
Penguin Books (NZ) Ltd
Cnr Rosedale and Airborne Roads, Albany, Auckland, New Zealand
Penguin Books (South Africa) (Pty) Ltd
24 Sturdee Avenue, Rosebank, Johannesburg 2196, South Africa
Penguin Books India (P) Ltd
11, Community Centre, Panchsheel Park, New Delhi 110 017, India

First published by Penguin Books Australia 2002

1 3 5 7 9 10 8 6 4 2

Copyright © June Dally-Watkins 2002

The moral right of the author has been asserted

All rights reserved. Without limiting the rights under copyright reserved above, no part of this publication may be reproduced, stored in or introduced into a retrieval system, or transmitted, in any form or by any means (electronic, mechanical, photocopying, recording or otherwise), without the prior written permission of both the copyright owner and the above publisher of this book.

Every effort has been made to trace and acknowledge copyright material, but this has not always been possible. The author and publisher would be pleased to hear from any copyright holders who have not been acknowledged.

Designed by Melissa Fraser, Penguin Design Studio
Typeset in 12/16.5 pt Granjon by Post Pre-press Group, Brisbane, Queensland
Printed and bound in Australia by McPherson's Printing Group, Maryborough, Victoria

National Library of Australia
Cataloguing-in-Publication data:

Dally-Watkins, June.
The secrets behind my smile.
ISBN 0 670 91078 3.

1. Dally-Watkins, June. 2. Models (Persons) – Australia – Biography.
3. Businesswomen – Australia – Biography. 4. Church work with refugees – Croatia.
I. Title.

746.92092

www.penguin.com.au

The secrets behind my smile

Contents

Acknowledgements vii

1. All that glitters 1
2. Sticks and stones 4
3. Drink and The Shadow 19
4. A new identity 28
5. Mannequin moments 38
6. Leaving Mother 49
7. Charmed, I'm sure 60
8. Open for business 72
9. Planet Hollywood 90
10. Four babies and a divorce 107
11. Travels with my children 124
12. Not just pretty faces 135
13. Rollcall 149
14. An affair with Asia 155
15. Quest for success 166

16	Friends like these	179
17	A final journey	191
18	The Shadow returns	200
19	Dynastic dreams	209
20	More to life than champagne	218
21	Dissolution and retreat	224
22	Miracles	234
23	Smiling through	247
	Epilogue: A new beginning	261
	Index	265

Acknowledgements

To write this book I needed the encouragement of my family and friends, who kept saying 'someone should write about your era'. To do that I had to write about myself.

I had to be honest about my whole life, which meant dredging up the unhappiness I had been hiding behind my smile. I didn't know how much it would hurt: at times it was more than I could bear.

Slowly I started writing in the strangest way, as if driven by an unseen force. Early one morning in Mudgee when staying with Marg and Warrick Gietz I woke up and felt compelled to start writing in a little notebook with a pencil.

Little by little over the next four years the past surfaced. Rolene Markson kept encouraging me and suggested Julie Gibbs of Penguin Books should look at what I had written.

Terry Dowling, the treasured teacher of Communications at my Business Finishing College, typed up my pencil scribbling. As an author of a number of published books, Terry gave guidance in this, new to me, world of writing. Thank you, Terry, for all the early morning talks before class, listening and encouraging.

Professor Ross Steele phoned often during this time to say 'Hang in there.'

Sally Begbie, my friend and travelling companion in the war-torn cities of Croatia and Bosnia Herzegovina, constantly gave encouragement, love and prayers. She is also a published author.

One of the first to read my early manuscript was Bruce Smith. He encouraged me to believe it was worthwhile.

Di and John Cant lent me their apartment on the Gold Coast of Queensland to drop out for a while and write; Colette and Max Hunt – their Bali home.

Clare Littlewood and Gianmania Beretta loaned me their villa on the Island of Filicudi, where the wonderful locals gave friendship. Aeolus, the God of Winds, wafted moods of the sea, and Maureen Daly cooked great meals.

The Tuscan farmhouse of Gemma Rossi Consumi at Consuma high in the Apennine Mountains gave cool respite from the August heat for more scribbling.

Thanks to Bert Skewes and third and fourth cousins who have come into my life and been a fund of information, including Keith Skuse for introducing other ways of spelling my mother's family name and tracing Skewes, Skues, Skuse back to the Domesday Book.

I am indebted to Louise Gee, who relived my life again and worked intensely with me to bring this book together.

When talking to Ita Buttrose about the pain I was suffering writing this book, she understood. She said it was like childbirth, it hurts, but as soon as it is over, the pain is forgotten. I can only hope so.

1 ALL THAT GLITTERS

A breath of lazy, hot air limped through the windows of my grandparents' house. The heat had stilled the bush but I was feeling restless. It had been a few years since Mother and I had left the stagnation of Watson's Creek in outback New South Wales to pursue our dreams in Sydney. We had returned in the summer of 1949 to the listless environment of my childhood for the Christmas–New Year holidays. There was little else to amuse me so I resumed my childhood ritual of walking with Mother to the post office to collect the mail and newspapers. We were eager to read up on the latest news and social happenings in Sydney. Mother had planned to cut out any pictures of me from these publications and paste them into a scrapbook.

Newspapers were a lifeline linking us to the rest of the world – and on this occasion there was my black-and-white face smiling back at me from the front page of *Truth* newspaper. My eyes ran over the text accompanying the photograph. The newspaper said I was Australia's model of the year for 1949 and the most photographed model in the country. Australia's fashion photographers had chosen me as the nation's top model. These were truly accolades to which all Australian models aspired. As a young girl, I had always held on to the hope that if I reached for the moon I might catch some stars along the way. Now it seemed some stardust was in my grasp. I had made it!

Professional models in this era were few and therefore instantly recognised like superstars. We were treated like stars too – feted by the press, admired and envied by women, and desired by men. Every fashion show was a gala affair. Everyone knew me by name and by face. Little did they know I started out in life as June Marie Skewes. Born in Sydney on 13 June 1927, I spent the next twelve years growing up in the bush, far from the limelight or even the dim lights of town. I was a long way from becoming the doyenne of modelling and deportment at the helm of the June Dally-Watkins Group of Companies, where I would remain for over fifty years.

That award proved to me that I had made it from the country to the catwalk, from being a 'nobody' to being a 'somebody'. So I sought out new adventures and opportunities. I figured that if I didn't reach for something I would always have nothing. So I became a pioneering career woman at a time when the only businesswomen were those who had a frock shop or hair salon, or who ran their husband's business. I opened the first modelling and deportment school, model agency and business finishing college in the southern hemisphere. I produced the first fashion parade of Australian models and designs to be shown overseas, Australia's inaugural fashion parade in the air (aboard TAA), and I was the first Australian to take a one-woman fashion show to the USA. Over the years, my business turned out eleven women who won titles in the Miss Australia quests, three Miss Internationals, one Miss World, one Miss Teen International, scores of other quest winners and hundreds of successful models. In 1993 I received an Order of Australia. I was delighted the honour was bestowed on me for my contribution to business. I much prefer to be recognised as a businesswoman than as merely a former model, because my influence on the world of modelling has been far greater than my role in it. Recognising this, the Australian Business Women's Network honoured me as Australia's Most Inspirational Business Woman in 1998 and inducted me into its Business Women's Hall of Fame. More than 300 000 women, men and children have come through my doors to be educated and nurtured, but my four children, along with my seven grandchildren, have been my supreme success. I've had every reason to smile, but often the bigger my smile the greater the heartache I've been hiding.

2 STICKS AND STONES

In the far-flung nest of Watson's Creek, the occasional Saturday night dance was eagerly awaited as the highlight of our lives. Neither distance nor a bracing New England winter could dampen locals' enthusiasm for a chance to meet so-called out-of-towners – folk from neighbouring hamlets. Indeed, there was little other social stimulation at Watson's Creek. In my early years, a five-kilometre walk to the hall at Upper Watson's Creek, where the dances were held, did nothing to cool our excitement. That was the distance from my grandparents' granite-pocked sheep property, Springvale – my childhood home. Later, another hall was built closer to Springvale that cut the distance by half, but it still meant hiking down what seemed to my young legs a steep slope from the homestead, crossing a creek and climbing another rise. On the trek home sometimes my mother and her brothers took turns carrying me asleep in their arms until I was old enough to make my own way under the guidance of the moonlight.

  I learned to dance as soon as I could walk, my uncles balancing me on their shoes as they instructed me. As these evenings wore on, I usually found myself bundled in a woollen blanket, left with other local children to sleep on the stage. There we were lulled to sleep behind sweet Uncle Blue (so named because of his red hair), who worked the piano keys to popular tunes of the day – 'Whispering', 'Goodnight Sweetheart' and 'Save the Last Dance for Me'. The women were mostly seated around the hall's corrugated-iron walls, waiting for someone to ask them to dance. There was always someone on hand to announce dances like the jolly miller, the barn dance and the foxtrot, perhaps to round up the stragglers outside who were happily quaffing wine or beer hidden in blackberry bushes or stashed in car boots.

On one of those nights, my mother was outside when I – all of six years of age and a bit of a show-off – climbed up on stage: 'Ladies and gentlemen, the next dance will be a quickstep.' Before anyone noticed, a man known to my family towered over me. 'Shut up, you little bastard,' he seethed. I didn't know what the word 'bastard' meant, but I knew from the big man's anger that it wasn't a compliment. Although it was much later that I came to understand the real meaning of this word that sadly underpinned my life, I felt embarrassed and bad. If the man wanted to put me in my place he certainly achieved that; my confidence wilted. Many years later I mastered public speaking and compered many fashion parades, but that was my first speech and I'll never forget it.

I grew up not knowing my true self. No one ever told me the circumstances of my birth, and sensing it was a taboo subject I never asked. Imaginative children would perhaps treasure such mystery and secrets, but to me mysteries were unanswered questions, and secrets were whispered innuendoes. Some of the grown-ups, even my own family members, treated me with disdain. Children taunted me with the name 'bastard'. They probably didn't know what it meant either, but I knew by their vindictive expressions that a 'bastard' wasn't a good person. 'Don't worry, Junie,' assured my mother, who also endured snide remarks from the locals and her family. 'Sticks and stones may break your bones, but names will never hurt you.'

The hush-hush surrounding my father and my identity became deafening and continued to echo throughout my life, occasionally rebounding with a force that silenced all happiness. So I masked my shame and buried my self-consciousness with a smile – something I've done all my life, both on and off the catwalk. No one knew how I really felt. I became a loner at school and was forced to seek solace in my own imagination. All alone I could daydream of other places and another life. My mother fed me her dreams, including a desire for me to be a 'somebody', which would be a way to rise above the drudgery of our day-to-day lives. Thankfully, Mother convinced me that I was not the social misfit that some people made me feel I was. She said I was different only because I was special. How clever of her. Her reassurance and love made me strong enough to rise above the taunts and those who hurled them. My head was held high.

In this era respectable women were expected to marry, raise children and stay at home, so to have a child out of wedlock was truly frowned upon. Single mothers became social and moral outcasts. Deep-rooted attitudes took longer to shake in the bush. Pregnant single girls disappeared to other towns to deliver their babies for adoption or submitted to backyard abortions. Similarly, alcoholism and cancer were swept under the rug. People of my mother's generation referred to alcoholism as 'the drink'. They'd say 'The drink got to him' or 'She couldn't keep away from the drink.' Cancer was referred to in nebulous terms. Despite the laid-back way of country folk, they were stoic people who covered up or denied some harsher home truths. Growing up in that kind of culture made me suppress many of my feelings. For instance, I have never told many of my friends that I am illegitimate. All my life I've been trying to unravel the shroud of my past, discover my identity and rise above the whispers. If the stigma of illegitimacy continued today, I would probably still hide my past. Nowadays, however, many people choose to have a child out of wedlock and there is no shame attached.

If my mother, Caroline Mary Skewes, were alive she might still be embarrassed by the public revelation of my illegitimacy. My mother loved company and had a quick wit, but it must have taken courage to turn up to dances with me in tow. Carrie, as her family called her, was a carefree 22-year-old when she fell in love, only to be abandoned by the man she loved after she became pregnant. She had longed to leave the bush for Sydney, but sadly found her way there when she was three months pregnant. Hiding her condition, she arranged to stay with her married, older sister Elsie until my birth. When Grandfather discovered the truth he wrote to my mother, 'Come home. We love you and we will look after you and the baby.' So she returned to Watson's Creek with me, a babe in arms. There was nowhere else for us to go.

My ancestors were Cornish. I like to think this heritage explains some of my tenacity, energy for work, and brave face whatever the reality. The miners in Cornwall were forced to work in insanitary and dangerous conditions underground and live in appalling conditions, so when the tin ran low some of them escaped the hardship by drinking until John Wesley helped them to abandon the drink and turn to Methodism. Many sought a new life in a distant country.

My great-grandparents, William and Elizabeth Skewes, were migrants from Cury, in Cornwall, England. They married in Sydney in 1855. News of a gold strike at Rocky River, near Uralla, sent the newlyweds, along with Elizabeth's two brothers and her mother, by boat north to Morpeth, then to nearby Maitland, where they bought a horse and wagon and made the arduous journey north. Life at Rocky River was so remote that it took three months for the bullock wagons, used to transport supplies from Sydney, to arrive at their destination. Often bushrangers robbed the wagons en route. Auntie Mercy told me how Great-Granny Skewes always had a bed made on the verandah of her house for the legendary gentleman bushranger Fred Ward, otherwise known as 'Captain Thunderbolt'. Sometimes she found the bed slept in and hay she had left out for his horse gone – along with some of her hens and eggs. Grandfather's sister-in-law, Old Mrs Northey, was adamant that Thunderbolt gave her a large amethyst and silver brooch that she always wore. According to some historians, Thunderbolt was not shot in 1870 and buried in a grave at Uralla – that grave, they claim, is filled by a horse thief named Morgan. The story goes that a policeman, who happened to be a mate of Thunderbolt's, deliberately misidentified the body, as did Ward's mother. Auntie Mercy told me Thunderbolt lived at Watson's Creek for a while because he was sure no one would look for him in such an inaccessible place.

One of William and Elizabeth's twelve children, James, tried his luck at Tingha, also in the New England region. He died there in a mining-shaft accident. In the late 1800s my grandfather Sam and his brother William headed south to the Moonbi Ranges to fossick for tin. They had some luck at Giant's Den Mountain, so named because according to local legend a Chinese giant dwelled there to protect the Chinese miners. In its shadow, the European and Chinese miners remained segregated, never imagining their tents and huts would one day develop into the small community of Watson's Creek.

Sam made the long journey on foot to and from the Den Mountain and Watson's Creek every week. He also dredged for tin in the creek on his allocated land, Springvale, but gradually turned it into a fine sheep property for his bride, Sarah Pennell, who came from Guyra, north of Armidale. Together they had thirteen children (one baby didn't survive), so Sam built a homestead from slabs of wood to raise his family. It was surrounded by fruit trees and a paling fence kept the livestock out. Later the family moved up the hill into a more impressive house he had built. Springvale had a foundation of cement blocks. Grandfather had made it from miner to country squire. So proud was my grandfather of Springvale that my mother called it 'his rock foundation'. To me, Grandfather was simply the rock of the family.

Life in the bush was a rough-and-ready affair, so Springvale was an enviable landmark in the area. We didn't have tap water, but we had our own bathroom, a stand-alone laundry structure complete with a wood-fired copper, a formal dining room that was rarely used, and a living room with a piano that only my mother played. The house had a verandah, which wrapped round the front and one side of the house and served as Uncle Les's outdoor bedroom. I always envied him. Mother and I shared a room and a double bed, while Les's bed commanded a view of the stars and moon. In reality, his sleeping quarters must have been unbearable when the mercury plunged below zero degrees in winter.

The homestead overlooked an orchard, the remains of the earlier house, a fowl house and a shed where we shod horses, repaired our own shoes and did other farm work. To the rear of the homestead my uncles had built a tennis court, and beyond that stood the slaughter yards where Sam killed our stock. We kept the meat in the cement cool-room. Day-to-day perishables were stored on the back cement verandah in the drip safe – a stack of shelves with the sides covered in fine gauze. On top of the safe, water dripped slowly from a metal tray down onto attached hessian strips that ran over the gauze. This cooled the passing air, and therefore kept the food inside the safe fresher. It was non-electric air-conditioning at its best!

The shearing shed and attached sheep and cow pens, situated closer to the creek, represented the property's nerve centre. Springvale really came to life at shearing time. Grandfather oversaw the operation and Gran, my mother and my aunties worked tirelessly to prepare meals for the shearers and roustabouts who stayed on the property. Wishing I were a boy so I could be like one of the shearers, I began to copy their swear words and tone. 'Don't use those bad words. Don't speak that way,' my mother insisted, stifling a laugh. At the shearing shed, I tried to impress the shearers and my grandfather by sweeping the floor and laying out newly shorn fleece on the sorting table. More than any other chore, I loved it when Grandfather lowered me into the press to tread down the wool. I was a capable, strong and healthy child, but if I made a nuisance of myself Grandfather sent me back to the homestead. I was hurt by his disapproval, but knew he loved me. There were many times when Sam made exceptions for me, even when, as a pre-schooler, I stuck his tax stamps to consignment papers and envelopes as if they were postage stamps and posted them through a hole in the fence. Instead of getting annoyed Grandfather proudly told our relatives: 'Mark my words, that child is going to make a name for herself.'

If farming work made me a tomboy, the same could be said of pretty much all country children. I practised target shooting at bottles lined up on a fence until I had the skill of a marksman, and I rode a horse. But I also played 'ladies' with my celluloid doll and imitated the models pictured in retailers' catalogues and magazines that my mother collected. I would dress up in my mother's clothes, light a candle or lamp and strike poses in front of the wardrobe mirror in our bedroom. Maybe that sounds vain, but I didn't think I was pretty. I simply wanted to look my best and take care of myself, just as my mother took care of the way she looked, moved and spoke. So I cleaned my teeth furiously at the freshwater tank outside the house and brushed my hair repeatedly to try to make it shine. Inadvertently, I was preparing for my career.

My mother also made sure I behaved like a lady. I was taught to eat quietly and daintily, sit up straight, stand tall, and have impeccable manners. How wise my mother was to know these attributes would help me make it in life. If I didn't pronounce a word correctly, spoke Strine, or used incorrect grammar, she'd slap me gently, even when I was a young adult. 'Don't say that, June, I've told you not to speak that way,' she'd lecture. I can talk Strine with the best of them, but it wouldn't have done me much good in the business world, travelling overseas or in certain circles. Although Mother didn't have exposure to those opportunities at Watson's Creek, she trained herself to speak in a refined tone that was more reminiscent of an English than an Australian accent. The locals thought she had a plum in her mouth. I can still hear a cousin drawl, 'Your mother's stuck-up. Who does she think she is?'

When I look back at photographs of my mother with her siblings, it's clear there was something different about her. Like me, she was the odd one out. Only Auntie Elsie had a similar style and sophistication. Perhaps that's why some women seemed jealous of my mother. They wore their centre-parted hair tightly back – too tired to make an effort or lacking the same aspirations for a more exciting life. My mother worked hard also, but dressed fashionably in clothes she had made using Gran's treadle sewing machine or had chosen from mail-order catalogues and were gifts from my grandfather. She had a flair for fashion and, as I grew older, encouraged me to take an interest in it, allowing me to select catalogue clothes that Grandfather paid for. He supported us both.

My mother modelled herself on images from those catalogues and magazines, and was up with the latest trends. When I was a baby, Mother wore her chestnut hair in a fashionable bob and later modelled herself on Wallis Simpson, the Duchess of Windsor. Two large rolls of hair framed her alabaster face and dimpled cheeks and the rest was fastened at the back of her head in a low bun. My mother was five foot, seven inches tall – an inch taller than me as an adult – slim, with shapely legs that often attracted comment. Indeed, New York model agent Eileen Ford told *Woman's Day* during her visit here in 1965 that the only 'wonderful pair' of legs she had seen in Australia were 'long, beautifully shaped, with slender ankles' and they belonged to my mother. By then my mother was a grandmother and understandably pleased as punch with the compliment. I was proud too.

Those catalogues and magazines of the 1930s greatly influenced my mother's style, manners and elegance and she insisted those traits rubbed off on me – something she reiterated when I was profiled on 'This Is Your Life' in 1976: 'She'd sit for hours going through the fashion magazines that came through the post and even as a tiny girl she would dress up in my clothes and parade and say, "Oh my! Mother, I do want to be a model or a mannequin when I grow up. I'd be just like Margaret Vyner."' Vyner, who grew up on a well-known sheep station near Armidale and became a successful model in Sydney in the 1930s, was my mother's idol.

In the days before television, department-store catalogues from Farmer & Co (later taken over by the Myer Emporium to become part of the Grace Bros–Myer department-store chain) in Sydney and Wakes in Melbourne, and magazines like *The Australian Women's Weekly* connected country women to the rest of the world. Despite the Great Depression, the *Weekly*'s first issue in 1933 had a circulation of 120 000 copies.

To collect these treasured publications, my mother and I walked two kilometres to the post office, where we lined up at the postmistress 'Auntie' Amy Howarth's window – a wooden square cut from the wall of her house. Auntie Amy was the proud owner of the only telephone in the area. The postman met the train from Sydney at Kootingal, fifty-one kilometres south of Watson's Creek, to collect mail and other provisions for the surrounding villages. He didn't live locally, so mail day was twice a week. With the exception of the occasional dance and tennis match at Springvale, mail day was about the most exciting thing that happened at Watson's Creek.

Escapism provided by those magazines helped my mother survive the loneliness of the bush and sparked her imagination. Her hands fluttered excitedly and her green eyes (like mine) lit up as she talked about what the future might hold for both of us. Her enthusiasm was infectious and, before long, I became a dreamer. I believe that's why I succeeded in business; I was always dreaming of my next big adventure. I still do.

I began to nurture the idea that I could become one of the women wearing the clothes in the catalogues or magazines. My first dream, however, was to become a film star. The moon became my confidante and naïvely I wondered on which star I would find the Hollywood I had read about, and how I would get there. Little did I know that one day I would spend time in Hollywood, and that I would exult in the moon as it hung romantically over the Colosseum in Rome; paused pregnantly over Filicudi, an Aeolian Island; floodlit the *Cristo Redentor* on top of the Corcovado Mountain, which overlooks Rio de Janeiro; inflated slowly from the sea in Bali; and boldly outshone Hong Kong's blaze of lights during the Chinese Moon Festival.

As a child, my favourite and most regular excursion was to Bendemeer, which was twenty-four kilometres from Watson's Creek along a bumpy, dirt road. Travelling elsewhere was problematic. Tamworth was too far away for regular trips and to the west of the Creek was Manilla, accessed by a tortuous track, which I feared would gobble up the bullock wagons that travelled along it. Besides, Bendemeer was a relative metropolis to us. It had a bakery, a general store and the Bendemeer Hotel. The hotel is still on Caroline Street and has a barbecue area that rolls down to the banks of the Macdonald River.

Usually one of my uncles drove Mother and me to Bendemeer when they wanted to watch a football game or cricket match. One of the reasons I enjoyed going to Bendemeer was because my mother seemed happiest there. We would visit her friends Celie and Ossie Warlow, who owned and ran the Bendemeer Hotel. She relaxed and laughed a lot and they enjoyed a few drinks. Ossie and Celie exuded an air of sophistication that told you they had been to Sydney. Ossie was dapper with a neat moustache. However Celie had gone to Watson's Creek Public School with my mother. Mother and Celie's close friendship was reflected in their similar style: from how they sat to the way they seemed to glide across a room. They wore clothes in floating materials, chiffon and silk, with pearls and crystal jewellery rarely worn by rural women. Celie made me feel special and I thought she was very classy, with a joyful, clear voice.

The night before we would visit the Warlows, my mother always curled my hair, tearing an old pillowslip into strips that she wound around sections of my waist-length, auburn-gold hair before knotting them all over my head. It was difficult to sleep on the tightly bound knobs and strands of hair that pulled at my scalp, but I wanted to look good for my mother and the Warlows. For a frizzy look, I brushed out the curls. 'Out' was the operative word. The more I brushed my hair the more it stood out! For these outings I wore my best homemade dress, a fake gold bangle above each elbow as was the fashion then, crystal beads, black patent shoes and knee socks that I would roll to my ankles as soon as I was out of my mother's sight.

My mother and Celie smoked, it seemed to me, ever so elegantly. If a gentleman were present, he lit the cigarettes that balanced daintily between their red-painted lips. Inhaling delicately, they tilted their heads slightly towards the ceiling and to one side before slowly exhaling silvery blue swirls of smoke through pursed lips. The cigarette was held between two slender fingers, the hand of which was flipped back, palm up, to expose a slim, feminine wrist. It was very Marlene Dietrich or Carole Lombard in style. The ladylike art form my mother and Celie seemed to make of smoking has long since died. Today, I see teenage girls and women dragging on butts in a desperate way as they walk along the street, deeply sucking deadly nicotine into their lungs. They litter, stamping their feet on butts or slovenly flicking still alight butts onto the footpath. A few years ago, one of my friend's daughters was visiting from Holland and remarked on the prevalence of prostitutes during the day in downtown Sydney. It dawned on me that the women she had seen standing outside city buildings weren't prostitutes but office workers on 'smokos' or work breaks. These women look as though they can't be bothered making an effort. Too lazy to stand tall, they must lean against a building wall.

Grandfather hated my mother smoking. 'That stuff will kill you. I don't want you smoking in this house,' he bellowed, if he caught a whiff of smoke coming from our room. 'I know you're smoking Carrie. I can smell the stuff. Get rid of it.' But as he sat on the verandah, it seemed for hours, studying the sky for rain, a hand-rolled cigarette often dangled half-finished from his mouth. To avoid these confrontations, my mother and my aunties smoked on our evening stroll from the house to 'the dub' – our twist on the rhyming slang 'rubbity-dub' for 'pub'. It was their evening ritual after washing the dinner dishes. The dub was our crude outhouse, a deep pit dug under a wooden box with a hole on the top to sit over. There was no such thing as toilet paper; we used newspaper. On these clandestine smokos, my mother and my aunties would conduct mock competitions to see who was the best cigarette roller. I demanded they teach me and, thanks to the regularity and necessity of these evening excursions, I became an accomplished cigarette roller. But I never smoked.

This kind of amusement reflected our quiet and simple existence. However, from time to time, a man from a neighbouring property or village broke the routine and invited my mother to a dance. She always insisted that I came along. We were a pair. As a child, I was my mother's best friend and we went everywhere together, even on her dates. With my mother's make-up and hair done by lamplight and both of us dressed in our best clothes, we'd sit on the verandah, watching for a car to come over the hill towards Watson's Creek. On occasion the time would pass, the dogs would begin to bark at the moon, and then I would sense her despair and disappointment. A proud woman, she didn't want others to know the sadness that engulfed her existence, but instinctively I knew when she was sad. It would be dark before she'd say eventually, 'He's not coming. We better go to bed.' Mother then dejectedly washed her face, took off her pretty dress and climbed into bed, the thought of more numbingly quiet nights ahead no comfort to her. Or she'd go to the piano and play with sensitivity the 1920s hit song, 'Whispering', and sing the lyrics of this, her favourite song. However, she didn't have anyone to whisper the words to her.

Perhaps her date had been waylaid or had a few too many beers at the Bendemeer Hotel. I don't think there was malicious intent behind these occasional no-shows. It was more likely the man thought, 'She'll be right.' This thoughtlessness made an impression on me. If I say to someone, 'I'll be there', I'll make every effort to turn up at the appointed time and place. When someone makes a commitment to me and then doesn't follow through I feel the same disappointment my mother must have felt on those nights.

Grandfather also instructed me in the importance of punctuality and keeping my word: 'Your word is your bond. Don't let anyone down. Don't let yourself down. Don't tell lies. Don't steal. A man's greatest possession is his time; we all have a limited amount of it. Don't waste other people's time or your own.' They were lessons I have tried to use in my career, but in my experience I have found that some people in business today place a higher value on aggression, deception and manipulation.

Grandfather was a highly principled, hard-working and intelligent man. At six feet tall, with a greying beard and a deep voice, Sam was an imposing man who set high standards for his children and was very strict. He was respected in the district and was relatively well-to-do. During World War II, Grandfather had enough money to clear a racetrack for a one-off event to raise funds for the war effort. People came from as far as Tamworth and Armidale and it was a grand affair.

Grandfather was my idol. I grew up calling him 'Father'. I loved him as a father and never considered that it wasn't possible for him to be both my father and my mother's father, until some of my cousins and the children at school set me straight. After that I didn't give him any name. I was 13 when my mother married and from then on I called my stepfather 'Father' and Sam 'Grandfather'. I think that hurt Sam as much as it made me feel awkward. On my birthday that year, he gave me a bible that I still cherish. At the time I wrote on its flyleaf: 'I set him up as an idol – from there he has never faltered –

he is a symbol of goodness, honesty, courage – someone to make proud of me and someone I'm proud to call Grandfather. I will always love him and he will always be my guiding star.'

Although Grandfather was my role model, he and Gran's relationship was the first of many joyless marriages I observed. I never saw them speak fondly or show affection to one another. Grandfather worked outside, came in for meals, then sat in his special chair on the verandah, watching the sky for rain. My grandparents also slept in separate bedrooms, with Grandfather having the more modest quarters and Gran the main bedroom. I loved sinking deep into the feather mattresses of Gran's bed and sometimes slept the night in it. From her bed, I could look through the double doors and survey all of Watson's Creek, especially when there was a full moon, which made the dogs bark incessantly.

I loved Gran although she was forever working. When it was time to kill a chook for Christmas or a special celebration, Gran pointed to the plumpest fowl in the yard and I'd set chase. My long, skinny legs quickly caught up with one of the birds, which I then presented to her. Once it met Gran's expectation, determined by poking its breastbone, she lopped off its head. I was amused to watch the beheaded chook running around, flapping its wings. Now I would be horrified. Once the bird collapsed, Gran plunged it into a copper of boiling water to loosen its feathers for plucking, stuffed it with seasoning, then baked it. If I close my eyes I can still smell those succulent chooks being roasted in the fuel oven.

Some mornings Gran had chopped the wood, stacked the stove, lit the fire, collected water from the tank outside and boiled it to make porridge – all before anyone else had risen. It was essential to have cut wood for cooking and heating, and it was supposed to be my daily job to collect it from the wood heap (which sometimes harboured snakes) up the back of the house and place it in the pantry wood box. One morning I was heartbroken to find my white fox terrier, Fluffy, hanging stiff and cold from the heap. Fluffy had jumped from the top of the heap and become caught on his chain. His legs couldn't reach the ground, so he died by hanging.

However, there was no time to grieve over dead animals on a working property. Gran made sure everyone did his or her chores. Her orders to my mother never stopped: 'Did you let the stove go out? Why isn't all the ironing done?' Ironing was my mother's most dreaded chore, especially in summer, because she had to stand near the stove where the iron was heated. She would hold a piece of rag around the handle of the heavy iron to prevent burns, but the heat transferred easily and often her hand was red raw from using it. Between all this work Gran and my mother argued, made up and argued again.

I can now understand the frustrations of both the women I loved. Grandfather knew about their intense fights, but no one intervened and mostly they were during the day, when the men weren't home. Coming home from school, I'd hear Gran's abusive comments. 'Get out of this place, Carrie. Why don't you leave? GO!' After their blow-ups, my mother and I sometimes escaped the house by visiting Auntie Ida's, where I was sent outside to play with my cousins. More often, however, my mother and I fled into the surrounding bushes, both of us crying hysterically. Fearing I was the cause of these rows, I shared in her emotional distress. After one raging argument, my mother ran into the bushes without me. When I found her, she had collapsed to the ground and was repeatedly hitting her forehead with a stick. She was screaming and out of control. I suppose my mother was so frustrated with her lot, she took it out on herself. I was only about eight years old and it scared me to see her like that. I struggled with her, 'Stop it, Mother. Stop it.' Gradually she calmed down and became quiet. The incident made me fearful of ever upsetting her. Maybe I saved her from serious self-harm and gave her a reason to live, but if it hadn't been for me she wouldn't have been stuck in Watson's Creek in the first place. We sat in the scrub for a long time – until darkness approached and the men were due home – before heading back. There was no escape.

3 Drink and The Shadow

Although I grew up as an only child, I was surrounded by eleven aunts and uncles. My mother was the third youngest of a brood of twelve, however some of her siblings had enough problems and children of their own to be much concerned about Mother and me.

Uncle Sid made a good start at scorching an entrepreneurial path. He built a wooden slab hut and ran it as a butcher shop for a while. His next venture required a two-day journey by horse and cart to Tamworth to buy bits and pieces, food and alcohol for his own general store. He made enough money to become the first person in our district to buy a car, which had running boards and detachable celluloid windows for cold and windy days. However, Sid became his own best customer as far as alcohol was concerned. In time he lost everything: his wife and children, his business and his precious car. Then, during drinking binges, he would turn up at Springvale in the night, shouting abuse as he stormed up and down the verandah and woke everyone. My mother and I would remain in the bed we shared, too fearful to move. The commotion ended only when Sid disappeared or all his alcohol was consumed and he had fallen asleep.

I suspect Sid brought alcohol to Gran. Their closeness made my mother upset and jealous: 'Why do you love Sid so much? I iron, cook and wash, and you treat me badly. I give you my life. I do everything for you and you idolise Sid who causes nothing but pain.' Yet often a parent worries and tends the bird with the broken wing more than the stronger one. Sid drank himself to death by the time he was 48.

Elsie was a beauty and the first daughter to break away from the family. A talented dressmaker, she lived a sophisticated life in Sydney and her homecomings were fashion eye-openers that made my mother envious. But the drink destroyed Elsie. I wonder if her marriage broke down because of it, or if her drinking bouts surfaced only after its collapse? In any case, her addiction forced her return to Springvale. I remember her pacing the house at night or disappearing for days. After one drinking session, when her absence dragged on longer than usual, Uncle Les hitched a ride with the postman on his weekly trip to a relative's property (ironically called 'Why Worry', which was sixteen kilometres from Springvale) to search for her. When he arrived, the property was deserted and Elsie was lying on a track near the house, dead. Her body had been exposed to the heat and flies for several days.

Auntie Thelma, Uncle 'Blue' and their three sons lived nearby in a three-room cottage, but they only ever used two rooms – the dining room with the wood-veneer suite and sideboard was reserved as a showpiece and only used for Christmas lunch. The boys slept in beds on the verandah, which had a large roll-up canvas blind to protect them on wet and windy nights. Occasionally I stayed over, sleeping in Auntie Thelma and Uncle Blue's double bed with them. I loved the attention and sense of family. Thelma was my youngest aunt and like an older sister to me, so I was saddened to learn she too became an alcoholic. Her drinking problem was evident only after she and Uncle Blue moved to Bendemeer. Whether her drinking began because Uncle Blue travelled for work or because she lived across the road from the hotel remains a mystery to me. Whatever the reason, it caused anguish for Blue and their red-haired sons. She literally drank herself to death.

Why were some of my relatives cursed with alcoholism and others not? Maybe the loneliness and boredom of living in the bush brought on this affliction. Maybe it was in their blood. Fearing history would repeat itself, from a young age I was wary of alcohol and developed an inbuilt warning system: if I had more than two glasses of wine I'd start to feel sick and stop drinking. A few times I've had too much to drink, but only to the point of feeling happy, like on my twenty-first and fortieth birthdays. I enjoy an occasional whisky, beer, or a glass of wine with a meal but stop at that.

Grandfather, however, hated the stuff. 'Keep away from that damn drink,' he advised me. 'It will kill you.' So too did some of my aunts and uncles. Uncle Jim married Pearl, bought a property near Manilla, and worked there until he died at 80. He hardly ever touched a drop. Pearl died of breast cancer when it was something shameful that people didn't talk about. Ida married her cousin Will Skewes and had many children, including two sets of twins. She was a great cook and her cream puffs were the best in Watson's Creek because she had a much sought-after milk and cream separator. Like the other Skewes women, Auntie Isabella was a clever seamstress and was appointed as sewing teacher at Watson's Creek school in 1921. Bella was a quiet, dignified lady, who hated alcohol. She married, had six daughters and ended her days in Tamworth. Oswald married Emily and lived a quiet life in Sydney, where Uncle Os worked on the wharves. Jack, the oldest of my mother's siblings, lived with his wife Edith at Watson's Creek until an old age. He hated alcohol too.

Uncle Len could handle alcohol and lived at home when I was a young girl. His mate was Mr Galom, an Indian travelling salesman who camped in our shearing shed whenever he visited with his horse-drawn wagon of wares. Fascinated by Mr Galom's lyrical voice and origin, we sat around his campfire as he made curry for us. Tentatively I ate the spicy meal, unsure if I liked it. Now I know I do. Lamb curry became a favourite easy-to-make meal.

Len had a go at running the general store, saving enough money to buy a car that he drove for hours with Mother so they could attend social events beyond Watson's Creek. My mother and Len were close in age and yearned for 'the good life'. For tennis games on our court, they dressed in creams and enjoyed drinks with friends. To watch these matches I'd climb up a large, weatherworn granite rock, which wasn't always safe to do, as a faint scar under my chin attests. Len was not only the top tennis player and cricket player of the district but also the top playboy. Handsome, tall, slim and clean-cut, he had the potential to excel in life, but things didn't work out for him. His marriage to Auntie Mercy failed and his children didn't maintain contact. I don't know why. He became a loner, living in a little shack on the creek bank and panning for tin. When he came to Sydney as an old man, my mother and I tried to care for him with the help of my friend, Dr Bob Melville, but eventually we had to place him in a nursing home. He was still a handsome ladies' man and we received complaints that he had chased female residents and climbed into their beds. Whenever we visited the nursing home, he'd be holding hands with one of the women. She always looked pleased. Len died alone aged 80.

Aunt Ethel married Bob Streeting, who also ran a general store for a spell. Their home was next to the school and Bob owned a Willy's Knight truck. I loved those times when all the Skewes piled onto the back of Uncle Bob's truck and went on excursions. It made me feel part of a family. Mother was happy too. On Boxing Day, Uncle Bob drove us to the Macdonald River near Bendemeer. My cousins and I would strip to our underwear and swing from the low-hanging branches of the willow trees into the river and play rounders or cricket. Ten of us once went to Yamba sitting on the back of the truck and slept in tents. It was the first time I had seen the sea. I enjoyed picnics with Ethel's children in the hills behind Springvale. Her son and I were the same age. When he died, aged 46, from an alcohol-related illness, his only possessions were a few clothes in a suitcase and a photo of me.

    Les, the favourite of all my aunts and uncles, walked with a limp and had a left hand contorted into a permanently closed fist. I had been told that he had been climbing through a fence when his gun accidentally went off and left him crippled on the left side. More recently my cousin Bert Skewes revealed that as a young man, Uncle Les had experienced an unhappy romance that triggered depression. Les sent a note to Bert's father, William, saying he was going to kill himself. When a search party found Les in the scrub with a bullet wound to his head William rode to Bendemeer to telephone the nearest doctor, based in Armidale, about ninety-five kilometres away. The practitioner was visiting a patient in Kingstown, west of Armidale, so Will met him on the way and they travelled cross-country to shorten the journey. The doctor became drunk on the way, so that, by the time he sobered up, it was three days before Les received medical attention. Without any anaesthetic, the doctor probed the wound with a boiled piece of fencing wire and concluded that removal of the bullet was too risky. Somehow Uncle Les survived.

    Les was a gentle soul who never married nor drank. His only outlet was work. I spent a lot of my time helping Les round up the calves and milk their mothers. In the orchard that Uncle Les tended I picked apricots, peaches, turnips and carrots, washed them in the stream and often ate them as I walked home. Les's ginger beer was just as irresistible. During the night I'd hear the corks on the ginger-beer bottles pop, indicating the sweet fizz was ready for consumption.

    Uncle Les always made time for me. He constructed a plywood box to catch birds that nested in the orchard. Holding a piece of string attached to a stick that raised one side of the box, I would wait behind a bush until a bird came to eat the seeds I had left on the ground, ready to snare it with a tug on the string. That was the idea – the birds were always too quick. In the evenings, Les and I would set rabbit traps and the following morning we'd walk around the property to collect the trapped animals. Unflinching, I'd watch closely as Les pulled the skins off the dead rabbits and placed the skins on a wire frame, which he hung on the shed wall to dry, ready for the rabbit man to come and buy them. The rest went to the dogs.

Les was so caring that even after I had become a successful model in the late 1940s he sent me money from the sale of his heifers. That's when my grandparents sold Springvale. In old age it had become too difficult for them and Les to manage, so they moved into a little weatherboard house across the creek that looked over to their former home. It must have been heartbreaking for Sam to leave Springvale – his life's work – and watch it wistfully from afar until he died aged 92. Only now do I understand his heartache. Sarah died aged 87. Les lived out his days on the verandah of that cottage until he was 78.

Although they were buried in the Methodist section of the Bendemeer cemetery, I wasn't raised as such. Sam gave me strong moral values, but I always felt spiritually deprived. Christmas wasn't a religious time but was significant because it meant a visit from the men of the district, who arrived in a convoy of cars on Christmas Day and brought with them a keg of beer before going home somewhat intoxicated for lunch. We never attended a church and thought Auntie Amy was strange because she and her relatives read the Bible and had Christian gatherings. 'There go them Catholics to Mass,' someone would say as a car disappeared from view over the hill. The Catholics lived on a property near Manilla and didn't mix with the Creek people. I thought Mass was a town and that Catholics were strange. They probably thought we were irreverent and ignorant. Now, when I return to Watson's Creek and people come to listen to my talks about Christianity at my cousin Bert's church gatherings in the old rusted corrugated-iron hall, I suppose the ones who don't come think the congregation and I are strange.

I didn't receive religious instruction at the Watson's Creek Public School, which began as a slab hut with an earth-beaten floor in 1885. In 1907, Grandfather led a petition for a larger school, weather shed, and a rain tank so the children wouldn't have to walk to the snake-infested swamp for a drink and risk falling down a mine shaft on the way. A year later a new, one-room school, seven metres by five, was built. My mother was among forty children who crammed into it for classes. The school's future seemed secure when it celebrated its centenary, though sadly, it closed in 1987.

I'm proud of my Watson's Creek education despite the limitations of having one teacher to educate first to sixth grades. This rudimentary education gave me a permanent hunger for knowledge and led me on various pathways of discovery. I wasn't a diligent student, but I could get my head around a subject quickly and was a good lateral thinker. Impatient with school, my mind would take me further afield. Mathematics and memorising dates didn't interest me as much as history and geography lessons did. I had untidy handwriting, which Grandfather insisted I improve: 'You have to have good handwriting because people judge you by it.' Now he'd be proud; I write all my letters with an ink and nib pen. Grandfather knew I had to make it on my own and my education was important to him. So was my teacher's wireless radio. Until Grandfather bought his own, he would visit my first teacher Ray Ramsay's home to listen to the BBC broadcast of the cricket from England at night and afterwards tramp home in the early morning frost.

School was at least a two-kilometre, rather lonely, trek from home. One day my mother decided to keep me company after school. I had stripped to my panties for a dip in the creek on the way home. I was only 7 and couldn't swim, which wasn't unusual for a country child. When I disappeared from the surface for too long, she realised I was in trouble and jumped in to rescue me. After that I didn't even paddle in the creek. Instead, I preferred to imagine that it was frozen and that I was ice-skating film star Sonja Henie, whom I had read about in the *Women's Weekly*. My imagination was always my saviour.

The boys at school nicknamed me 'Phar Lap' because of my speed and when we played cricket I was dubbed 'Don Bradman'. I loved competing against them because I was motivated to try my best. If I didn't always win, at least I knew I had given it every effort. During one school cricket game, a handsome man dressed in a suit and hat beckoned to me. Gingerly, I went to the school fence where he stood and noticed a lady was sitting in his car. The stranger gave me a brown paper bag filled with brightly coloured lollies, the kind not available at the general stores in Watson's Creek or even Bendemeer. Then he was gone. I ate all the lollies before I went home, because I didn't want to get into trouble for accepting them. I had remembered the man from an earlier visit to Springvale. My mother, grandparents, Les and I gathered on the verandah to speculate about an approaching car; we hadn't been expecting anyone. When the driver pulled up everyone's chatter stopped abruptly. The man was slick in appearance, wore two-tone shoes, a baggy cap and smoked a pipe. Grandfather spoke sternly to him and didn't invite him inside. Everyone else remained silent. The man kept looking at me, but we weren't introduced. I sensed he was someone important, though I didn't know he was my father. This shadowy man was to come in and out of my life without warning. The next time I'd see him after this schoolyard visit was as a successful model in Sydney.

My mother never talked about my father – ever. I was to learn my father was Bob Monkton. He first laid eyes on my mother when he and a mate turned up at Watson's Creek in a flashy car in the spring of 1926. Apparently on a rabbit-hunting trip from his home town of Armidale, he stayed at the Creek for several weeks, during which time he seduced my mother. In her eyes, Bob was worldly and exciting. He had been educated in Melbourne and travelled widely, or so he told her. My mother had been no further than Tamworth.

Marriage might have been in Bob's mind when he took her to meet his sister Maude in Armidale, but somehow my mother found out he was already married and returned to Watson's Creek, a disgraced woman. Someone told me Grandfather paid him to stay away, but there's no way I can verify that.

4   A new identity

'There's Junie, she's going to high school in Tamworth.' I felt smug to hear the locals' envy instead of scorn. No one from Watson's Creek had ever been to high school. Boys stayed on the farm; girls helped their mothers at home until they married. Despite never having attended high school herself, Mother assured me it would be an exciting adventure. It was to be our ticket to Tamworth and out of Watson's Creek.

Another way out was marriage. My mother was watching a football game on the field adjacent to the Bendemeer Hotel when Major David Dally-Watkins walked in to the hotel. David was the sales representative for Penfolds Wines, so the Warlows introduced him to my mother. David was thirteen years older than Mother and had a military presence, a trim moustache, and an authoritative manner. He had signed up as bugler for the Boer War until his mother secured her 14-year-old son's discharge, and so he had to wait until World War I for his chance to see some action. David drove a flashy motorcar with glass windows that rolled up and down, unlike any cars seen around our way.

David fell in love with my mother and began courting her, with Gran and me accompanying them on bush picnics. Mother expected David to be like other men who had disappointed her, so when he went away for work she doubted he'd keep his promise to return. But David was true to his word, so my mother agreed to marry him when he proposed. I don't know whether my mother loved him, but she was 35, opportunities to meet single men were limited, and she desperately wanted to get away from Watson's Creek.

So we were suddenly in Sydney where my mother and David married in the Methodist Church on William Street, Kings Cross in 1940. Mother began to call herself 'Kay' instead of 'Carrie' and from that day 'June Skewes' no longer existed. My mother told me to keep my past a secret and pretend David was my real father. So I became June Dally-Watkins, although it wasn't until 23 February 1943 that David formally adopted me. Despite its somewhat surreptitious origins I am grateful David gave me his family name. It made me less upset when I saw that no details were supplied in the space next to natural 'father' on the adoption form. I tried my best to be a good daughter to David.

David had three children from his previous marriage. When we moved into a comfortable rental home at Willoughby with his two adult children, Toni and Arch, we had an instant family. I shared a bedroom with Toni, sleeping in a single bed next to a window that overlooked a lovely garden. I spent a lot of time there daydreaming, feeling homesick for my grandparents and Watson's Creek. I liked the idea of being in a family, but felt alone, ill at ease and didn't know how to behave with these strangers. Arch and Toni were kind, but I don't think they were happy with this intrusion into their lives, because our time together was short. I wish we had stayed in contact. Now it's too late, because they're no longer alive. On 'This Is Your Life' I was introduced as the only daughter of Kay and David Dally-Watkins. Can you imagine how that upset Toni and Arch? They complained about the misrepresentation to the program, whose researchers had been briefed, not surprisingly, by my mother. During the show I worried what might be revealed or who might surprise me from behind the automatic sliding doors, but I remained composed. By then I was an expert at concealing my true feelings.

When David's career began to falter, Mother, David and I moved into a house at Chatswood with a share-kitchen and bathroom. I slept on the verandah, which had a tarpaulin to conceal my quarters from the front street. I thought sleeping outside was terrific – it reminded me of Les's and my cousins' outdoor bedrooms at Watson's Creek. Mother and David's bedroom opened onto my verandah and we ate all our meals in their room. The confined space ensured I was always within earshot of the accusations my mother aimed at David: 'Why didn't you come home earlier? What were you doing? I can't trust you. Go away, you're only going to hurt me.' Mother was suspicious of David as she was of all men. She expected to be betrayed and subconsciously wanted to destroy her relationship with David before she could be hurt. My reaction to these rows was to daydream, wander the streets and pretend they weren't happening. Maybe Mother was so used to arguing with Gran that she didn't know how to conduct a relationship successfully. Gradually, quarrelling became the way she related to all those closest to her.

I'm not sure how my mother and David's relationship ended. Mother probably pushed David away and he probably gave up. I missed him, his protection and having a father figure. When David left us, he joined the reserve of officers in regional New South Wales for the rest of the war and never remarried. Tragically a runaway lorry injured fifty-eight people, including David, during the 1948 Anzac Day Parade in Sydney. David died shortly afterwards in hospital. I was sad to hear of his death, but neither Mother nor I went to his funeral. I don't think Mother was heartbroken that her marriage was over, but we never talked about it. Nor did we ever discuss tricky personal issues, menstruation or sex. Only a warning that men were not to be trusted was issued regularly: 'Keep away from them or they will ruin your life.'

We struggled on and formed new alliances. I loved Willoughby Girls' High and years later entered its Hall of Fame. Keen to make friends, I joined the Girl Guides and Mother made my uniform. I felt proud and important to belong to a group – to be a 'somebody'. Being a *persona non grata* still haunted me. It took most of my life to realise I could never shake the ghosts of my past.

I don't know how Mother became friends with Em Loftberg who lived in a mansion at Mosman with sweeping harbour views, but my mother had such elegance that she attracted friends who were much better off financially and socially than she. I had never been in such a grand house. Even though the windows were plastered in brown paper because of the war, I imagined I was in Hollywood as I descended a spiral staircase or looked out from one of the balconies to the harbour. One sleepover we had there was unforgettable. It was the end of May 1942 and I was staring at a full moon from the balcony outside the bedroom I was sharing with Mother. Suddenly, an air-raid alarm sounded and continued longer than usual. We gathered, wondering what was happening, when the Loftberg boy ran home yelling, 'Quickly, the Japs are coming. Get under the stairs.' We hid, listening to the vague wireless reports of an explosion, until there was an announcement that the incident was over. Japanese midget submarines had entered the Harbour and shelled Sydney's eastern suburbs. One had exploded at Rose Bay, and we were told no one was injured. Later we learned that some nineteen navy personnel were killed when the ferry *Kuttabul*, which was used as a barrack ship, was torpedoed. The submarine incident was enough to send us and many other Sydneysiders packing. Grandfather pleaded by telegram: 'Bring June home. Sydney is not safe. The Japs are coming. Love Dad.' There was no way my mother would return to Watson's Creek, so we took the steam train to Tamworth.

We listened to the wireless for news of the war, but, as a teenager in Tamworth, it was as if the war didn't exist. I didn't have family involved and I became preoccupied with boys and attending Tamworth High. Tamworth was like going home. There was a comforting sense of familiarity that had been missing in Sydney. Nothing much had changed since we had last visited in Uncle Sid's car. There were the wide streets, green spaces and expansive skies I had longed for in Sydney and we were nearer to Watson's Creek and Springvale.

As a war refugee the fact that my mother was a single parent didn't raise too many eyebrows. In any case, it was true that her absent husband was away on duty. We moved into the widowed dentist Mr Newman's modern home in Upper Street and, in return for board, Mother looked after it and his primary school-age children, Terry, Wendy and Michael. Mother and I shared a bedroom with a window that separated our beds.

Tamworth brought happy times for me. For starters, there was no one with whom my mother argued. Mother and I each made new friends and became reacquainted with those who knew Grandfather. Like Cyril Cahill, the pharmacist, whom Grandfather admired because he still drove his old car when he could afford a newer model. Mother met up with wealthy graziers she knew from around Watson's Creek and Bendemeer when they came to town. Mother would join her friends for a whisky or sherry and sometimes a silver-service lunch at the Central and Tudor hotels. Meanwhile, I found some freedom. Sometimes I'd tell Mother I was going for a walk and then I'd tour the different churches in town. I didn't understand denominations so I went to all the churches and enjoyed the ambience and the singing. I was at peace and didn't feel lonely.

Tamworth introduced me to the silver screen and I discovered the film stars I had only read about until then: Jean Harlow, Clark Gable, Marlene Dietrich, and so on. Moving pictures were beautiful and romantic. The violence and sex pervasive in today's films didn't exist. Going to the picture theatre for the Saturday matinee or evening session was my week's highlight. At interval, my mother and I each had a milkshake at one of two adjoining cafés run by Stratis Vellis. Jack Kouvelis owned the Capital and Regent picture theatres and Harry Kouvelis managed them. Jim Contagos ran the Civic Restaurant, where we treated ourselves to fish and chips wrapped in newspaper. He came to Australia as a teenager in 1937 and fought in World War II. All these men had come to Australia from Greece with nothing. They never complained and worked hard to become successful small-business operators. I admired them.

Tennis was the 'in' sport in Tamworth, so Mother saved to buy me a racquet; we never asked Grandfather for money. This made me determined to be the best player at school and make Mother proud, so I challenged the champion tennis player at school, Una Joseph, one of the daughters of Bertie Joseph who founded the *Northern Daily Leader*. Una let me win a few games and then swiftly wiped me off the court. My sporting ambition was always greater than my ability.

After school, my best friend Joan Cooksley, who had also left Sydney because of the war, and I headed straight to Rackham and Paul's to buy a cream horn – a flaky pastry shaped into a cornet and filled with fresh cream. If I was really hungry, I bought a one-penny meat pie. After that we'd stroll along Peel Street, the main street in town that was lined with department stores: P.G. Smith's, Fosseys, Money Savers and Thacker's. Only Treloars exists today, but it has undergone a makeover from the days when it had a cash-cage in which money was placed for payment. A pulley system whizzed the contraption to the next floor where the accountant received payment, then shot it back with a receipt and change.

My school captain Muriel Cable, Joan and I spent much of our time checking out the boys. Mother would never have allowed me to go out alone with a boy, but she didn't mind me talking to one over the fence at home. Desperate to catch the boys' attention, I insisted she shorten the skirt of my black uniform. I didn't consciously flirt, but showed off at the public swimming pool, a favourite boy-spotting place. I never achieved my aim to be the best swimmer at school, though trying made me reasonably good and, keen to catch the boys' eyes, I concentrated on improving my style. Instead of using the diving board, I dived from the side of the pool with as pretty a style as possible. At the pool, my girlfriends and I drooled over Ian Handley (who put on a diving performance to impress the girls), Tamworth High's diving champion Neville Girdler and Bill Cousens. I wanted Bill to notice me, but he had eyes only for Marg Graham. They were meant for each other, shared a love of music and were part of the Tamworth Musical Society. Not surprisingly, their son Peter Cousens inherited their talents and became famous throughout Australia and in London as a musical theatre performer.

On the way to the pool I walked past Joe Faulkenmire's music and sport store to see if his younger brother Ken was there. I had a huge crush on Ken, who had dimples, dark curly hair and olive skin. He seemed interested in me too, later admitting to splashing about in the pool to attract my attention. Ken gave me my first kiss as we were walking through Anzac Park on the way home from school. After that, he showed no interest in me. I was devastated. Ken had set eyes on and eventually married June Ridd, whose family had a large property. Nevertheless, Ken gave me a wallet-sized photo of himself and I had the audacity to give him an A4-sized professional photo of me taken by Jan Solomons – a male photographer who ironically had married a lady christened 'Neville'.

Jan Solomons' photographs of me changed my life. One day Jan came across us on the street and told my mother that he thought I was photogenic and that he would like to take some photos of me. She was flattered and excited that a professional photographer had noticed her daughter. Mother trusted Jan's eye, having known his father Bertie, who used to run the studio. Bertie had taken photos of my mother, often as a bridesmaid but never as a bride. It was suspected he fancied my mother, and her brothers and sisters teased her about him.

The night before my photographic sitting, Mother tied my long hair in rags and shaped it into long curls. Jan promised to telephone us when the photos were ready. We waited three weeks, fretting that the photos were a failure, before Jan told us to come to the studio. Many hand-painted, large portraits of me filled his shop-front windows. The hand-colouring (an art that died out when colour film was invented) explained the delay. 'The corner of Upper and Brisbane streets never looked the same again,' Jan later told 'This Is Your Life'. 'The results were so good I recommended to her mother that she be taken to Sydney to enter the modelling field.' I don't know whether Mother thought I had model potential, but, when Jan raised the possibility, she didn't hesitate: 'Let's go.' We left Tamworth with nothing except Jan's photos, our clothes and a little money my mother had saved. I left school aged 16 and enrolled in the school of life. I have not stopped learning since.

It was 1944. The Allies were winning the war, so it was safe to return to Sydney. We stayed at a hotel on Anzac Parade in Kensington. Our room was small and the bathroom was down the hall. Accommodation was almost impossible to come by due to the war. The noise of the traffic and the drinkers who spilled out onto the street after the six-o'clock swill and stayed drinking in the gutter made it difficult to sleep. We were poor and we hated it.

Quickly my mother began to organise. With the war having reduced the demand for advertising, there was little need for models, except for appearances in mail-order catalogues. Modelling was almost non-existent as an industry. My mother said modelling would get me nowhere: 'You should enrol in a secretarial course.' She thought it would lead to a secure job. Grandfather thought modelling was an unrealistic notion too. However, I thought secretarial school would be dull and refused to be swayed. So Mother found work for both of us at Mousoley's dress shop in Market Street. She joined the sales staff and was in her element working among the fine gowns bought by society ladies. I was trained as a junior window dresser. The Mousoleys were a fine Lebanese family and treated their staff like family, but I betrayed their trust. At the end of one day, I borrowed a black dress with a blue inset on the bodice without their permission. I had been invited on a date and intended to return it the next day. However I slept late, forgot to bring it back and hoped the Mousoleys wouldn't notice it was missing for one day. Mrs Mousoley confronted me and I told her what happened. I still feel ashamed. I learned then that I could never get away with anything. It was a good lesson.

In a lunch break from work one day, Mother and I visited Farmer's department store, which straddled the corners of George, Market and Pitt streets. Mother decided to ask if I could model for them. In new outfits Mother had sewn, we took the store's lift (then controlled by a lift driver) to the advertising department. Mother did all the talking at the interview. With my puppy fat, my homemade dress and no make-up I thought I looked more like a milkmaid than a model, but perhaps that's what made me different from the others. I had a wholesome freshness, thick light brown hair, rosy cheeks and good teeth.

When Australian models started working overseas, the European model agencies also liked their natural, outdoors look compared to the sophisticated, bony appearance of the Continental models. These days aged 17 would have been a bit late to start such a youth-obsessed career. What's more, I'm five feet six inches tall – lofty for a mannequin in my day, but not Amazonian enough by current standards. Now five feet nine inches is regarded as the absolute minimum height for a girl to work as a model. In my day, models were required to be SSW – a standard size ten. Although my figure was the requisite shape, I was not a beauty like some of the models of my era, so I was amazed to hear, 'Could she model a hat tomorrow for our catalogue?' Could I! I was thrilled at the thought of the catalogue reaching the locals at Watson's Creek. I was paid ten shillings and sixpence (equivalent to one dollar and five cents) for a half-day's work, and thought I had hit the jackpot. The money I earned from that first modelling assignment in 1944 remains my proudest financial reward.

I took a day off work at Mousoley's to present myself at Squire Morgan's studio, located on the rooftop of a city building. I wore my own clothes for the shoot and a light application of lipstick, which Squire used as a focal point for the camera lens. Squire was an experienced black-and-white catalogue photographer and had just begun to work with colour film. In hindsight, it was an incredible experience to pose for colour photos in 1944. Colour photography was a new medium and the camera shutter was slow, therefore the model had to remain very still. Kodacolour film for prints, the world's first true colour negative film, had been on the world market for only a couple of years. A combination of improvements to the speed of film and breakthroughs in camera technology over the next few years would change modelling forever. But, in those days, fashion photography was a rigid affair, relying on clever lighting and interesting backgrounds for outdoor shoots. When film speed increased and electronic flash was invented, models could move, dance, leap.

I thought posing for a photo would be a cinch. It proved exhausting. Squire used a studio-mounted camera on a tripod, which was heavy and therefore remained in the same spot. A steel-rod stand with a vertically adjustable curved metal clamp was fitted at the back of my waist and neck to help keep me from moving. Squire then adjusted the overhead, boom and back lights, and ducked beneath a black cloth that concealed the camera to check the focus. He readjusted the lights, checked the focus again and from under the black cloth I heard: 'Okay, close your eyes, tilt your head, lift your chin slightly, hold everything, wet your lips, steady, open your eyes . . . smile.'

5   Mannequin moments

My first fashion parade is vivid in my mind: Mother beaming at me from the audience; me not knowing how to walk as a mannequin, as ramp models were called, and trying my best to copy the other girls, who probably knew little more about professional modelling. 'June, you were wonderful. You were the best,' Mother assured. I knew I wasn't, but was determined to become the best – for her. From the outset, my mother was a driving force in the rise of my career. I had only secured the in-store engagement with Farmer's because she wasn't prepared to wait and see if it would fulfil its promise to contact me for another assignment. As the forthcoming season's fashion parades approached, she approached them again. Her determination for me to succeed influenced the way I approached modelling as a serious full-time career and this didn't abate even when I thought I had made it to the top. It made me strive to become a 'somebody' as a way for both of us to overcome the shame of our past. Just as strong a motivator was the financial need to provide enough money to support us both. While some girls approached modelling as a stopgap until they met Mr Right, my mother's experience made me aware that I couldn't rely on a man to come along and provide for me.

Deportment schools and model agencies didn't exist; mothers stayed at home to take their daughters' bookings. There was no such thing as model portfolios used to tout for work, so I waited for people to contact me. With only a handful of models working in Sydney, I became known quickly to the management of department stores and advertisers, but it took about six months to make modelling a full-time occupation. In the meantime, my mother's income supplemented my earnings and I took a job as a part-time make-up artist at Charles E. Blanks – a cinema advertising company. I had only just begun to apply my own make-up, but that was good enough for them. I loved meeting the film actresses used in the commercials.

Charles E. Blanks also sponsored me as an entrant in the 1945 Miss Australia Quest. As part of a fundraising component to the quest, entrants sold one-shilling badges that featured their portrait as a way to raise funds for the war widows' appeal. I was busy working during the day, and without a network of people to help off-load the badges I didn't sell as many as other entrants. I became convinced I was wasting my time and withdrew before any elimination round. What a relief! At that stage, I lacked the confidence to withstand the scrutiny of being judged by strangers. Yet, in years to come, I would judge for that quest and many others.

Fashion catalogue work initially provided my bread and butter. The results of some of my early modelling assignments didn't appear as photographs but as artists' sketches. These were mostly line drawings, though some were tonal and coloured and the resemblance was apparent. Gradually bookings for newspaper and magazine advertisements increased. The latter included posing for intensely coloured cover photographic portraits for various publications, including *The Australian Women's Weekly* and *Woman's Day*. For one of the *Weekly*'s covers I was featured wearing a red-and-white checked apron and cheerily making a blue cake in a matching blue kitchen fitted out with the latest home appliances. I believe it's an image that documents the new era of consumerism, the emergence of white goods, and post-war society's idea of a woman as the glamorous stay-at-home wife. Although the kitchen was where I was most comfortable at home and I aspired to provide a good home life for a family one day, at the time of that photograph I had no idea how every career move I made in fact rebelled against the homemaker image.

For some early assignments I wore little make-up. I learned to hurriedly apply Vaseline over a light lipstick to give my lips a gloss and to my eyelashes to make them lustrous. Mascara came in a cake form and needed to be applied with water. As water often wasn't available in a photographic studio, I would spit on the mascara brush, which made the mascara gooier and stick better to my lashes than a water mix did. I would still use that mascara if it were available today. It was wonderful, except for the brown rivulets that trickled down your face if you cried! Gradually I began to use blush and foundation and eye shadow. There weren't any model 'tricks' to add to our tote bags. False eyelashes and hairpieces did not come into vogue until the 1960s. Bras may have been padded, but cosmetic surgery was unknown. Models had to be naturally beautiful. Nor were there stylists, hairdressers and make-up artists to ensure we looked the part. We supplied and applied our own make-up and hair products, stockings, shoes and accessories, which we stuffed into tote bags and hatboxes to take with us for each assignment. Transparent headscarves were an essential part of this kit. In the rush of changing clothes during a parade, we put scarves over our heads and tied the ends under our chins, so no matter how fitted the clothes were we didn't disturb our make-up, hair or stain the garments. I still use one at home.

Making sure our tote bags were well stocked and our clothes and shoes were up to scratch took a substantial bite out of our earnings. If we were doing a commercial photograph, whether it was to sell a refrigerator or a brand of cheese, we were expected to supply our own clothes. If it was a fashion advertisement to sell a dress or hat, we

TOP This baby photograph of me with Mother was taken by Bertie Solomons. He was the father of Jan Solomons, who photographed me when I was 16 years old and suggested I should go to Sydney and model. (*Photo by G.A. Solomons, Tamworth*)

LEFT Aged 3, wearing my mother's bangle and necklace in my grandmother's garden at Watson's Creek and practising my future model pose.

RIGHT By age 6, I have my own bangles, imitating my mother. My hair has been put in rags overnight and brushed out into a frizz. (*Photo by G.A. Solomons, Tamworth*)

A rare Skewes family photo. Grandmother and Grandfather with nine of their twelve children. Sam died age 92, Sarah, aged 87. (Clockwise from the back row at left: Jim, Oswald, Bella, Len, Thelma, Jack, Kay (my mother), Sam, Ida, Sarah, Elsie)

LEFT My mother on the banks of the Macdonald River, Bendemeer, elegantly smoking. (*Photo by David Dally-Watkins*)

RIGHT An Identity Studio photo taken walking along Market Street in Sydney, wearing my Willoughby Girls' High School uniform. My friend Lorraine (right) married an American soldier and never returned to Australia. They say she died of loneliness and a broken heart.

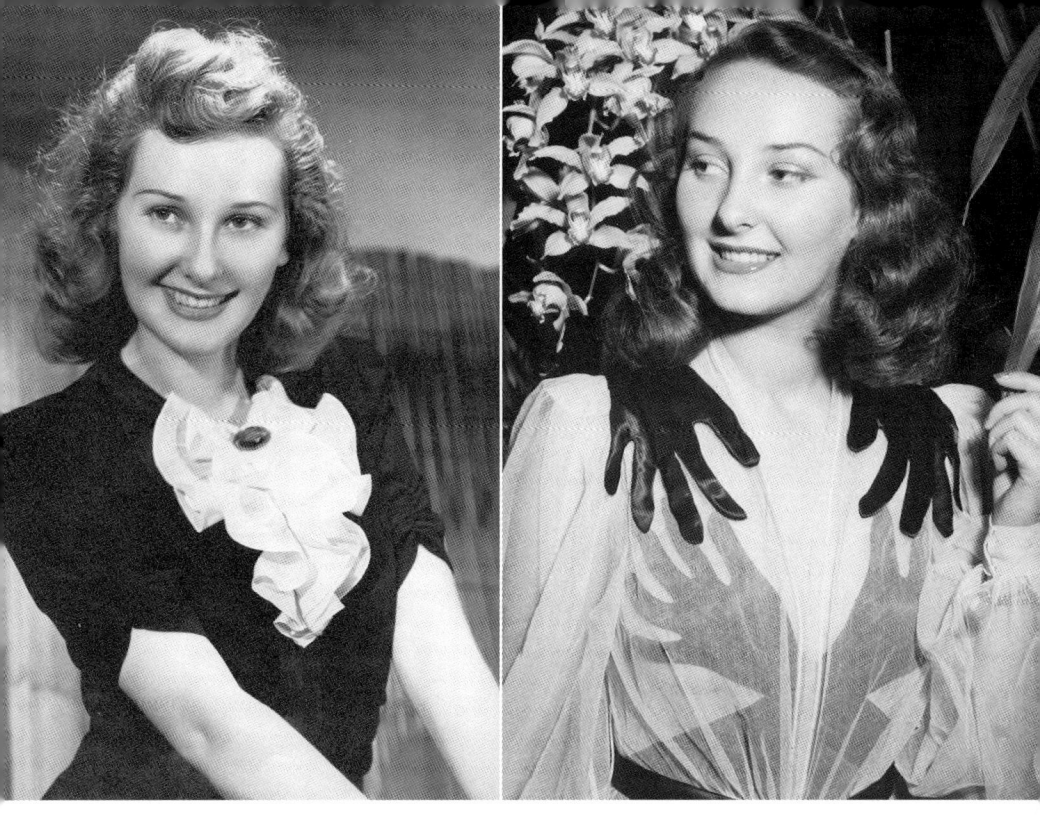

TOP OPPOSITE As a 16-year-old Tamworth High School student, my course in life was changed when this photo was taken and Jan Solomons suggested a career in modelling. My long hair had been put into rags overnight and next morning wound around my mother's finger into curls. (*Photo by Jan Solomons*)

OPPOSITE Mother and I return to Sydney after our war sojourn in Tamworth.

LEFT At age 17, my modelling career was just beginning. (*Photo by Barry Louden Photography*)

RIGHT Innocently modelling 'The Gasper' negligee and night dress in Mark Foy's Mannequin Parade, aged 17. I had not realised that the appliqué on the gown looked like black satin hands – no wonder the audience gasped.

TOP This is another of my early modelling photos. I am growing up. (*Photo by Barry Louden Photography*)

LEFT 13 June 1945. My 18th birthday formal photo was taken at Monte Luke Studios, Castlereagh Street, situated opposite the old Australia Hotel.

OPPOSITE A photo that emphasised the country girl's natural look, taken by the famous photographer, John Lee, when I was 18.

TOP LEFT Little did I know how this shot was going to be used.

TOP RIGHT As it turned out, I was actually posing for a cigarette advertisement. The cigarette and smoke were drawn in later and the watch rubbed out.

LOWER LEFT Fellow fashion-show models, Joan Fahey (at left), Marguerite Marr (centre), and I (age 18), with our chaperone, on our way to Brisbane for Curzon's Department Store parade in 1945.

Model's tote bag

Basic necessities

* See-through headscarf
* Skin-tone underwear
* Waist panties
* Strapless bra
* Black bra and waist pants
* White and skin-tone bikini pants
* Skin-tone half-slip
* One bikini
* One one-piece swimsuit (Maillot)
* High-heel sling-backs for summer
* High-heel beige pump shoes
* High-heel black pump shoes
* One pair gold or silver evening shoes
* One pair flats in fashion
* Two pairs pale pantihose (10 denier)
* One pair black pantihose (10 denier)

All in good condition with fashion changes each season. Watch fashion changes each season.

* Box of tampons – use when modelling swimwear
* Underarm deodorant
* Perfume
* Collection of scarves – small and large
* Collection of costume jewellery – ear studs
* Collection of belts
* Leg tan lotion
* Make-up kit
* Hair accessories

supplied our own accessories. Therefore, the way we dressed and looked attracted the interest of other women. They looked to us for advice, and because there were so few full-time models, we became familiar faces and household names. The cult and promotion of the celebrity was yet to develop, so we were truly unassuming superstars who, at the same time, were very real to Australians.

Gradually clients employed stylists to attend photo shoots to make sure the models looked just right; and dressers were on hand at department-store parades – once to my detriment. During a parade at Curzon's department store, a dresser zipped up the side of my frock and in the process ripped off a mole. As I made my way down the catwalk, blood oozed through the dress. That wasn't, of course, the only time something went awry during a parade. Farmer's had constructed a grand staircase from which swimwear-clad models were to descend. The moment I put my wedge-heeled shoe on the edge of the top step I slipped. As I slid on my bottom to the base of the staircase, a shell bracelet I was wearing broke and the tiny shells bobbed down each step with me. What else could I do but pick myself up, smile and continue, thankfully to the sympathetic applause of the audience. Once Betty Girling, my madcap friend with the flame tresses, didn't see the end of a catwalk and simply walked straight off it and into the audience.

Fittings for manufacturers' showroom parades were the least glamorous part of my work, requiring me to stand for long periods while garments were adjusted in size, with much changing in and out of them between the clothing racks. In contrast, I looked forward to working in department-store parades. They were exciting, lucrative and lavish, hour-long productions that became major social events. With each parade my full turns, half turns, entrances and exits improved. Detail was important to me. I would carry a long-handled umbrella, holding it to the front with one hand directed up the stem and the other downwards to create an attractive angle. When I came to a standstill at the end of the catwalk, I placed the tip of the umbrella on the platform, held the handle with an arched wrist. I studied how to remove gloves gracefully as I walked and smiled at the audience, and how to hold a skirt to make it swell like a sail. I trained myself to take off a coat without exposing the lining, trail it gently behind me, then place it over the crook of my arm, slightly behind my body so as not to distract from what I was wearing. A sports jacket was flung jauntily over one shoulder. Collars and pockets were touched lightly to draw attention to them. Every movement had to be graceful and feminine: walking so the legs moved only from the thighs down, holding the body still and straight, and moving arms from the shoulders, but not the shoulders themselves. To give the appearance of a long neck, I imagined my head had been pulled from the top of my ears and the centre of my head was trying to touch the ceiling. Projecting expression was important, but I baulked at doing anything outrageous. I was quite self-conscious though I smiled more than the other models. It wasn't stagecraft, just radiation of the enjoyment I felt from this work. Very often my mother was in the audience so I would give her a smile, then extend that greeting to welcome every other woman in the audience, as though each one were my mother.

 David Jones' parades on the seventh-floor of the city store were elegant affairs. Women wore hats and gloves, delicately ate cucumber sandwiches and sipped tea whilst mannequins walked elegantly around a circular catwalk. Romantic instrumental background music accentuated this refined salon scene. I always requested the band or pianist perform Charles Trenet's 'Mamselle' or 'La Mer' for my walk on. It made me feel as though I could glide effortlessly. Often 'A Pretty Girl is Like a Melody' was played.

 Curzon's always used me for its Brisbane and Sydney parades. Its owner, Ashley Buckingham, told me I was his favourite model and advised me in a fatherly way about my career. His flirtation was harmless and I enjoyed the way he treated me like a lady. Feminism has quashed this kind of rapport between men and women, but for what purpose? I'm sad about many things the feminists introduced.

Mark Foy's department store, the grand exterior of which remains on the corner of Elizabeth and Liverpool Streets, had the most inventive parades and outlandish sets. But they were still a far cry from the shock tactics of modern fashion shows – one recently resorted to setting rats loose on the runway to scurry between the legs of scantily clad models. Mark Foy's ideas of creativity extended to a group of models walking around the perimeter of an ice-skating rink while skaters went through their routine on the ice. Foy's garments were also daring for the time. Modelling a full-length night dress and negligee for a parade, I heard gasps of astonishment from the audience. I had no idea what the commotion was about. Now I do. Black satin hands appliquéd onto the bodice of a cream net top appeared to be groping my breasts. The press referred to the gown as 'The Gasper' and someone complained to a newspaper that I was disgusting for wearing it.

Innocence is the enemy of many models. Early in my career, a photographer who was much older than I was told me to take off my clothes and give him a kiss during a photo session. I refused and quickly left his studio. I didn't tell anyone about it, even Mother. I thought it was my fault, that there must have been something bad about me that had provoked him. I understood the difference between a sleazy proposition and when a photographer told me to imagine something romantic, like being in the arms of a handsome man, as a way to encourage emotions that would be reflected through expression and the eyes onto photographic film. Expression is all-important in photographs to show that there is someone 'at home'. Already less relaxed and free-and-easy than other girls my age, this incident only made me more reserved around photographers. Some of them thought I was haughty even after one of the models came to my defence saying, 'June's not stuck up, she's just shy.'

When I began modelling there were no model agents whose role is to protect the interests of the models. All the fashion photographers were men who could sway a client to use or not use a particular model. This gave the photographer significant power over the model. The arrival of model agencies and the supermodels of today have helped change the balance of power, though there are still unprofessional operators who dwell on the industry's edge, ready to take advantage of unworldly girls. Thankfully, I was privileged to work mostly with decent, professional photographers, many of whom became life-long friends.

Among them was the charming and brilliant Max Dupain, a truly talented photographer. Max kindly told *The Sunday Herald Magazine* in 1949 that I had the characteristic features required of a model: 'facial symmetry, fine skin, eyes clear and wide-spaced, good teeth – and a naturalness of expression'. Gervaise Purcell was another one of my favourites. He took many of my portraits, mostly for hat advertisements. Gervaise had been an assistant to one of the early greats, John Lee, whose wife Sandra was probably Sydney's first unofficial stylist, helping the models with their hair and make-up and adding some glamour to the shots by providing a marcasite brooch or a pair of earrings to set off a garment. Gervaise defected to Monte Luke's studio in Castlereagh Street, which was ultimately taken over by John Hearder, where everyone who could afford it had their family portrait or wedding photos taken, just as everyone had an Identity Studios' photo of themself walking along a city street. Identity Studios usually stationed a photographer on Market Street, who snapped passers-by and gave them a ticket with which they could order a photographic print. Noel Hickey was even-tempered and every model's friend. Some of my earliest photos were by Barry Louden.

The quirky Reg Johnson juggled the Jantzen swimwear account and photographing cancer patients' operations for surgeon Dr Alan Lilley at the Royal Prince Alfred Hospital. Dr Lilley was deeply interested in photography and accompanied us on many shoots along with

Eric Longley, who modelled occasionally to fund his way through medical studies. When one of his professors saw Eric's photo with me in a publication, Eric was promptly given an ultimatum: modelling or medicine. Seemingly, the two were mutually exclusive. Reg eventually left the fashion world to pursue medical photography full-time, but while he had the Jantzen account, he was able to indulge in his favourite pastime: waterskiing. It was no coincidence that Reg usually chose the Hawkesbury River for location shoots. Standing in swimming trunks, his muscular body dripping wet, Reg would take the required shots, then disappear up the river before the next photo session and a picnic lunch. It was always a great day to work with Reg and his wife, Jeannie, who managed his studio. Reg tried to teach me to waterski, but I wasn't very good and, like his other favourite swimwear models – Dorn Fraser (not the former Olympic swimmer, Dawn) and Fairy Folkes – I didn't want to get my hair wet and redo it, as well as ruin my make-up and have to reapply it for the next shoot. When on location shoots, if there were no public toilets, models changed in the back seat of the photographer's car or behind a tree or a boulder, sometimes screened by a towel held up by another model.

Like today, the fashion industry worked one season ahead, so we'd suffer in swimsuits in winter and fur coats in summer. For swimsuit photos with other photographers, I went only as far as Bondi or Tamarama Beach where the rock formations created an interesting backdrop. For other location shoots, I was photographed in Hyde Park and the Domain. There was no such thing as going interstate or overseas for a photographic shoot!

Scamp was another swimwear label I modelled. Its manufacturer Ben Turner had been a pioneering parachutist whose factory supplied parachutes for Australian soldiers during World War II before he converted the production line to turn out swimsuits. The engineer in Ben was easy to scratch. Whenever Ben visited my mother, he'd talk for hours, if we let him, about the technical feat required to produce the perfect swimsuit. Although Scamp swimwear was considered somewhat daring, the bottoms of its two-piece costumes always covered the navel and had a half-skirt attached across the front. I never modelled a bikini. Only a few years later some of my models were chased off Sydney beaches by inspector Aub Laidlaw who measured the distance between bikini bottoms and tops to assess a costume's respectability.

Veteran *Women's Weekly* photographer Bob Cleland took many of my professional shots. During World War II he and Ernie Nutt produced the first colour photos for the *Weekly*. Bob and I worked well together in the *Weekly*'s studio on the lower ground floor of the Grand United Building in Castlereagh Street – where I was one day destined to have my deportment school and model agency. 'You've got to be the unsexiest model in Sydney,' he'd say teasingly. 'I can't understand how you can be successful when the other mannequins are more beautiful.' He was right. I suspected Ray Leighton, a leading photographer with a curt nature, who my mother said taught her new swear words, thought the same of me. Noting my adaptability as a model to the *Sunday Telegraph*, Ray commented that I was 'as good for toothpaste as she is for gowns'. Somehow, it just didn't seem like a compliment. Once he wrote on a professional photo he had taken of me, 'To my favourite model' – but I bet he said that to all the girls.

Laurie Le Guay had a formidable artistic reputation, but I didn't find it easy to work with him. He was gruff and I was convinced he didn't like me. Some models would answer him back, but I was sensitive to his abrupt manner. His wife, Anne Price-Jones, certainly knew how to answer back. As the supervisor for fashion photography at Farmer's, Anne would speak her mind when she was watching over the photo shoots for Farmer's advertisements at Laurie's studio. They would transform the studio into a war of words. Their volatile marriage didn't last as long as the enduring photographs they produced together.

My friendship with various photographers continues, thanks to a group of retired News Limited photographers who formed a social group, the Tutsitala Club. The boys invited me to become one of two female members (the other was Adele Hurley, daughter of the famous Antarctic photographer Frank Hurley). Male press photographers had been notoriously wild, but over the years they have mellowed. The club's former president, Ron Iredale, and partner Melva are great mates of mine. Ron photographed many models from my agency as 'page three girls' in the *Daily Telegraph*. They were in safe hands with him. He affectionately calls me 'Miss' and I like it.

6   Leaving Mother

When Mother and I could afford it and there was a lull between modelling assignments, we returned to Watson's Creek by overnight steam train. With the sweaty smell of steam and soot that covered our faces came the promise of escaping the constriction of my mother's constant companionship. Alighting the train at Kootingal, we'd meet the postman who took us by car to Watson's Creek. On these journeys Mother and I would talk about ambitious plans for my career. Mostly these short spells from Sydney gave me time to regenerate, take in the country air and go without make-up. However, these trips became fewer as bookings for modelling jobs and mannequin parades filled my schedule.

    In Sydney, we moved from the hotel at Kensington to a one-room, share-kitchen and share-bathroom at Rushcutters Bay. My mother had her heart set on living in Sydney's leafy, established eastern suburbs of Vaucluse or Bellevue Hill. She wanted people to think I was a born-and-bred Sydney eastern suburbs girl. She knew that if I spoke well, had good manners and was well presented, I could mix with anyone and people wouldn't be able to tell that I had started out at a one-teacher bush school. She believed if we could make it from Watson's Creek, we could make it anywhere.

On the tram home from the city to Rushcutters Bay one day I recognised the beautiful model Pat Firman. She looked desperately sad and I later discovered that Pat used to live in Java and had an unhappy marriage to a Dutchman who had ill-treated her until she escaped and returned to live with her mother at Rose Bay. We became friendly through modelling, with Dorn Fraser once billing us as twins – a transparent ruse as we clearly had different family names and didn't look alike. What Pat and I shared in common was the burden of absent fathers, no siblings, and being the centre of each of our mother's worlds. We didn't discuss our situations, but instinctively understood each other's lives. I caught a glimpse of my mother whenever I visited Pat and her mother, Mickey, at their Rose Bay home. Mickey was proud of her only daughter and both financially and emotionally needy. I too was beginning to feel trapped by the nature of a one-to-one relationship with my mother. To escape the confines of our small quarters I had begun to rise at dawn, get dressed and sit in Rushcutters Bay Park until it was time for my first modelling job of the day. Regardless of Pat and Mickey's relationship, it didn't stop Pat's success and she became a founding television panellist on 'Beauty and the Beast'. At the height of her television career she found a lump in her breast. She died in her forties, her beauty ravaged by disease. In hindsight, perhaps it was each of our mother's dependence and focus that determined our lives.

As my career took off, Mother and I moved again, this time into a small, sparsely furnished one-bedroom flat in an apartment block at the Kings Cross end of Williams Street. It was a move away from the ritzy eastern suburbs, but the flat was affordable – almost impossible to come by so soon after the war, and we didn't have to pay key money. An old lounge and oversized table and sideboard dominated the small living area, the kitchenette was big enough for only one person, and our single beds were separated by a narrow space. We had a gas stove and placed small, round asbestos mats between the stovetop and cooking pots for gentler cooking. When my grandfather sold Springvale he sent us enough money so we could afford to replace the icebox with a refrigerator. Most importantly, the flat had a telephone beside which we kept an exercise book for noting my modelling appointments.

Our flat overlooked Brougham Street, where a hotel, now called O'Malley's, stood. After the hotel closed at six o'clock, we would often hear its drunken patrons fighting and using bad language on the street. The Cross had a dark side of illegal card games, brothels and a growing drug trade of which I was naïvely unaware. Nevertheless the Cross was like a village then, with tree-lined streets and Art Deco buildings reminiscent of Paris. Some of our neighbours were of Italian, Middle Eastern and Armenian origin, sharing their traditional recipes and friendship with us. Cooking was my way to relax and be creative, so on weekends I would test their recipes.

Mother became a good friend of our neighbour, Rosie Howarth. We were all proud – and Mother and I a bit envious – of Rosie's daughter, Joan, as we watched her romance with Geoff Plater unfold. From our flat window Mother and I would see Geoff, a World War II veteran, pull up in his smart car to take Joan on a date. Geoff came from a highly regarded pioneering family. The Plater family owned the historical Ranelagh Estate at Darling Point, which has since been pulled down and replaced by a large apartment block of the same name. When Geoff and Joan married, they lived on the estate, and their daughters could just go through a hole in the fence to their school, Ascham.

When Mother and Rosie Howarth secretly entered me in the Twentieth Century Fox competition for Miss Kangaroo, the title seemed a dubious honour. The prize, however, certainly was an attractive escape – a trip to Hollywood to help promote the romantic adventure *Kangaroo*, which starred Maureen O'Hara, Bud Tingwell and Chips Rafferty. The judging was held at the Trocadero dance hall in George Street. I wore a dark tulle skirt, cinched with belt, and a white V-necked, sleeveless top that was one of Mother's last-minute homespun efforts. A panel of five judges asked predictable questions like, 'Why do you want to go to Hollywood?' I wasn't nervous. Rosie and Mother had convinced me I'd walk, if not hop, away with the title.

As it turned out, I came runner-up to Loretta North, a sweet, fresh-faced country girl who had begun to work as a model in Sydney. Mother was furious about what she believed was an unfair decision. She said one of the judges told her, 'We didn't give it to June because she can make her own way to Hollywood. She can make her own way in life. The girl who won would not otherwise have that opportunity.' Not placated, Mother and Rosie spent hours penning a nasty letter, giggling as they were doing it, to one of the judges, Sid Albright, who was then head of Twentieth Century Fox in Australia. Little did she realise that Sid would be our neighbour years later, when we moved to our grand apartment in Lower Beach Road, Rushcutters Bay. Though I could have done with that trip to the USA, the judges were right to give it to Loretta. I was already successful and becoming Miss Kangaroo opened doors for the lovely Loretta. After her American trip, she continued to work as a model in Sydney, but sadly eventually succumbed to multiple sclerosis. I never entered a quest again.

Another way Mother showed her support for me was to proudly cut out pictures of me and paste them into scrapbooks. Mother and I would stay up late on Saturday nights to wait for the Sunday newspapers to hit the streets around midnight at the Cross. The Sunday papers were full of advertisements, and therefore usually photos of me. Feeling guilty about Mother's unglamorous life and my success, I was thrilled when I helped to secure a photographic modelling assignment for my mother. She held a cake of Knight's Castile toilet soap for a print advertisement. But it was to be a one-off experience. I resolved that if I made it to the top, Mother would be there with me; we were a team. She had made sacrifices for me, so whatever success I had I wanted to share with her.

As time passed, Mother became a virtual prisoner in our flat. If my mother went out, she risked missing a booking, so mostly she stayed in and sewed clothes for other people to while away her time and earn extra money. We bought a new electric Singer sewing machine, but she never let me sew – even a button on a shirt. 'You can't do that, I'll do it.' This was one of the many methods she used to secure a foothold in my fast-changing life. One outlet for my mother was to gamble. She'd phone her favourite starting price bookmaker to place a bet on the Saturday afternoon races. SP betting on horse races was a popular pastime for many people. Mother and I sometimes flew to the Melbourne and Caulfield cups wearing our best home-made outfits. On race days I knew if Mother had lost she'd be cranky and, conversely, if her horse had stormed home, she'd be elated – 'June, let's go out to dinner.' I went with the flow.

Another escape from her confined life was to socialise with me and my friends. As a child, I had gone where my mother went. Now as I approached adulthood and was eager to accept social invitations from men and make friends and gain an adult's independence, she continued to accompany me where a young woman would not normally be seen with her mother – on dates to restaurants and night-clubs, to my girlfriends' weddings, and with my friends to parties. Sharing my life perhaps empowered my mother and salvaged some of the youth and dreams she had lost when she became a single parent, but it also made her possessive. Not free to develop friendships on my own terms – a necessary part of moving towards adulthood – without her interference, judgment and presence, it became difficult for me to live my own life. Normal as it is for parents to be concerned about their children's friends and romances, her negative experience of relationships with men fed a neurotic fear that I might fall victim to the same fate. 'Be careful,' she cautioned repeatedly. 'Don't be intimate with men. Don't trust them.' Those warnings became so ingrained in my psyche that I grew to distrust men romantically.

Already abandoned once by someone she loved, my mother was terrified I'd leave her too. I can hardly remember her going out socially without me. Isn't that strange? In an irrational state, she would bar the doorway just as I was ready to meet someone, 'You're not going out.' A row would ensue, and by the time she allowed me to pass, I was too unhappy to enjoy myself. Mother would be waiting for me when I came home, fuming if I was later than 11.30 p.m. If my mother couldn't keep me a prisoner at home, she surely bound me emotionally. I reasoned that I was having the life that she should have had and that I didn't have the right to be happy because she was deprived of that right by her circumstances. Emotional abuse was unheard of then.

It was never discussed, but Mother, like many parents, wanted her daughter to date a man with good career prospects from a respectable family of the same religious background, even though she never visited a church. Most of my admirers fitted her requirements, partly because of the social scene in which I moved, but I was also aware that it meant less interference from her and less anguish for me. Sometimes, if my mother approved of my admirer, she allowed me to see him alone. Mostly, however, it seemed easier to bring my mother along and keep the peace. Her presence might have seemed unusual to others, but it didn't seem odd to me. When young men asked me on dates I told them I could go only if they invited my mother. They politely acquiesced and the invitations continued to flow. In her favour, Mother was an attractive woman and comparatively young in spirit. Once she accompanied me and a young dentist, Len Keyte (who years later became my family dentist), to the elegant nightspot Romano's. A social pages photograph of the three of us appeared in the newspaper with the comment: 'Will wonders never cease? Take, for example, dining under lamplight at Rom's on Thursday this amazingly youthful mother . . . believe it or not, June's mama, Mrs K. Dally-Watkins'. She also had a wicked sense of humour that made her good company. For instance, on a date at a restaurant, the three of us were enjoying the gourmet dish of the time – cream of asparagus soup – when the fake flowers attached to Mother's hat fell into the soup. Though she quickly plucked the flowers out and wrapped them in a napkin, the dye left mauve and pink swirls in the soup. My date and I cracked up and my mother joined in.

Nevertheless, her resentment continued to build and she began to take her frustrations out on me. Some people undoubtedly envied my lifestyle, but they had no idea of the tough times I faced. It became almost impossible for me to get a decent night's sleep, which was all-important to achieve a bright-eyed look for a modelling assignment the following morning. In the middle of the night Mother would get out of bed, go to the kitchen and pace the living room. When she returned to our bedroom, she would be steaming about nothing or over something I had done or not done. Criticism of me and of my friends was flung across the room at me, along with a hairbrush or other objects kept on the dresser. 'You're having a good time, but I didn't at your age. I've given up so much for you. I hate you!' she'd scream. Eventually her fuse would extinguish and she'd collapse into bed. The morning after, Mother behaved as if nothing unpleasant had occurred. She never apologised or acknowledged these paroxysms of rage. I followed her lead. I wanted whatever state of mind she had been in to go away, so through this undercurrent of tension I smiled, nervously.

Whilst we lived in each other's pockets, we kept secrets from each other. Yes, we were good at that. So I didn't tell Mother when my father loomed at a David Jones' afternoon tea parade. I had seen a man and woman sitting among the audience, looking at me with familiarity. I don't know why, but I suspected the man was the shadowy figure who had appeared out of the blue and disappeared just as quickly from Watson's Creek. To the audience I would have appeared unruffled, but inside I worried that he would wait to see me after the parade. He didn't, but seeing Bob once again left me an emotional wreck.

It was easy to blame this stranger who was my father for my mother's actions and behaviour. His rejection of her undoubtedly injured her heart and I told myself that he had left her soul broken too. What I didn't understand fully then – and have taken the rest of my life to acknowledge – was that my mother suffered a personality disorder. Now it would be called depression. Mother had a harder lot in life than I did, and, when she was consumed with unhappiness, she would console herself with a drink. It was the alcohol that made her mood swings so poisonous. I often wondered if she took to drinking to keep dark thoughts at bay. Every day was a battle for both of us. I admire how hard my mother tried – and without any professional help for many years – to overcome her problems. But they were battles she couldn't always win. In the privacy of her home, she surrendered to the demons in her mind and I lived with their effects. In the company of others, she summoned all her energy and will to fight the illness, go to work, and make others laugh. Perhaps she could control herself better on social occasions because they gave her a legitimate excuse to have a drink. People would say, 'Your mother's wonderful. Kay's so proud of you.' She never gave me those kinds of compliments. My mother never told me she loved me.

Strangely, the effort Mother made not to humiliate me in public, to mask her unhappiness, and to strive for my success were her greatest acts of love towards me. All the same, her emotional illness at times made her manipulative, paranoid and impossible to live with. Even though Mother's illness no doubt tortured her, it devastated me, and ultimately my family. That said, I don't want her to be perceived as a bad woman. Indeed, the good times we shared outweigh the bad memories. I never raised my mother's illness with her. Nor did I share my concerns with others. Mother had a way of winning people over that would have made any revelation of the reality of her condition seem farcical. It seemed easier to keep my concerns to myself and bottle up the cocktail of emotions that went with them.

One person who knew the hard times my mother gave me was my dearest friend and only confidante Helen Meehan (later Helen Newham). Helen was only a schoolgirl when she first saw me in a mannequin parade at Farmer's department store. At the various parades I had become aware of the gaze of this 15-year-old, who apparently had pinned pictures of me to the inside of her school locker door. Seeking beauty advice, she began to stay after the parades to talk to me. After I replied to a letter Helen had written to me, we met for afternoon tea and became friends for life. On Saturday afternoons, Helen and I would play tennis or go to the movies. I'd worry about what mood I'd find my mother in when I came home. Helen could sense my anxiety and somehow I could talk to her about my mother whereas I couldn't trust anyone else. Helen, it seemed, was always there when I needed to cry or have a few laughs to forget the oppressiveness of my home life. She even came with me to speak to a doctor about my mother's problems, though we went away without any useful advice. Once I ran away from my mother and the Kings Cross flat to stay with Helen and her parents at their hotel, the Town Hall, on the corner of Park and George streets.

Thankfully, my mother liked Helen and made some beautiful clothes for her. Sometimes Mother and I would go to Castle Hill (in the days when it was the countryside) and stay with Helen and her family at their stud farm, which came with the rare addition of an in-ground swimming pool and tennis court. In return, I introduced her to the vibrant social scene that was opening up to me as I became well known as a model. I also dragged her along on some of my dates. Helen's presence lightened the pressure of having to deal with Mother on these occasions, and sometimes the unwanted attention of my date!

A young English friend, Ben Brown, also broke through the wall of pretence I had erected around my mother and myself. 'June, why don't you get away from all this?' Ben suggested, after finding me in tears one day. 'My brother and his wife live in Melbourne and I'm sure they'd let you stay with them. Give yourself a break and get away.' I packed all my clothes, courage and anger, and with money I had saved from modelling took the train to Melbourne and, because of my great unhappiness, walked away from a promising modelling career for a while. I told Mother I was leaving Sydney, but I didn't tell her where I was going and only phoned her during the year I lived in Melbourne. In my absence, she made money by sewing clothes for people.

The Browns took sympathy on me, without me having to discuss my personal problems with them. They had two young daughters and I shared their five-year-old's bedroom in their simple fibro-and-brick home in Croydon, which was then sparsely populated. Often on weekends I'd take long walks or a bus ride alone through the Dandenong Ranges. I wasn't lonely. It was a peaceful change from the flare-ups with Mother. I took a sales job at Myer's exclusive Incley Salon – this entailed a long walk to and from the railway station in darkness. On my approach home, I always felt relieved to hear 'Dad and Dave' on the wireless, a sign that my journey was nearly over. It wasn't long before the Incleys asked me to model one of the gowns they made for Melbourne's wealthy ladies. The chairman of the Myer Emporium, Sir Norman Myer, persuaded me to model for their in-store mannequin parades and newspaper advertisements. Allegedly, Sir Norman had a roving eye though he was married, so I never accepted his invitations. In any case, I had begun to make new friends. I dated wealthy Toorak bachelor Lyndon Duckett and attended hill-climb races of vintage cars with his friends. Lyndon and I nearly crashed in his car in one of these races, which brought home the saying, 'My whole life flashed before my eyes.'

Eventually the guilt I felt over abandoning my mother drove me back to Kings Cross. On my return, we were both wary around each other and Mother was on her best behaviour. She approved of the calibre of friends I had made in Melbourne, including Rod Myer of the retailing family, who took me nightclubbing when he was in Sydney. As was usual for us, there was never any discussion about why I had gone away.

7 Charmed, I'm sure

My modelling career in Sydney resumed easily and proved to be a nice little earner, but only due to the long hours I worked. In one week I earned about £85 at a time when the standard pay for a shoot was a guinea (£1 1s). It was impressive, but hardly the equivalent of the fees supermodels can command today. Remember Linda Evangelista's famous comment that she wouldn't get out of bed to work for less than $US10 000 a day? At 19 years of age, my newfound affluence enabled me to splurge a small fortune on a new cream Morris Minor 1000. 'Junior' was delivered while I was modelling interstate, so Helen drove it to the airport with Mother to surprise me. They put a ribbon around the car and wiped off any spots gathered from the drive with their handkerchiefs. Not only was it rare for a woman to have her own funds to buy a vehicle, it was less common for a woman to drive a car. If a family owned a car, it was usually the son, and not the daughter, who had permission to drive it. Gradually this attitude changed and by the mid-1950s I was writing a monthly column directed at a new breed of drivers – women – for *Wheels* magazine. For me, having a car meant I could drive with Mother to visit Watson's Creek.

My financial success pleased my grandparents. Some relatives now tell me they were impressed by what I had achieved, but didn't let on at the time.

In 1948 I was chosen, with leading French and Sydney mannequins, to debut the first collections brought over from Paris. Mary Hordern – then fashion editor of *The Australian Women's Weekly* and sister to Gretel Bullmore who had married the magazine's owner, Frank Packer – was responsible for this coup. As a leading socialite, Mary hosted truly enchanting evenings that, like the 'New Look', reflected the return to glamour in the post-war period. Mary invited me to elegant cocktail parties at her home, where the guests behaved with impeccable manners, wore black tie, full-length gowns and dined on French-inspired delicacies washed down with champagne. A French fixation thrived. Following Dior's collection came designer Pierre Balmain, for whom I modelled. The wives of prominent businessmen representing French companies opened haute couture salons: Germaine Rocher, Madame Pellier and milliner Henriette Lamotte in Sydney and Lillian Whiteman of Le Louvre in Melbourne. Local dressmakers and manufacturers also cashed in on the interest in all things French.

Christian Dior sent fifty designs to Australia for a series of parades to aid the post-war 'Food for Britain' appeal. It was the first overseas collection to be shown in Australia and Dior's first collection ever to be shown outside Paris. The collection defined the New Look of French fashion: lavish amounts of sumptuous fabrics, hand-span waists, full skirts and rounded shoulders. An eighteen-inch (forty-five-centimetre) waist was necessary to squeeze into Dior's designs. I didn't have too much trouble qualifying – I had lost my milkmaid look by then – but I worked on improving my waistline to ensure I was selected for the coveted parade. Every day for a couple of weeks, I slid one arm down my thigh, raising the other arm to my waist and repeating the manoeuvre on the other side. Then I placed my hands on my waist and twisted side to side. I repeated these exercises about one hundred times a day. It wasn't a strenuous regime compared to how some women exercise today. With the bonus of youth and walking everywhere, dieting wasn't a consideration. In any case, everything I ate was healthy – lots of grilled meat and boiled vegetables. In the lead-up to the parades' audition, Mother measured my waist: I made the cut.

As a young woman I didn't appreciate the perfection of the Dior garments as much as I do today. I modelled the signature gown of the collection called 'Dolly', which was made from about one-hundred metres of white silk organza and one-hundred metres of white lace over tiers of ice-blue taffeta. The detailed embroidery and care taken to create the collection was impressive. Gowns were made in two pieces to emphasise a feminine, nipped-in waist. An extra piece of material was added to the bodice to make sure the skirt held it in place. Skirts were full and layered with petticoats to further accentuate the waist, fitted with firm waistbands and always belts. Undergarment manufacturers created a waist whittler or 'waspie' – a waist-specific girdle that became a standard accessory in some models' tote bags while the fashion lasted. Large angular hats looked like mini-flying saucers and gloves accompanied superbly tailored daytime suits. There were no zippers on any of the clothes; the openings were closed with hooks and eyes or studs, each over-sewn with cotton thread that matched the fabric of the garments.

The models and I applied our own make-up and styled our hair. Long hair was considered untidy and distracted from the detail of the garment, so we wore it up and away from our faces. When I was later chosen to model the garments in Perth I had my long, wavy hair cut in the French style – about two inches short all over. I loved it and the newspapers began to comment on my trendy hair and the clothes I wore off the catwalk. Mother, on the other hand, had loved my long thick hair and took a while to get over the shock of my new image when she met me at Sydney airport.

The other models chosen for the Sydney Dior parades were June Bennett, Beth Campbell, Pam Clemson, Narelle Findlay, Dorn Fraser, Valmai Hoy, Coralie Kelly, June Mallett, Nola Rose, Lois Stephens and Prudence Thomas. I don't recall any backstage bitchiness amongst the models, though we were all pretty envious of Lois Stephens whose shiny blonde crimped hair, tanned skin and confident, come-hither look were magnets for men. Commenting that Lois was the most attractive of all of the models, men would talk, whilst in the company of other models, about how exciting they found her. She had the richest boyfriends too – the property developer Eddie Kornhauser among them – and her tote bag bulged with silk stockings, expensive perfume, lingerie and other presents from admirers. Lois married the wealthy Sydney developer Tom Whittle and divided her time between Darling Point and a condominium in Honolulu. In recent years she's fought back from a stroke and looks as lovely as ever. We're still friends.

Dorn Fraser was the only model working in Sydney to be married and have a baby – Jennifer is one of my godchildren and the first baby I ever nursed. Despite Dorn's efforts, her marriage didn't work out, but she was lucky to win the love of Captain Joe Griffith, a World War II veteran. After the war, he became a pilot for the Dutch airline KLM. They arranged to be married at one in the morning at St Stephen's Church because her divorce only came through at midnight and they had to leave that day for Holland, where Joe was based. How I envied Dorn's happiness and long marriage. Now a widow, she lives in Farnham, south of London. For eleven years during my business finishing college's grand tours of Europe, Dorn, Joe and I would meet for lunch in London. Though we are close, as with most of my friends, I have never shared my deepest troubles with Dorn.

What happened to the others? I don't know the fate of all these beautiful women. Some found good fortune, others hardship. Coralie Kelly had black hair and a peaches-and-cream Irish complexion.

Everyone was envious when Coralie snared the rich, good-looking grazier Bill Fagan. Coralie had come from a suburban, working-class family in Sydney, a world away from the Fagan clan's landed gentry status in the Bathurst district. She found it difficult to adjust to life in the country and in time she returned alone to Sydney. I had envied June Mallett's closeness to her family. She married businessman Ray Hope, who owned Hope Refrigerators, Electrical Equipment and White Goods. They lived in Brisbane, where she died of cancer. Valmai Hoy married an American cosmetics executive; June Bennett became a doctor's wife; and Pam Clemson married happily the second time around. Nola Rose won the Miss Pacific quest, and was one of the first Australian models to find work in England. She went on to run the impressive Du Pont parades in London, so whenever I was there I caught up with her. Sadly, she has died of breast cancer.

After the Sydney Dior parades, June Mallett, Dorn, Lois, Nola and I were sent to show the collection in Perth at Boans' department store. None of us had travelled so far before and in those days it was an overnight flight in a DC3 plane that was cold and uncomfortable. Perth welcomed us as celebrities and we lapped it up, staying at the Esplanade Hotel that overlooked the Swan River. The bachelors of Perth were eager to show us a good time. For Lois and me that meant a double date in which we endured an upside-down view of Perth from a small, open-cockpit, one-engine plane. Never again!

I was more impressed by Bob Ledger, a quieter gentleman with a kind round face. Bob managed Carris Bros jewellery store in Perth and we dated again when I visited Perth for other modelling assignments and in Sydney when he came to buy stock. When Bob took me somewhere fancy, like Romano's for dinner, he slicked back his dark hair and dressed in a three-piece suit with a white handkerchief in the breast pocket. Mother liked him, but probably only because she knew that he was ultimately returning to Perth! He was several years older than me and wanted to get married, but I was determined I wouldn't marry until I was 30. I had never seen an indication of a happy marriage, so it was something I wanted to avoid. I was also suspicious of men, even that fine man.

In any case, my social calendar was full and other men were vying for my attention. Courting took place at fine restaurants like Gleneagles. Romano's restaurant and nightclub was very popular, with a marble bust of Napoleon at the entrance to give it an air of sophistication. I visited the exclusive Pickwick Club on social occasions and for parades. My favourite venue was Prince's, which you entered down stairs from Martin Place. Its intimate round tables dressed in white linen cloths, circular dance floor and Craig Crawford's band gave Prince's an elegance that I believe has been forever lost. Silver-service, three-course meals and waiters in tails were *de rigueur* at these places and we thought we were very swish ordering *bombe Alaska*, crepe Suzette and anything flambéed from a French-only *à la carte* menu.

If I was going out for a night of dancing I usually wore a full-length gown teamed with a corsage that my date would give me. After midnight, the places to dance were the Hayden or The Roosevelt. At The Roosevelt there were showgirls, but as far as I was concerned it was innocent fun. Little did I know that prostitutes and criminals frequented this notorious nightclub. These clubs were filled with smoke, and wherever I went virtually everyone smoked except me. I was questioned and put down for this and a couple of times I tried to smoke – but I would forget that I was smoking and leave the cigarette to burn in an ashtray. I didn't like the taste or smell of cigarettes and the smoke hurt my eyes, though you wouldn't be able to tell that from some of the cigarette advertisements I innocently posed for.

Sexually, it wasn't an easy time for either men or women. The rules of romance and relationships were full of contradictions. For example, a woman was raised to believe that if she weren't a virgin a good man wouldn't marry her. This wasn't always the case, as I knew some women who had pre-marital sex and they weren't left on the proverbial shelf. Living together before marriage was considered improper and, in any case, rare. A man who had been seriously courting a girl was expected to offer marriage. However, some proposals were based on the pretext of seduction. Many young women lived at home and intimate moments with their boyfriends were snatched mostly in the back seat of a car. At the same time, there was the kind of man known to drive his date to a lonely spot and force her to submit to his sexual demands or give her a hard time for rejecting him.

Word would circulate as to which girls slept around and who didn't. I fell into the latter, vestal category, but that didn't mean I was more prudish than other girls. When one beau gave me a solid gold bracelet, I showed it to Grandfather during a visit to Watson's Creek, hoping he would allow me to accept it. He didn't and it was obediently returned. Often I missed out on meeting quieter men who lacked such self-assurance. Whilst I was selective and cautious, I managed to have many boyfriends and they were all respectful of my morals. I'm proud to say some of them and later their wives became lifelong friends.

There was Hilton Nicholas, whose family's pharmaceutical company developed Aspro. We stayed friends for a long time. Along came Margaret Whitlam's brother Bill Dovey, a tall, eligible law student who followed in his father's footsteps to become a judge. Bill and I mostly went swimming at Neilson Park together. Another boyfriend was Justin Hickey. He was knighted and amassed a fortune on the Gold Coast, only to lose it. Sir Justin and his wife Barbara remain good friends. I dated a mature English air marshal, Lord Sholto Douglas, but was never serious about this aristocrat. A wealthy playboy George Falkiner had his eye on me, but I wasn't swept away by him or his grand sheep station, Haddon Rig, in New South Wales. Jack Radford was a dear boyfriend. Jack and his younger brother Glen were profoundly deaf from birth but had learned to speak. We used to enjoy weekends together with friends from the Sydney Ski Club at Thredbo.

When I visited the family's Point Piper mansion for tennis parties, little did I know that years later I would return to it when my friend Susan, then married to Sir Frank Renouf, had claimed it her Paradise D'Amour. By coincidence Susie's legal counsel, David Price, is another former boyfriend of mine. David was the first to call me 'Dally' because I was one of four models in Sydney at the time with the name 'June' (the others were Bennett, Massey and Mallet). Our friendship began quite by chance. Trying to escape a downpour on a weekend away from Sydney, my mother and I made a dash for cover to the Camden Valley Inn, where David, then a law student, noticed me struggling to open the door and chivalrously came to our rescue. David remembers my mother fondly, but when I asked him if he thought she was protective of me, he replied 'was she ever'.

My social network expanded as I began travelling for regional and country parades. Fellow model Susan Middleditch, a pretty blonde English model who ultimately became a nun, and I became known as the 'flying mannequins' when we were chosen by *Fashion* magazine to test the suitability of a range of winter garments for travel purposes. To assess the garments we were sent on a six-day whirlwind trip around Australia flying with Trans-Australia Airlines. Our findings were hardly rocket science, but we had a great time. We reported back to the magazine that checks and stripes travelled better, looking fresher and more striking on arrival than plainer fabrics. Susan and I were also chosen to attend the grand opening of Hayman Island.

A bumpy flight in a DC3 to Brisbane marked the beginning of each fashion season. Usually Betty Girling, Joan Fahey, Marguerite Marr, Robbie Robinson and I made the journey from Sydney for Curzon's parades. Betty married Ron Eaton, a former prisoner of war in Changi, who became an executive with P&O Shipping. In Betty's endeavour to keep up her friendships she developed a telephone fetish. Betty can be driving along a road, see a public telephone and be compelled to make a call. She loves to chat. We have remained close.

As newcomers to travel, the models and I were impressed that our accommodation at Lennon's Hotel, then a new multistoreyed brick building in the middle of town, employed maids to service the rooms daily. I loved Brisbane's country-town ambience, the heat, and discovering the taste sensations of avocados, pawpaw, custard apples and passionfruit. The people were friendly and keen to show us the best of their State in a relaxed, low-key way. Over the years I have watched Brisbane grow from a country town into a fine city. Many people think I am a Queenslander and live in Brisbane, and I'm proud to think they do. I barrack for the Broncos and I love the casualness and warmth of the people. I feel at home there, but I have always thought of myself as a person of the world, not of Sydney or even Australia.

Curzon's representative and our chaperone was June Jones. She wasn't much older than us and allowed us to make the most of these visits. Brisbane's Stan and Olga Jones, of the established printing company Jones & Hambley Stationers, also took us under their wing. They loved having mannequins and other celebrities visit their Queenslander-style home at Clayfield and their weatherboard, beachfront holiday house at Surfers Paradise. Sometimes I slept at their home and enjoyed their fussing over me and being part of a family. After a visit to the coast, we would stop at the landmark pie shop at Yatala before returning to Brisbane.

Staying at Lennon's, we met all the visiting VIP bachelors. One of my visits coincided with an English cricket-team tour. I took the dashing and skilled English batsman Dennis Compton to the Jones's so he could avoid female fans who were trying to sneak into his room at Lennon's. All Dennis wanted was a good night's sleep, which he got in their empty nursery. The Jones's 10-year-old Wendy had fun telling her school friends how Dennis had left behind his blue linen boxer shorts. I liked Dennis, who was ten years my senior, but not romantically. I met Australian Test cricketers Arthur Morris and Keith Miller in Brisbane too. I dated Arthur in Sydney, but our respective commitments ensured nothing serious could develop. On another Brisbane trip, I struck up a friendship with the American tennis greats Pancho Gonzalez and Donald Budge, and we spent the weekend at the Jones's holiday house. Pancho and Don gave me a signed tennis racquet that my daughter Lisa took to show at her school one day. It never came home.

One lifelong male friend I made in Brisbane was Kurt, whose family set up the wool business Lohmann & Co in the early 1900s. Born in Germany, Kurt moved to Australia in 1937, but was interned for five and a half years during World War II. On his release, he was working for his family company as a wool buyer when he boldly approached me at an acquaintance's home where I had gathered with a group of models for a barbecue. I think Kurt best recalls our first meeting: 'I was sitting on the floor, gazing at this beautiful young woman. She removed her shoes because her feet were tired from working in a parade, so I took the opportunity to massage them for her. She was a bit surprised, but she remained very relaxed, very charming and knew how to handle people, especially men. She was a pretty good judge of men. If they started to be too friendly, she would give them a very charming heave-ho.'

Back in Sydney, Kurt was staying at a hotel in Kings Cross and began to call on me. Mother approved of Kurt and we started dating. He wooed me with a very rare gift – a brocade evening cape, which he had brought back from Japan. I wore it over a white, full-length, organza gown when he took me to the opera. In another attempt to impress me, Kurt arranged to pick me up in the city in his new car, a sleek convertible Armstrong Sidley. He remembers jumping at my request for him to give some of my friends a ride: 'It was a beautiful summer's day and there were five beautiful models sitting in the car, some of them sitting on the back. They were all laughing and playing up. As I drove up Williams Street I thought I was Father Christmas.'

My hectic modelling schedule was a convenient way to stop

a deeper relationship with Kurt. If I had a modelling assignment the next morning I aimed to be in bed by about ten, so, towards the end of an evening with Kurt, I delivered my usual excuse that I needed eight hours sleep in order to look my best the next day. It wasn't just a line; sleep is the fountain of youth. According to Kurt, I was living only for my career.

> That was no problem for June. She knew exactly what she wanted. She would never have more than half a drink, if she even had that. She had this famous saying 'Not before married life', which I thought was very good. I might not have liked it all the time, but I appreciated that, and at the time a young man honoured that. She was very conservative, straitlaced and very well brought up. There was no funny business.

After spending an evening together, Kurt would escort me home and Mother would allow him to come into my bedroom and give me a goodnight kiss. Then he'd sit in the lounge room and have a whisky or two with Mother. Kurt couldn't help but notice my mother's hold over me.

> Kay was very nice, but a very determined lady. She was very protective of June. I just sensed it. It was just the way she wanted to rule and govern every step of June's life, which June didn't like, because she was a very determined young lady. So there was some friction there, but I never wanted to interfere. June was very careful and discreet about not saying what she thought about her mother. Being well known and good-looking, June had a lot of admirers so I can't blame her mother for being protective. I knew that often the best way to charm a young lady was to approach the mother, so sometimes I might have invited her mother along. I think her mother approved of me. I never had any arguments with her.

The wife of the manager that Kurt employed warned my boyfriend that to marry a model would be lowering his standards, but he proposed to me anyway. I wasn't ready to settle down, but Kurt was. He ended up marrying into Austrian royalty, and all the while I had thought I was his princess!

8   Open for business

Having reached the pinnacle of my modelling career by 1949, when I was named 'Model of the Year' and the 'Most Photographed Model of the Year', it seemed possible to conjure and fulfil other dreams. Instead of basking in the success of my new status during that Christmas holiday period at Watson's Creek, I worked day and night to bring to fruition a business idea that my mother had conceived. Mother had foreseen an expiry date on my modelling career and the need to forge a new path to secure our financial future and capitalise on my success. After the parades, Mother had noticed how women of all ages often asked me for advice: what dress they should buy, what to wear to a particular function, where I had my hair cut, how to apply make-up, how to become a model, and so on. Having read about two charm schools in New York run by John Robert Powers and Harry Conover, and Lucy Clayton's school in London, she suggested my next adventure: to open the first such school in the southern hemisphere. 'I can't do that. I wouldn't have enough confidence,' I protested. 'Of course you can. You would be good at it. No one could do it as well as you, and young women need it.' My mother wanted to give young women the opportunities she'd never had.

Mother had a knack of lifting me with her enthusiasm, so there I was in the middle of the Australian bush working out how I would teach young women to become ladies. With no one to follow or books to use for research purposes, I had to develop my own program for the school. I wrote down all I had learned the hard way: the mistakes I had made, the hurdles I had overcome, and how I had reached the top of my profession. Documenting this body of knowledge proved to be the best and most lasting investment I've ever made in my business.

Taking advantage of my high profile, I settled on calling the school the June Dally-Watkins School of Deportment. I didn't want to call the business a 'charm' school – I thought that sounded too flighty. I wanted the school to be taken seriously and provide guidance that would last a lifetime. To achieve this, it was important that subjects addressed how to improve the person as a whole. Therefore subjects on social and business etiquette, good manners, personality, speech and being the best you could be were balanced with good posture, grooming, diet, make-up, hair and exercise advice. I worked out a series of lessons, their duration and set a fee of £10 10s for an eight-week course. This was raised to £15 15s a little later.

'To be poised, gracious and charming is the inherent right of every girl and every woman,' I wrote in one of the first series of brochures for the school. The course was marketed to women of all ages. For the young girl it was a practical finishing school; for the office worker it was important to be well groomed as their appearance and behaviour were under continual observation; for the business or professional woman of the future it was an investment in their career; and for the homemaker and matron, a door to a broader field of new interests. In an early promotional pamphlet, I warned, 'The housewife is in greater danger than others of becoming careless about her appearance and looking older than her years.' I also appealed to the 'wife of a career man' to enrol in my course. 'As her husband advances she is often expected to meet and mingle with his new associates or business friends and their wives.' In my mind, this still holds true. The secrets of good grooming and deportment have opened doors of opportunity, secured jobs, and found partners and friends for many of my past students.

It was important to avoid overhead costs, so I accepted an offer from a friend for the evening use of his photographic studio, which was up one flight of stairs in an office building on George Street, next to the General Post Office. I told the newspapers about my venture and, after a small story was published, Mother took several inquiries over the phone. We opened for business on 2 February 1950 with twelve students. Within two weeks the number had grown to twenty-five. Classes were offered only after office hours, which enabled me to work as a model during the day. Since I continued to model, the business had a good cash flow and it kept my profile high, which was good publicity for the school. Later that year I teamed up with local models and four American cover girls in the Neiman Marcus American Fashion Parades in Sydney. Andrea Johnson, who ran her own modelling agency in the USA, told the press my 'well-bred look' would 'go over big' there, but I was determined to stick to my business plan so as not to let myself or my mother down.

After modelling all day, I met my mother at the studio at 5 p.m. and taught from 6 p.m. until 7.30 p.m. Mother would bring me a home-cooked meal, talk to prospective students, receive payments, and note attendances in an exercise book. As our student consultant for twenty-five years, Mother used her enthusiasm to great effect as a saleswoman. It gives me joy when someone tells me, 'Your mother enrolled me. She was a lovely lady' or 'I'll never forget her' or 'She was so beautiful.' This is how I like to remember my mother: the way many saw her. It is a comforting memory. Had Mother had greater opportunities in life and fewer personal troubles, there would have been no reining in her potential. Her business foresight was sharper than mine. When our first cohort of twenty-five students completed the course, I planned to have as many graduation certificates printed. 'Don't be silly, June,' Mother said. 'It's cheaper to have printing done in large quantities. We should order 300 certificates.' I wasn't so sure, 'We'll never use that many.' More than 300 000 students have since gone through the school, and now we print certificates and diplomas in-house.

    I felt happy to move on from modelling, and couldn't wait for the weekends to finish, so I could return to work. Teaching was right for me and I was right for it. It came naturally and I loved it because I believed in what I was teaching and enjoyed sharing my know-how and giving guidance to anyone who wanted it. Despite the youthful exuberance of some of the school-leavers who were my first students, they were used to discipline at school and in the home and were always eager to learn. I was determined to remain in control to win their respect, even if deep down I wasn't always feeling cool and calm. At only 22 years of age, I felt completely responsible for the students and took them under my wing to nurture their talents and charm. Now, whenever some of us get together, we laugh about how serious I was in this endeavour. I was friendly with the girls, while expecting their respect, so they called me 'Miss Dally'. In those days students would never have addressed a teacher using their Christian name. 'Miss Dally-Watkins' would have been too formal, so 'Miss Dally' was a good fit. It is a name that has stuck to this day with students and some friends calling me 'Dally'. I like the name, it sounds affectionate. Nowadays, if I were 22 again, I wouldn't object to students calling me by my first name, but I was brought up to never refer to someone so casually. That said, I think young people, as a sign of respect, should refer to a senior person by their surname. I also think it's impolite for a stranger, such as a salesperson, to call anyone by their first name. And I don't like the honorific, Ms.

    In classes, I encouraged students to develop key relations with other people, broaden their interests, increase their business and social poise, remember names, make introductions correctly, speak with a pleasing voice, and listen attentively – to listen is to learn. Knowing how to conduct and groom yourself builds confidence. To know the rules of etiquette is to feel quietly confident within yourself. It means you can enjoy life more fully and accept invitations without the insecurity that you might do or say something wrong. I believe etiquette still has an important role to play in society, despite today's more relaxed unwritten code of behaviour. If manners are used just to impress others or to climb a social ladder, they could be seen as merely superficial overtures. However, if manners are employed genuinely, they make people feel comfortable in your company. Manners show kindness and consideration.

I would tell the students, as I still do today: 'Your body is the house you live in and if your house is neglected and not looking its best people won't want to approach it and will think badly of the person who lives in it. People respond to good grooming. When they get to know you better, they might discover you're not a fine person, and a sloppy person may have a finer character than a well-presented one, nevertheless people make the initial judgment on your appearance. You should have direct eye contact. You need to develop a well-modulated voice and be polite. Say "Yes" or "No" and not "Yeah" and "Nah". Someone who doesn't sound interested in others, won't be interesting to others. And remember to refer to people by name.'

In Posture and Figure Correction classes, I assessed each student's posture as they walked, sat and stood, how they held their hands, and how they placed their feet. I had the girls follow my guide to perfect posture alignment:

Feet together and straight forward; ankles pressed together; knees straight; bottom muscles squeezed tight and tucked under; pelvic bones up and forward; stomach muscles pulled tight and into waist; ribcage held high allowing lungs to expand; shoulders up, back and down; shoulder blades into back; head on top of spine; back neck muscles long, chin held in slightly; arms relaxed at sides, elbows bent slightly, inner wrists against body, thumbs forward; imagine a straight line down the centre of the body; another straight line across the shoulders and another one across the hip bones; legs walk from the thighs; arms swing from the shoulders.

I'll admit it wasn't always easy for some girls to adhere to the Miss Dally way of doing things, but it paid off for those who did. A person with a fine carriage can turn heads when they enter a room; it's as if their good posture announces their arrival. Good posture can also give someone a more youthful appearance, improve body shape and health, and bring life to what someone's wearing. It can alleviate muscle tension and fatigue, and correct positioning and use of the diaphragm improves speech. Posture, along with refinement, gives someone style. It has nothing to do with money.

I also devised step-by-step tips to help the students adhere to my regime. For example, there was a fourteen-step guide 'to greet each day the Dally way'. It went like this:

1. Shower, and shampoo hair or place it in a shower cap.
2. Blow-dry hair, towel dry or finger dry.
3. Put in heated rollers or similar.
4. Apply body moisturiser, underarm deodorant, talcum powder, and spray skin perfume all over body (or enact Step 12).
5. Check toenail enamel.
6. Put on underwear and dressing gown.
7. Apply make-up, except lipstick.
8. Eat breakfast and clean teeth.
9. Finish dressing.
10. Style hair.

11 Apply lipstick.
12 Apply perfume to wrist and behind ears.
13 Check nail enamel.
14 Smile and have a happy day.

This may all seem like commonsense, but, in the era before magazines were full of such practical self-help hints, this kind of information was vital for some women who had no-one else to advise them on grooming. After starting the day according to my guide, students received instructions for a night-time beauty regime. I advised the students to go to bed early, if they wanted to look their best. If they had a late night, I told them to make sure the next one was early. Sleep and relaxation are the best ways to rejuvenate mind and body. It allows skin, mind and soul to rest. You can apply all the creams in the world, but nothing will restore the ravages caused by lack of sleep and an unhealthy lifestyle. Nevertheless, as some insurance against the effects of ageing, I have always dabbed some lanolin around my eyes at night.

My mother and I both had an eye for fashion, so Wardrobe classes were a natural extension of what we inherently understood. The classes taught how to create an effective wardrobe on a limited budget, the effective use of colours, how to dress to highlight the body's best attributes and hide problem areas, and forthcoming fashion trends. The lesson was devised to give students an idea of how to construct an affordable and adaptable wardrobe for different seasons. My personal wardrobe reflects what I teach. I'm obsessed with style and quality, not flashy labels to impress people. I buy clothes to mix and match and to dress up or down depending on the occasion. Money doesn't buy fashion sense or style. I still wear some of my daughter Carel's Italian designer hand-me-downs!

In Make-up classes, students were taught how to apply cosmetics to enhance their appearance and which colours were most flattering for their complexion. I complimented the girls when they looked good and

I suspect they knew when I thought they could look better. Rather than dictate how they should look, I found it more effective to give them subtle hints, like: 'It's important to keep your shoes in good condition', 'I think a pale lipstick would look great on you, why don't you try this one?' I always tried to keep criticisms general and not draw attention to a particular student's dress or appearance. Skin and hair care and hairstyling were also taught in the Deportment course. If there were a way to improve someone's appearance, I was keen to address it. It could mean helping a student to choose glasses frames that flattered her face. Some people are born beautiful, but, I believe, with the right technique, a positive attitude and self-discipline it is possible to change and enhance anyone's looks.

I wanted students to stay healthy and wholesome without being overweight. I advocated a positive approach to food, so students thought of a diet as a way of living rather than something a person went on only to lose weight. For students with specific weight issues, I suggested a weight-gain or weight-loss diet. The 'model diet' the school recommended required eating eggs and grapefruit daily, along with other low-fat foods. I've been fortunate to never have a problem with controlling my weight. The stress and activity of being a working mother kept me trim in my younger years. Now, if I have put on a couple of kilos from over-eating and lack of exercise, I will follow the 'model diet' for a couple of days and I'll admit the appeal of eating eggs and grapefruit wears off pretty quickly. I also practice gentle stretches in the shower and take a walk, mostly to and from the office, every day.

Some of the students who came through my doors over the years suffered from eating disorders and a poor self-image, so it was important to develop a good relationship with them and their parents if we were going to try to turn around these problems. First, I would approach the parents to see if they were aware of their daughter's problem. In some cases, parents relied on my influence over their daughter to change the girl's eating habits. They would say, 'Miss Dally wouldn't want you to skip meals.' Our school also participated in research that aimed to gain a further understanding of anorexia nervosa.

The school was more forward thinking than some would assume. Throughout its lifetime, the school has adapted to the times. In the 1950s, yoga classes were introduced, although yoga was little known in the western world. Classes were streamlined for pregnant women and new mothers, offering correct pre-natal and post-natal exercises, and dietary, skin and hair-care advice.

In the 1970s, a Men's Executive course was introduced and one of the teachers was former model Angela Belle McSweeney, who came from one of Australia's most prominent racing families. Her parents Molly and Tony McSweeney have remained treasured friends. Angela reintroduced 'Fashions on the Field' at Royal Randwick and was invited yearly to do the fashion coverage for the BBC at Royal Ascot, England. The Men's Executive course aimed to turn timid males into confident gentlemen. It is now structured to appeal to both sexes. To help students improve their speech and develop drama skills I introduced acting workshops. For this purpose, I have employed industry people, from veteran entertainer Lionel Long in the 1980s to television soap actors and in more recent years Judy McBurney.

In 1988, I launched the first business finishing school in the southern hemisphere. It thrives today as a college for young people and has evolved with the times. The graduates are much in demand. They have all the attributes an employer requires to represent their company.

Over half a century after I developed the original curriculum, it is still being used in my Brisbane and Sydney schools, albeit with modification and modernisation. Why is this? Well, human beings don't essentially change and so I find that the techniques I used at the outset in the 1950s still work today and the same principles apply. My school offers basic worthwhile guidance to take both men and women attractively, confidently, happily and successfully through life. People today, as in the 1950s, will automatically judge you through the senses: sight, sound, touch and smell. So healthy and well-maintained skin, hair, hands and nails, good posture, a smile, and eye contact are always essential. A well-modulated voice and good voice tone, correct grammar, and laughter are the ingredients to make a pleasant sound. Cleanliness and smelling nice are appealing, so perfume or after-shave, breath freshener and deodorant are vital to a pleasing presence.

Knowing how to present yourself well in order to create a positive image is not expensive. It requires a motivated self-respecting person to obtain and maintain, but it lasts a lifetime. Expensive clothes are not necessary. I have always believed in a basic mix-and-match wardrobe in colours that work best for the individual. It is the person that matters, not the designer labels.

I try to encourage the students to understand there is a depth to each one of us. A refined, well-spoken and well-groomed person can go anywhere in the world and mix at any level. It is the depth of beauty that counts. Over the years, I have seen physical beauty fade and bodies expand. Personality, charm and depth of character never fade. True beauty resides in the soul of a person. What good does a facelift do if it is depended upon to give a sense of wellbeing? Lines give character. We have all earned them. Confidence comes from accepting who we are and working on the things that truly matter. To be the best we can be in all things is important and we should never stop learning.

I have learned that the most important attributes are free. A smile lights up the face and the eyes. It makes us feel happy. It also changes the tone of our voice. A smile doesn't only have to be seen; it can be heard, so smile into the telephone. Good posture too is free. It gives us a look of confidence and importance, and protects our bodies from shrinking and growing out of shape as we grow older.

We all have the ability to improve our voices. We should tune in with our ears and constantly listen to, and correct, our manner of speech and voice tone. Voices should be low, not high-pitched. They should flow clearly and distinctly out of the mouth, not hit the roof of the mouth and come out the nose. Voices can be compelling or repelling.

The English language is beautiful and should be protected. I feel sad about the intrusion of Americanisms into our language and conduct. I prefer 'yes' to 'yeah'; 'child' to 'kid' (which is, after all, a baby goat). I love to hear 'thank you' and 'please'. Little by little words are being abbreviated and are in danger of being lost altogether. Nowadays it seems no sentence can be uttered without the word 'basically' or sounds such as 'um' and 'ah'!

Although times have changed, my advice in the 1950s resembles what many motivational speakers still promote today. Make-up products and the method of application have improved. Fashion changes each season and a plethora of skincare products have been introduced, so instruction in these matters reflects that. I believe my etiquette and deportment advice is timeless, keeping men and women in good stead for surviving and shining in any social or work situation. I have also reintroduced evening classes that, along with the classes held on Saturdays and during school holidays, attract students aged 10 to 70. The subjects I put together at Watson's Creek are now included in the current courses: Personal Development, Professional Development, Corporate Success, Business, Receptionist Skills, Acting and Modelling. I have, in addition, an incredibly productive and unique Business Finishing College.

In addition to the school's longevity, its graduates have always been the best proof that what I have taught works. Within the first year my graduates had taken first, second and third places in the Miss Australia Quest in New South Wales and the success was repeated in Queensland in the following year. The awards kept rolling in, and the business kept churning out more beauties. As veritable walking advertisements for my school, these remarkable women deserve a chapter of their own.

I am still striving hard to convince people that beauty and brains can go together. It is very important to be a constantly switched-on person. Drugs, alcohol and cigarettes are not needed, in fact they switch us off, and they age us as well.

The first course in Sydney had been successful, but my mother feared there would not be enough students to keep it going continuously, so she suggested we start a course in Brisbane. We ran our first Brisbane course in June 1950, and were given free use of old Mr Poulsen's photographic studio in Queen Street, at the centre of town. 'Old Mr Poulsen', as we called him, and his son Harry were most kind to us. I can't imagine such generosity in business these days. The classes were well received and we decided to alternate between the two cities.

I had also spied a new business opportunity. With the school attracting so many natural beauties and transforming ducklings into swans by the time of graduation, and with increasing requests from advertisers to recommend models, I saw a gap in the market begging to be filled. I was convinced a modelling agency would benefit models, clients and myself. It seemed to be an obvious spin-off from the school. An agency also would liberate the models' mothers – like mine – who had stayed at home by the phone to take their daughters' bookings. I sounded out the department stores for their response: 'An agency will never work. We like phoning the mothers and having a chat with them.' Undeterred, I was convinced they would come around to my way of thinking. The war was not long over: the advertising industry was growing, fashion shows were becoming popular, and department stores were beginning to boom. So I took the risk to open the first model agency in the southern hemisphere only a year after the school had begun. It didn't take long for the advertisers and retailers in Sydney to appreciate the convenience of booking models through an agency. The Brisbane market was considerably slower to change.

Our first teacher in Sydney was the diminutive Jill Ferris – there are many students from the early years who remember her fondly.

With students graduating to become models, it made sense to develop subjects that would equip them with the basics to work in the industry. Students enrolled either in the general grooming Deportment course (now called Personal Development) or a new stream I developed to turn out potential models: the Model course. This gave them the basics of the Deportment course as well as knowledge of how to walk for parades, pose successfully in front of a camera, work with photographers, model make-up and engage in the business of modelling.

In the 1960s, closed-circuit television was installed at my schools so students could obtain on-camera modelling experience. These students were encouraged to approach modelling as a serious career option. Assembling a model portfolio, I told them, was like opening a shop and window-dressing it with something wonderful that people wanted to buy. If my mother and I felt prospective students had real potential and they were interested in modelling as a career, we recommended the Model course. No one was overlooked and no one was ever made promises unless I was sure they had the elusive 'it' factor.

I have always advised against modelling unless the person is outstanding. Only about two in every one hundred are suitable for modelling. My philosophy remains that it is better to be gently upfront with a student, even at the risk of bruising their egos, than for them to undertake the Model course and find out the hard way.

If the candidate has the basic requirements of a model (height and bone structure), they have a chance of a career as a model, but success in this pernickety industry can't be evaluated with a tape measure alone. It takes a good eye and a lot of experience to assess someone's potential as a model and even then it doesn't guarantee a long career in this youth-obsessed industry. The fashion world has become increasingly fickle about what constitutes beauty. A popular look one season can be unfashionable the next; but, in the main, the industry has a preoccupation currently with the physiologically rare type: the lofty, reed-thin supermodel.

With the agency off the ground, the need for larger premises in Sydney was urgent. Mother and I approached Tom Deamer, on the advice of a photographer friend John Nesbitt. Tom was making the most of the post-war shortage of rental space by leasing a rabbit warren of business premises on the ground floor of the Grand United Building in Castlereagh Street. He was beautifully eccentric and produced cinema advertisements and short films in his studio, which seemed to be constantly under renovation. We convinced Tom that we needed only a small permanent space for an office. He was sold on the idea of allowing us evening use of his film studio, which his daytime tenant, Old Mr Brown, had adapted to become a second-hand-wares shop. 'You can have that corner for the office,' Tom said, pointing to a small area in the foyer. At the end of each trading day Mr Brown's gallimaufry of goods would be placed against the walls to create floor space and returned to their rightful place before he opened for business the next morning.

Someone lent us a large black desk, which took up most of the corner space. We built a partition of three-ply wood from wall to wall. Our makeshift office came complete with a door that locked, but the following day we forgot the key, so Tom climbed over the petition to open it. In our haste, we had also forgotten to apply for a telephone line, so a neighbouring tenant kindly allowed us to use their phone until they received so many inquiries they couldn't answer their own business calls. Until the new phone line was installed Mother had to stay at home to take phone inquiries. 'You'll never get this off the ground,' Tom warned. However, we soon proved him wrong and won him over. During school evening graduations in the studio, Tom enjoyed showing the audience of mostly students' parents, one of his films while the students changed into their next set of clothes to parade. When we finally outgrew his space, Tom would visit my new place of business and we'd talk about old times. I miss him. He died, like many others have, as I was writing this book.

I now desperately needed a secretary. The mother of one of my students, Mrs Eastman, told me that her teenage daughter, Yvonne, had recently graduated from Miss Hayles' secretarial college. 'You can have her for £4 a week,' Mrs Eastman offered. There was no space for Yvonne in the desk-filled corner office, so I placed her at a small desk outside the corner office in the passageway where the other tenants would walk by as she slowly struck the typewriter keys using only two fingers. There was a wonderful mixture of people in Tom's rabbit warren of offices. I will always remember the tall, handsome and distinguished Hans Heinrich Vladimir Sergie Krull von Alderstein. He married Marion, who as Marion von Alderstein has produced her own etiquette book and written for *Vogue* magazine.

Almost two years after opening, the Sydney business was growing like Topsy and the office was bursting at the seams. It occurred to me that, if I had a financial backer, I could find a new home for the business and employ a teacher so that I could study how overseas charm schools and model agencies operated. I decided to ask Frank Packer whose business, Consolidated Press, was across the road from mine, to come on board as my business partner. As the publisher of some of the magazines that my models and I had helped sell as cover girls, I hoped he would be interested in the proposal I outlined in a letter to him.

> The demand for enrolment in the school is now more than I, and with the studio space available, can cope [with]. There are more than seventy new girls on the waiting list for 1952, not taking into account possible developments in other directions such as classes for married women, children and young girls coming straight out of school. With additional space available during the day and evening, it would be possible to employ more teaching staff as every class is conducted at the moment by me personally. There is also the possibility of a good demand for a correspondence course

for girls living in the country. In time and with the right staff the school could continue to grow in Sydney and in Brisbane and perhaps other States. Many girls have made inquiries about dressmaking classes, which could be an extra course after the deportment class has been completed.

At the time, the course cost twenty-five guineas per student and I had sixty-nine girls enrolled. I estimated the school's earning capacity in January 1952 would be £173 a week. I put it to Sir Frank that he invest assets equal to half the current net earning capacity for three years (£84 a week for the school and £20 a week for the agency), a total of £7800 over three years. In exchange, I wanted a salary of £18 a week and after six months, four months' leave of absence overseas. Sir Frank never replied.

As the model agency and school grew, Tom came to the rescue and agreed to lease us a space across the foyer, thus making the tenants' foyer much smaller. We used blond wood-veneer walls and opaque glass panels to divide the space into three small offices. There was further relief when we secured the use of a large storeroom across the hallway. At last we had a floor-to-ceiling door to our own space, which created four offices and a reception area.

I hadn't given up on the idea of going overseas to visit the charm schools in London and New York, but I had to employ staff to make it happen. I had personally groomed Pat Woodley to become Miss New South Wales in 1951. In the absence of a Miss Australia that year, Pat had travelled overseas as an ambassador for the country. On her return, she agreed to take on my teaching responsibilities while I made my first overseas trip. Pat had previously worked as a domestic science teacher and I admired her devotion and the way she took note of everything I said. So when an industry friend told me Pat was looking for space for her own deportment school and model agency, I went cold with disbelief. When Pat turned up to observe another class

I confronted her. Without so much as batting an eyelid she admitted her plan to set up a rival business and walked out the door. I buried my fury as though nothing had happened because I had students waiting, who had paid for their lesson and this time was theirs. The show had to go on and, of course, I was used to covering up. At least the secrets of the past had taught me this survival skill!

For a while the Pat Woodley School of Deportment (even the name was not very original) was quite competitive with my school. After all, Pat had observed my classes and taken notes. However, her modelling experience was not as extensive as mine. Her school no longer exists. Nonetheless, I took Pat's departure as a deeply personal wound. This was a new business experience for me. It was still an era when a person's word was their bond in business. Nowadays, I would expect such practices in business, protect my intellectual property, and consider legal action. I didn't contemplate taking legal action at the time and, with the exhaustion of working day and night, I felt beaten anyway. This was my first taste of betrayal in business, but it wasn't to be the last.

I had been toying with the idea of opening a school and agency in Melbourne, so I made a trip there to seek the advice of one of Australia's leading fashion photographers, Athol Shmith. I had dated Clive Shmith who managed his brother's accounts. I respected Athol and had done some modelling with him in Melbourne, so I felt comfortable confiding in him. 'Melbourne's not ready for your business,' Athol suggested. 'Why don't you try again in a year or so?' Within six months, Athol and his wife, the beautiful mannequin Bambi Tuckwell, had opened a business that was surprisingly similar to mine. When Bambi left Athol to marry the Queen's cousin, the Earl of Harewood, someone else took over the business. Then another deportment school opened in Melbourne and I knew the market couldn't cope with a third player.

I don't regret never opening a school in Melbourne because

LEFT Photographer Ray Leighton commented: 'She is a model as good for toothpaste as she is for gowns.'

RIGHT I was becoming a more sophisticated model by age 19, as captured here in a photo by Rob Hillier of the Hillier chocolate family in Melbourne.

BELOW An instance of the photographic artist's skill is evident in this hand-tinted advertisement for Rexona Soap: 'Her flawless skin won romance... The moment he saw her, love welled in his heart.'

OPPOSITE Christian Dior Parade at Prince's nightclub and restaurant in 1948.

TOP LEFT Christian Dior Show at David Jones in 1948. Waists had to be eighteen inches.

ABOVE This was the outstanding gown of the Christian Dior Show. 'Dolly' was made from one hundred metres of white silk organza and one hundred metres of white lace over tiers of ice-blue taffeta.

LEFT Out for a ride at the sand dunes, La Perouse, in 1949 in my first car, 'Junior', a Morris Minor 1000.

OPPOSITE This sophisticated shot was taken in 1949 by Max Dupain. My hair is now cut short in the latest fashion.

TRUTH, SUNDAY, JANUARY 1, 1950.

Most Photographed Model Of The Year

OPPOSITE The absolute signature June Dally-Watkins' model pose on display at a Surfers Paradise fashion show. The gown is by John Hayles.

LEFT The *Truth* announcement that I was the most photographed model of 1949. (*Photo by Tony Leal of John Lee Studios*)

RIGHT When wearing hats, such as this basket-style hat with veil, hair was always swept out of sight.

TOP In the basement studios of Laurie Le Guay (in the foreground) and John Nesbitt. I am adjusting the collar of a gown being fitted on Jeanette Elphick (aka Victoria Shaw), aged 16.

MIDDLE Here I demonstrate the June Dally-Watkins full turn to a class in 1950. Classes were held in Old Mr Brown's makeshift studio in the Grand United Building at 149 Castlereagh Street, Sydney. In the morning the old wares, which we had moved aside to work, came out for sale.

BOTTOM At Old Mr Brown's, an exercise class works at reducing waists.

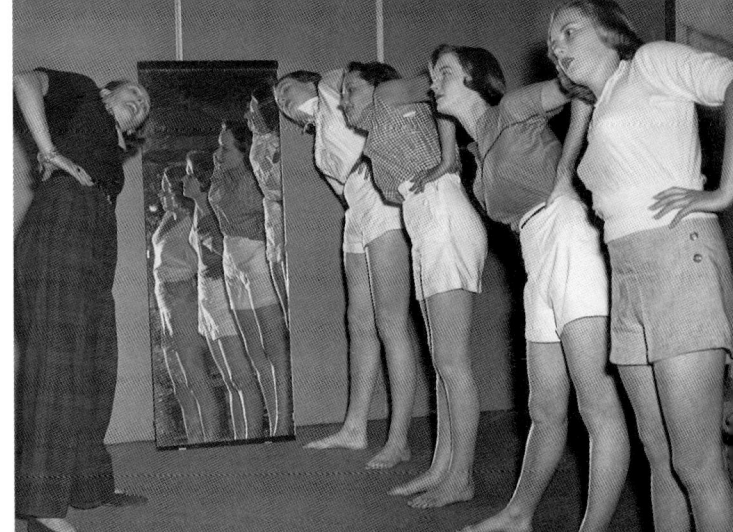

I may not have invested as much of my time in Brisbane where the school has flourished and where I have developed enduring friendships. Brisbane was my chosen city and I found a permanent base in the heart of the city on Edward Street next to the Shingle Inn – a Brisbane landmark famous for its cakes and old-style comfort food. One of the regular photographers my business used was Geoff Dauth, whose sideline was photographing the dead for their surviving loved ones. His studio was conveniently near the morgue, but it never seemed to make the models uncomfortable. With the business well established in Brisbane and Sydney, it felt like the right time for a break. In Sydney, I took on Marcia Hatfield and Jose Goldberg to run the business. I was more than ready for a new adventure.

9   Planet Hollywood

I devised the idea of producing a one-woman fashion show to help fund my travels as I visited the model agencies and charm schools in the USA and London. British Commonwealth Pacific Airlines (BCPA later became Qantas) accepted my proposal and gave me a return ticket to the USA. Leading Australian designer Frank Mitchell had supplied a collection for me to model, which served as my travel wardrobe as well. In those days, young women didn't usually travel alone, and not many Australians travelled abroad, but I was financially independent and eager to discover new places, learn and make friends. Mother, Helen and a group of models came to the airport to farewell me. I was 25 years old and about to embark on the best year of my life. Over the years, when people have inquired about my age, I've told them I am 25 because it makes me feel good to remember this fabulous time and the freedom I felt in casting off my responsibilities for six months. I believe a lady should not be expected to declare her age; it's only a number anyway. We are what we feel and I still feel 25.

My first stop was Honolulu, Hawaii, where I was met by BCPA ground hostess Eileen Weedon. (It was she who had arranged my itinerary and booked my fashion shows.) Looking back, my solo stage effort was as ambitious and as comical as a one-person band. As both compere and mannequin, I spoke to the audience about the next outfit I was to model, disappeared backstage to frantically change clothes, then reappeared trying not to look frazzled as I walked amongst the seated audience. The weather was sultry, but seemed to reach boiling point by the time I changed into and out of my twentieth ensemble. Despite the delay between changing garments, my debut was well received, as I reported back to the girls in the office.

> Well, kids, I'm a hit. The parade last night at the Edgewater Hotel was probably the biggest success I have ever had. When I started there were about 200 people in the audience: all the dress designers from the island, representatives from the States, socialites, etc. The dining room was booked out, also the bar, which is on the terrace, and there were people sitting around the pool. By the time the show was over there were about 300, which says a great deal for the success of the show, as I modelled the clothes myself and lasted from 7 p.m. to 8.30 p.m. . . . The setting for the parade was terrific – just like a movie setting – Hawaiian music in the background, exotic flowers strewn everywhere, people sipping the most interesting cocktails . . . It gets dark very quickly here, so when I started at 7 p.m. showing the casual wear it was very light, the sun still showing through the palm trees, and as I changed into the cocktail and evening clothes, the lights lit up the pool and the surrounding trees.

The local designers were fascinated and full of praise for Frank Mitchell's collection, which was quite distinct from American fashions at that time. I had many offers for the garments from the audience – and at any price, too! A few days later, I was guest model in a luncheon parade at the Royal Hawaiian Hotel.

It is the most fabulous place one could ever model. The show was held in the Surf Bar where lunch is served buffet style. The audience comprised tourists from all over the world. They come straight up from the beach to eat here – their clothes are mostly gay and exotic Hawaiian prints. I paraded Ceil Chapman and other terrific gowns. We paraded from the Surf Bar (the walls are all glass and slide back) out onto the Lani, which is the terrace, just a step from the beach. I was announced as the guest model from Australia and received quite an ovation, as Australians seem to be very popular. The shop which put on the show is called Mary & Jane – situated in the Royal Hawaiian Hotel. They gave me a beautiful pair of diamanté earrings, much to my delight. Elizabeth Arden's salon at the hotel did my hair for the show. Elizabeth Arden herself sat next to me having her hair done. The powder room where we changed was out of this world. It is called the 'Pearl Room' – namely because the drapes in the room are made from ceiling-to-floor lengths of pearls. They also hang from all the lights. Cute little Hawaiian girl attendants helped us to change and supplied us with masses of tissues to prevent perspiration, as it was a hot day . . . An Hawaiian firm, Paradise Sportswear, gave me a sarong, aloha shirts, a Chinese-type dress, a cotton sundress and Chinese pyjamas.

As an Australian model, I was something of a novelty and therefore newsworthy. I received positive press coverage for my plan to set up what I called a lend-lease model scheme to exchange my Australian models with those in Europe and America. I met with Models Hawaii, one of Honolulu's top agencies, to strike an exchange deal. I brought with me a large collection of photos of Australian models to help sell the idea, and was told the Australian girls generally were considered more attractive than American models. They had naturalness. That was the beginning of model exchanges worldwide.

From Honolulu, I flew to San Francisco where I had an entrée to the right people, courtesy of a letter from the Hawaiian-based BCPA representative to the secretary of one of San Francisco's top columnists. Her praise was most flattering.

In our midst here now is a most vivid personality from Sydney, Australia – Miss June Dally-Watkins, Australia's foremost and most-photographed model, who has taken Honolulu by storm . . . Her 'one-woman' fashion showing here at the Edgewater Friday evening was a terrific thing – everyone loved it and the place was jammed with . . . the elite of the Island. You would especially have enjoyed the bubbling atmosphere that was created by the one, Miss Dally-Watkins. Her flair for modelling is free and rather exciting to watch.

She has with her an Australian-designed wardrobe which is pretty darn sharp, versatile and smart as the dickens.

And which the Honolulu designers and buyers approved of – most definitely! I must say the designs brought New York and Paris to Waikiki – if for only one evening – darn it!

Interested? Good! I shall go on – June will arrive in San Francisco, Wednesday, 23 July (Plaza Hotel) to make contacts to both boost Australia and learn from America . . . I have given June your name and address and she in turn will contact you. I told her your capacity at the *Chronicle* and that you not only know S.F. and San Franciscans like a book, but practically run the Village. I thought of you as being a most logical person to help welcome a cousin to the home-shores . . . The gal is definitely news and your boss might even find a bit of interesting journalistic material to write up – lend-lease and that – but you shall see.

Taken in by San Francisco's social set and promoted by BCPA, I appeared on television as a guest on 'The Marjorie Trimball Show' and modelled Frank's designs. It was my first encounter with television, which would take another four years to reach Australian shores. Naturally, it was exciting to be exposed to this medium in its pioneering stage. Perhaps expatriate film celebrities may have appeared on television, but certainly I was the first person to show Australian fashion on American television.

Before I left for Los Angeles I telephoned Orry Kelly, an Australian who had become successful in Hollywood designing clothes for Australian actress Merle Oberon, Joan Crawford, Norma Shearer and other Hollywood stars under MGM's control. I was lucky to have met Orry on a recent and rare visit to Sydney, and he had told me to contact him when I arrived in the USA. I gratefully accepted his invitation to stay at his Beverley Hills home.

I didn't go to Hollywood intent on becoming a film actress, but it was a buzz to finally discover the Hollywood I had thought as a child was a star in the night sky. All the same, it seemed about as far away from Australia as a celestial formation. Hollywood oozed sophistication and brashness that had not reached Australia's isolated shores. It was a shock to find out that many would-be actors were willing to recline on the casting couch in order to get a break into movies. Sex and sexuality were not discussed in Australia. Hollywood reeked of the stuff, but film-studio bosses went to great lengths to keep scandals from public knowledge. How times have changed! Nowadays, controversial trysts have become promotional tools to publicise new films. I knew I wasn't fast enough for Hollywood, but it didn't stop me from enjoying my time there.

Orry was happy to show me off and introduce me to his friends: the inner circle of Hollywood's top echelon. After a few introductions my social invitations snowballed – everyone wanted to meet 'the Australian'. The American fascination with and warmth shown to visiting Australians continues today.

I knew nothing about homosexuality, but soon twigged that

Orry was different. When actress Ethel Barrymore invited us to a dinner party at her home she and I were the only female guests amongst a group of mostly mature men, including the songwriter Cole Porter. The director and playwright George Cukor was also a guest. I was almost speechless to be in this famous group's company. My amazement with the revelation that men could prefer each other to women amused Orry, but my innocence also made him protective of me. When an attractive man started calling at his home to ask me out, Orry told him to stay away from me. 'Beware of him, June, he is married and bisexual.' I didn't know what 'bisexual' meant, but didn't want to appear even more of a fool by asking.

Orry would take me to lunch and dinner at 'in' places like Romanoff's – the famous restaurant of the stars and would-be stars in Hollywood. Seating depended on how famous you were. Orry was always given a place up front so anyone walking in spotted him immediately. All the stars knew Orry and came by our table for a chat, so I met actors John Wayne, Cary Grant, Judy Garland, Ray Milland and Herbert Marshall and many more. Sometimes Orry drank too much and argued with friends. After an altercation with Merle Oberon, Orry gave me a gold watch. 'Here June, take this thing. I don't want to be reminded of the bitch.' It was engraved, 'To Orry Kelly, with my undying love and friendship, Merle Oberon.' A few days later, Orry regretted his actions and asked for it back.

I knew the girls in the Sydney office would love my news about the who's who of tinsel town, so I sent photographs and wrote:

> It is almost unbelievable that so many wonderful things could happen to one girl in just ten short days in Hollywood. My first evening was rather a quiet one and I felt the usual pangs of homesickness. On reading the newspaper, I noticed a column by Gordon Currie, and immediately wondered if it was the same one I knew in Sydney. [Gordon took photos of the rich and

famous and sold them along with bits of gossip to the newspapers. He also had a syndicated radio program, which was broadcast in Australia.] On phoning the paper I discovered it was. So I phoned his apartment the next morning and renewed an old friendship with him and his wife, Eve . . . then the whirl started.

They asked me to go along with them the same afternoon (Sunday) to a party for Marilyn Monroe. It was held in the garden of the beautiful home of Ray Anthony, the famous band leader. From the moment I arrived my eyes were popping. Across the pool in purple flowers was written the word 'Marilyn'. Ray's full band was there, and as we stood and ate caviar and other fabulous food with the choice of any drink, Ray's band played – for the first time in public – the new song 'Marilyn'. It is a beautiful number, bound to be a hit.

At 5 p.m. Marilyn was due to arrive, and everyone was interested to know how she would make her entrance. We eventually saw a helicopter circling above and, believe it or not, that was how she arrived! The helicopter set down on the lawn near the pool, doing its best to remove some of the guests and beach umbrellas as it did so. Marilyn was wearing (here's where my eyes nearly fell out) a fuchsia-coloured jersey dress with not a stitch underneath – absolutely nothing – or so it appeared. She was very friendly and sweet to talk to, and has a very pretty face. While on the subject of dress – immediately I arrived, I felt overdressed. I was wearing as you can see by the picture, my Frank Mitchell silk dress, also a brassiere and stockings – neckline about three inches too high, and a bow which was covering too much.

I was photographed with Mickey Rooney, who did several numbers on the drums with the band – he is terrific and a cute little chap, much nicer looking than in the movies. Also met Tennessee Ernie Ford [a country and western singer and movie actor].

That night, I was introduced to the other side by Orry

Kelly. We had dinner at a very exclusive restaurant 'La Rue'. Here Orry introduced me to George Raft, Jimmy Stewart, Charles Laughton, Tyrone Power, George Sanders, Linda Christian. It was a wonderful evening with Orry the perfect host. He also introduced me to Mrs Jerry Wall, wife of the producer, who is the smartest woman I have met or seen in Hollywood, and also Stanley Marcus of Neiman Marcus in Dallas, Texas...

During my week here, I have done three television shows, a radio appearance on 'The Bob Hope Show', and had my whole Frank Mitchell wardrobe filmed to be used on TV. This was a wonderful experience, as the film men really know their business, and it was so easy to work with people like that directing. The film will be used on television throughout the US. On one show I was selected as 'The Woman of Distinction' for a coffee ad.

It was after this show on Sunday night that I met Jughead the Ostrich – a very clever bird. He and his master, Jean, have a TV show and Jean asked our party to have a drink after the show. We took Jughead along too. The man behind the bar nearly collapsed as we all walked in and sat up at the bar. Before long the bar was crowded, and we had a wonderful time watching the expression on people's faces as they came in the door. Later we went off to buy hot dogs on the corner of Hollywood and Vine – so we took Jughead along too...

I have visited all the interesting nightclubs, and went to see Nat King Cole and the Bell Sisters on stage. Nat King Cole is the most terrific person I have ever heard sing, and now I'm quite a fan of his. The hit here right now is called 'Half as Much', sung by Rosemary Clooney.

Anyone who imagines Hollywood as we see it in movies would be sadly disillusioned. It is not nearly the glamour spot you would imagine. Movies are strictly a business and a hard business. In my opinion, Australian girls would go home broken-hearted after six months here. There are so many girls waiting for a break into the movies, and they will use any means to get it. Meeting the stars is a great thrill. It is so exciting to be talking face to face with people you have watched so many times on the screen. All the stars I have met, I have found to be so natural and charming. They are just ordinary human beings who have chosen that line of business to make a living ...

Now I am looking forward to the next leg of my journey — across the States to New York. It will be so interesting to visit the model agencies and schools there, and learn more of their progressive ideas. My very large file of Australian models has caused a tremendous stir here. The girls' pictures were shown on television, and now everyone wants to see the girls in the flesh!

In New York, at the invitation of John Robert Powers, I visited his charm school to observe classes and learn from the business that had discovered many famous faces, including actresses Gene Tierney, Ava Gardner, Joan Crawford and Lauren Bacall. Mr Powers, as everyone called him, was many years my senior and I felt honoured to learn from the master. His business had an arrangement to sell Revlon cosmetic products, so trying to emulate his business I found my way to the Revlon head office on Fifth Avenue. With great bravado, I introduced myself in the hope of becoming the exclusive Australian agent for Revlon. 'You've come just a little too late. We gave David Jones the agency a week ago. Have you heard of them?' said an executive, who called me nothing but 'Dolly' during our meeting. Nevertheless, my school and agency have used Revlon products in classes ever since.

I was introduced to Sherman Billingsley, who invited me to his famous nightclub, the Stork Club. As I recall, Sherman was a bit of a rogue and leered at me during the evening. However, the experience of entering a glittering world where starlets stalked millionaires and where the famous and infamous mixed, from politicians to actors and royalty, was worth it. Anyone who was anyone went to the Stork. It was the perfect way to cap off my American visit.

Arriving in London, I was transported from the brand-spanking new world to the old world where butchers wore long, striped aprons and boater hats and hung sides of lamb and beef outside their shops. I stayed at the Cumberland Hotel and caught up with two Australian models with whom I had worked, Nola Rose and June Massey. The talented photographer David Moore took photos of me when I modelled for the house of Hartnell, the Queen's dressmaker.

Although I was able to bring back to my school the knowledge I gained from my exposure to the fashion industry and modelling overseas, work wasn't my priority while I was in London, so I didn't seek out other assignments. I was there to soak up the sights, theatre and meet people. Through Hollywood connections I had a blind dinner date with the English actor Michael Rennie, who found fame in *The Day the Earth Stood Still* and *The Robe*, among other films. We had only dated a few times before he proposed marriage. I was flattered, but found his preoccupation with his beauty tiring.

The director and playwright Garson Kanin and his wife Ruth Gordon, an actress and screenwriter, cabled me to contact their friend Spencer Tracy who was in London at the time. Garson and Ruth co-wrote several films, including the Tracy–Katharine Hepburn hits *Adam's Rib* and *Pat and Mike*. When I called Spencer he asked me to meet him in the foyer of Claridges Hotel where he was installed. At the appointed time, I saw him descend the hotel's marble staircase, glance at me and look away as if to seek out another face. It was obvious he had not been given a recognisable description, so I introduced myself and he seemed surprised. No wonder! Over afternoon tea he told me that Garson and Ruth had played a joke on him, saying I was an older actress from Australia and thought I would make a good mother for Debbie Reynolds' character in his next movie.

It was awesome to be with Spencer – he was already very

famous, with hit films like *Father of the Bride* and *Pat and Mike* to his credit. We went to the ballet at Covent Garden with Bettina, the most famous Parisian model of the time, and her lover, the playboy Prince Ali Khan IV (the former husband of screen siren Rita Hayworth and son of the mega-rich Aga Khan who reigned over millions of Shiah Ismaili Muslims worldwide). Afterwards, we were escorted backstage to meet the prima ballerina Dame Margot Fonteyn. Spencer showed a romantic interest in me and there was a spark between us that culminated in a kiss. I found Spencer handsome, but he was leaving for the USA by ocean liner and I was going on to Paris. At that stage I knew he was separated from his wife and two children, who lived in New York, but I didn't know that Katharine Hepburn was his lover. We arranged to meet again when I returned to Los Angeles. In the meantime, he sent cryptic telegrams: 'Word from Kanins/they meeting ship/are you too/how goes work and health which questions should cover all/love ballet man.' Not long after I landed in Paris, another note arrived: 'Trying get through/long delay quoted/maybe early morning/after letters you are mean to disappear/Have run off with handsome stranger if not when coming? Lovely house, homely man waiting/much love Uncle Sam.'

Visiting Paris for the first time was a good distraction from Spencer and the city easily wooed me. Just to buy a baguette and tuck it under my arm as I strolled along a tree-lined boulevard felt like a special occasion. To be invited to preview the forthcoming season's fashions at the haute couture autumn parades most certainly was. As mesmerising as it was to be amongst the fashion elite, I was in a daze at Balenciaga's show for other reasons. The parade was held in an intimate salon that had no air-conditioning. Guests perched on uncomfortable and impractical gilt chairs. As the lights bore down upon me, I began to feel woozy, so I left the room and fainted. When I recovered my head was in someone's lap and I was being fanned and encouraged back to consciousness by a lovely voice. I opened my eyes and thought I had died and gone to Hollywood heaven; my supporting angel was film star Claudette Colbert.

One of my escorts was the gorgeous Jacques, who owned a swish brasserie, La Rosarie. I could have had a romance with him, but I didn't want one to start that I knew I would finish. Jacques took me to a chic nightclub where we drank champagne – which remains my favourite pre-dinner drink. I was shocked to see women dancing with each other and kissing. I knew the word 'lesbian', but was naïve enough to think lesbians were simply quirky women who amused themselves by dressing as men. I hadn't ever considered that women could love each other romantically or have a sexual relationship. Once I realised this, I felt uncomfortable whenever a woman brushed up against me on a boulevard in Paris, and that happened more than once.

My new friends from Hollywood put me in contact with people working on the Bing Crosby film *Little Boy Lost*, being made at the Palais de Versailles outside Paris. They told me I could get on the film set if I agreed to pose as a journalist from Australia wanting to cover the filming for publicity back home. However, the plan was flawed; Bing didn't want a journalist there. When I revealed who I was and where I was from, curiosity got the better of Bing and I was made welcome. I think he expected me to hop onto the set like a kangaroo. He asked me to stay for lunch, during which time I sat beside him for a sing-a-long with the cast and crew. I was having such a good time that I soon overcame my self-consciousness about singing in such talented company, even forgetting that I was completely tone-deaf. My four children are harsher critics. Whenever I sang around the house over the years, they would cover their hands over their ears and urge me to stop. 'But I've sung with Bing Crosby,' I would offer. That didn't impress them. 'Try to whistle,' they'd plead. I couldn't do that in tune either.

Next destination: Rome. The scenery was absorbing as the train hurtled from France and through Switzerland towards Italy, but I was not prepared for the ancient wonders of Rome, which was romantic, clean and safe. My love affair with Italy has continued and been passed on to my children, particularly Carel, who lived there for more than four years, and Lisa, who is settled in Florence. I now have two Italian-born grandchildren, Natalia and Leo, and all my seven grandchildren call me 'Nonna'. I love it.

I checked in to Scalata, a boutique hotel at the top of the Spanish Steps and directly opposite the exclusive Hotel Hassler, where Gregory Peck was in residence for *Roman Holiday*. My Hollywood matchmakers arranged for me to meet Gregory. He invited me to attend the end-of-filming dinner party. Although a bundle of nerves, I eagerly accepted and hung on every word of Greg's well-modulated voice. I've always been a pushover for an attractive voice and Greg's had won me over. Audrey Hepburn had already moved on to work on another film, so I was placed between the star and the movie's director, William Wyler, in a seat that would have been occupied by Audrey had she been there. I have always admired her and in my own humble way I have followed in her footsteps. She was an ambassador for United Nations International Children's Emergency Fund in her senior years and now I'm an ambassador-at-large for Crossroads International – a no-frills charity that provides goods to the needy around the world.

The chemistry between Greg and myself was apparent to both of us at that first dinner. During the next week Greg romanced me and showed me the great vistas and monuments of Rome, including St Peter's, the Trevi Fountain and the Colosseum. We had our own Roman holiday. The locals seemed unaware of his celebrity status and so we could enjoy quiet dinners and get to know each other better. He took me to the Roman Forum and kissed me there in the moonlight. We walked hand in hand up the Spanish Steps and he kissed me goodnight and left me at the front of my hotel. He was a true gentleman of deep character. I didn't know whether to be relieved or disappointed.

I wanted to let myself fall in love with Greg, and we could have had a deeper involvement if only I had let my guard down. It was as if I had reached another one of those stars and didn't know what to do with it. Greg, on the other hand, was ready for a serious relationship. He had separated from his first wife and seemed lonely. He asked me to accompany him to Paris, but I was reticent to take this holiday romance to the next stage. I didn't know how to handle an intimate situation and I doubted that Greg would be interested in me beyond a fling. I would not have known how to make love anyway. There were no sealed sections in women's magazines giving explicit instructions on the intricacies of sex and it was never discussed with girlfriends or my mother. All the while, Mother's warnings surfaced from the back of my mind: 'Don't throw yourself at a man, he'll take advantage of you. Don't trust men. He will respect you more if you don't sleep with him.' So I resolved to show Greg that I wasn't easy and told myself that I preferred to win his respect as a friend. Now, I regret not taking up his invitation to meet him in Paris, not only because of what could have been, but because my decision was based on fear.

So what was my excuse to Greg for declining his proposition? Some modelling commitments with the designers, the Fontana sisters, whose clients included Ava Gardner, Audrey Hepburn and Grace Kelly, followed by a visit to my long-time friend, Dorn Fraser, who was living in Amsterdam and expecting another baby. I didn't want to disappoint Dorn. Keeping my word and being punctual was ingrained into my psyche as much as not sleeping around, so I held fast to my travel itinerary. Letting someone down took me back to the days when my mother and I would wait in vain on the verandah at Springvale for a gentleman caller who never showed. I didn't tell Dorn about Greg when I stayed with her, but she knows now. While Greg was in Paris he met the woman who would become, and still is, his wife – Veronique – and their marriage has stood the test of time. Greg briefly came back into my life in 1959 when he was in Melbourne making *On the Beach*. At his invitation, I visited the film set for the day and we reminisced about Italy. We parted, never to see each other again. In the early 1970s, I came home from work one day to learn from my son Marc that 'a man called Gregory Peck phoned and left his number'. We spoke to each other by phone, but did not have a chance to meet. If I had my time over again in Rome things might have been different, but that's the tide of life.

After I had extricated myself from Rome and Greg's embrace, I travelled alone to Sorrento and to the Isle of Capri before heading to Amsterdam. On the boat trip to this still unspoiled paradise, a young woman, who was among a group of women in smart, masculine clothing, gave me the eye. This time I understood her body language and appreciated the value of travel as an educator. Although I enjoyed my own company and the peace it gave me, I found it easy to make friends too. Many Europeans had never met an Australian and knew little about Australia. In the company of Italian tourists and a young Australian, Len, who was also travelling alone, I explored the island.

At the end of my grand tour of Europe, I flew back to New York. Friends had put me in contact with a man called Bud Lucky Junior (yes, that was his real name), who showed me Washington, DC, Monticello and Williamstown. He proposed to me, but once again I had a convenient exit from this potentially awkward situation – I was homeward bound and homesick. Before I left he gave me *The Prophet* by Kahlil Gibran and wrote in it, 'To June, so you'll never feel lonely again.' I don't know what became of Bud and it saddens me that we never met again. Sometimes life rushes us along too quickly and we have to swim like crazy to keep afloat, losing some friends along the way.

Back in Los Angeles, Spencer had a car and driver meet me at the airport. He had also organised my hotel accommodation and began to turn up his efforts to seduce me: 'Why stay at the hotel? Move in with me while you're in town.' Maybe Spencer would have cherished me, but I wasn't about to take the risk of finding out. By now I knew of his relationship with Katharine Hepburn and was curious as to why she never appeared or attended any of the social gatherings that I went to with Spencer. Spencer never mentioned Katharine or his wife, so I played it safe and didn't refer to them either. After I rejected Spencer's advances, he continued to treat me well and respect me. He even arranged for one of his cars to be at my disposal. It was the first time I had driven an automatic car and it came with a remote control to open his garage door. I'd go around the block to his house again and again to test the remote control, such was its novelty value.

Spencer seemed proud to have an Australian to introduce to his friends and took me to dinner parties in the company of Humphrey Bogart, Lauren Bacall and James Cagney. We were also entertained at the Beverly Hills home of George Cukor, a producer and director of some of the Hepburn–Tracy films. I might disappoint some readers, but I never witnessed the Dr Jekyll–Mr Hyde mood swings brought on by alcoholic binges for which Spencer was known in Hollywood circles. Nor did I have anything outrageous to report from the various dinners I went to in Hollywood. Everyone was very normal and unpretentious. The only star I met who didn't live up to my expectations was the too brassy and barely dressed Marilyn Monroe.

I visited movie sets through a contact at Paramount Studios and met a series of actors, including Cary Grant, John Payne, Jan Stirling and Colleen Gray. These were brief encounters, but unimaginable today in terms of the ease in gaining on-set access to chat and be photographed with actors who were in the middle of filming. Bing had asked me to call him at Paramount when I returned to Los Angeles, but when we met again he was distraught because his wife Dixie was dying of cancer. My long acquaintance with Bob and Delores Hope had its origins on this trip. I established a rapport with arguably the world's most famous comedian over lunch, after being a guest on his radio show.

Of all the invitations I received during this sabbatical, the most tempting was an MGM proposal to run a personal development school for the studio's starlets. MGM's Benny Thau invited me to visit the studios and made the attractive offer. He was intrigued by my nationality too. One evening at his home, Greer Garson telephoned and Benny handed me the phone so she could hear my voice. I didn't mind; I was enthralled to hear Greer's lilting tones. I consider her voice, along with Greg Peck's and James Mason's, as the most attractive voices I've ever heard. When I didn't jump at the studio's job offer, MGM mogul Arthur Loew, who had tried unsuccessfully to court me, got Australian Betty Bryant to work on me. Betty became famous as the love interest to Chips Rafferty in the Australian war film, *Forty Thousand Horsemen*. 'Arthur doesn't want you to leave,' she insisted. I declined the offer again.

I don't regret walking away from this opportunity and leaving Hollywood. Instead of dwelling on what I might have achieved there, I prefer to think of what I have achieved in my own homeland. I might also have found it difficult to keep up with the fast crowd in Hollywood. At the time regular commuting between Australia and the USA was unthinkable and, in any case, I was unprepared to give up what I had already established at home. However, the overriding factor that made me reject MGM's offer was the thought of my mother. I knew she missed me and needed me. It was getting close to Christmas. Mother had sent me a copy of an invitation for a welcome-home party she had planned in my honour. And she wrote about our new ground-floor apartment on Lower Beach Road near the Harbour. We were now truly in the eastern suburbs. It had taken hard work and perseverance to get there. If I stayed in Hollywood I knew I would have to uproot her and bring her to me. On my flight home, I travelled in first class, which had pull-down bunks attached to the walls, but I couldn't sleep. As the aircraft droned loudly, reservations about heading home crept into my mind. When the plane eventually landed in Sydney, it was to the thud of reality. There was no welcome-home party.

10 Four babies and a divorce

In my six months' absence overseas, the only man back home that I had missed had fallen in love with someone else. With the exception of Gregory Peck, I had not allowed myself to fall for anyone. Of all the young men I dated, I felt serious only about John Paul, a sandy-haired bachelor who was about my age. He and his business mates Kell Hutchence, the father of former INXS lead singer Michael, and John Mingay were the impressive young men around town. John Paul's business, Younger Garments, produced fashionable clothing. I was invited to their Cocktails with Chic parties held at the stylish Pickwick Club and I became good friends with all three. I began to spend weekends sailing with John and visiting mutual friends, property developer Arthur Little and his wife Thelma at their Palm Beach home. However, by going overseas I treated this young man as I had others; I severed ties before I could be hurt. Perhaps, I had been too reserved with John. Then there was the possibility that he never loved me. Either way, I never tried to find out.

On top of the disappointment of a lost romance, after so much time away from Mother I found it difficult to resume living under the same roof. Our new apartment at Rushcutters Bay was attractive with views of the bay and park. It had two bedrooms, however Mother insisted on keeping the second one as her sewing room, meaning we were still sharing sleeping quarters. When an old boyfriend from Melbourne offered me the use of his father's rooftop penthouse in Darlinghurst I braved Mother's predictably cool reaction to move in. I lived there alone for the next six months.

Rekindling my social life came easily and for the first time I felt ready for a relationship with someone special. From the moment I caught the eye of John Clifford across a crowded room at an acquaintance's home, I was smitten. The Italians have an expression for it, *colpo di fulmine*, which means 'a bolt from the blue'. His dark looks and resonant voice reminded me of Gregory Peck. He looked sharp, dressed in tennis whites and a navy blazer, having spent the afternoon on the Royal Sydney Golf Club tennis courts. The fact that John had lived abroad also appealed. He had completed a Royal British Navy traineeship in England and, as a midshipman with the British Navy, had visited Ireland, Europe and the West Indies before becoming a lieutenant in the Royal Australian Navy. Before the party had finished, we left. John gave me a tour of the frigate, HMAS *Shoalhaven*, on which he was based and we spent the rest of the evening in the officers' dining room.

Our courtship was snatched between John's commitments at sea and mine on land. In the interim, I admired a photograph I kept of him by my bedside. He was so very handsome. His return to dock heralded romantic rendezvous, including one in Brisbane, where he had leave from HMAS *Australia* to meet me for a date at the Doomben races. When 'The Twist' made its debut in Australia John and I danced at Chequers nightclub in Goulburn Street, and we saw Nat King Cole at The Stadium at Rushcutters Bay. Our friends and John's parents, Jess and John, were quick to tease us about getting married. After three months of intermittent dating – a period that hardly gave us time to really understand each other, let alone determine compatibility – we walked up the aisle.

Until then, I had been reticent about the idea of marriage, evident in my rejection of several proposals. I had maintained I would stay single or at least wait until I was 30 before I made a lifelong commitment to a husband. This was a period when a woman was considered an old maid at 22 years of age. I was 27, so my attitude was unorthodox. My mother's unhappy experience with men no doubt had worked its influence, but I also didn't want to lose what I had: a successful career, earning more money than most other men I knew, overseas travel, and meeting exciting people. I had no reason to long for a husband solely because one would provide financial security. Also I hadn't liked much of what I had seen of others' marriages.

Having confided in John about a lingering sadness from my childhood (and that was about as much detail as I did disclose about my illegitimacy), and then being accepted by him, the fear of rejection because of my past dissolved. Trust took its place and I allowed myself to fall in love with him. My career didn't seem to be a problem. Most wives didn't work in those days. John, however, had no qualms about me pursuing my passion, even in the event of motherhood. I figured that any child we might have would be better off with a working mother who was happy than with one who resented being at home. By preserving my career, I hoped it would be some insurance from becoming like some stay-at-home mothers, including mine, who felt bereft when their children grew up and left them. These women's identities became lost in marriage. Surrendering my business name wasn't a consideration either. I had seen wives work alongside their husbands in a business, yet all the glory went to the man because the business was in his name. In any case, John recognised the value of my name. In private, for his and my children's sake, I happily became Mrs Clifford. I remain so to this day. I have only had one marriage, although a friend told me she was at a dinner recently when someone said, 'Oh, June Dally-Watkins has had at least four husbands.'

Unfortunately, but not surprisingly, Mother didn't warm to John. Any man I chose to wed would inevitably have met with her criticism. Mother felt I belonged exclusively to her and John represented a wedge between us. He had a Catholic upbringing too, which presented another problem for someone like Mother who had been raised to think Catholics were strange. In those days churches and society frowned upon 'mixed marriages'. Indeed, in the Catholic Church it was the practice for a couple of mixed religion to marry behind the altar. John and I were probably among the first to be married before the main altar at St Mary's Cathedral in Sydney. I remember the priest wanted me to have more instruction in Catholicism to which my bridesmaid, Helen, says I replied: 'Get me now or I might change my mind about getting married!' I agreed to follow the Catholic doctrine and raise our children as Catholics, but I didn't convert to Catholicism until my youngest child, Lisa, was born nine years later.

Mother presented a cheerful face for my wedding but, knowing that she didn't approve, I found it difficult to truly enjoy every moment of that day. On the eve of my wedding, we had been preparing savouries and sandwiches for the reception at her home and had an argument, over what I can no longer remember. I fled the situation and was later found by John sitting in my car, sobbing. Even so, everything felt right in the world on a sunny afternoon on 27 June 1953. Uncle Os gave me away. I wore an ankle-length, ballerina-style tulle skirt and a bodice of guipure lace. The dress was lined with soft pink and I wore high-heeled court shoes that had been dyed to match. Sweet Helga Marling, an accomplished milliner from Hungary, made my headdress – a divine, heart-shaped hat with a short pale-pink veil attached. Scores of onlookers packed into the cathedral and congregated outside, along with the press, as John and I exited the church through a naval guard of honour. Our wedding made front-page news and wedding photographs appeared in magazines. My dear old mate John Hearder took our album photos. About thirty people gathered for the reception, including John's parents, who had travelled from Melbourne. I'll never forget John's father patting me on the head and saying, 'Don't worry, son, as soon as she has a family she won't want the business.'

Our honeymoon at a house on the edge of the Hawkesbury River was brief and not romantic in a champagne-and-roses way or glamorous compared to the places I had travelled. John and I started our married life just as unpretentiously. We rented a basic, ground-floor flat at Woollahra, in an apartment block that Arthur Little owned. When friends came to visit we didn't have sufficient chairs, so they sat on lots of cushions. It was fun. Washing clothes was only minimally easier than at Watson's Creek. I used a stick to remove the clothes from a gas-heated copper, transferring them into tubs where I wrung them out, then carried them outside to the clothesline.

Early in our relationship there were plenty of good times. On Friday nights, we took turns treating each other to dinner, keeping the choice of restaurant a secret until we arrived at the appointed destination. Sundays were reserved for lawn parties with friends. Helen was always there, as well as John's naval mates and their wives, Ted and Lorraine Jones, John and Liz Brooker, and Geoff and Sheila Woolrych. We cooked sausages and chops on a portable barbecue and drank beer until a trend in all things Italian swept us along. We thought it was adventurous and sophisticated to eat spaghetti bolognaise; we didn't know other pastas existed. We bought food from a delicatessen for the first time. Taking a tip to use garlic, I added raw cloves to a salad and shocked our inexperienced taste buds. We took empty bottles to the Italian importer, Fiorelli, in Surry Hills, to have them filled with cheap wine and sherry from wooden casks. John and his mates thought it would be economical to buy a cask and have a bottling ceremony on our lawn. By the end of the day, most of the bottles were half empty and our teeth and tongues were stained purple. It became stylish to use empty, round-bottomed Chianti bottles as candleholders and I even became upset when a zealous housekeeper removed built-up wax that I had intentionally melted over a bottle for decorative effect.

My business was flying high, literally. I had just successfully produced Australia's first fashion parade in the air. Trans-Australia Airlines (TAA), like other businesses keen for promotion in the post-war commercial boom, was receptive to my proposal for an in-flight parade. So, during a flight from Sydney to Melbourne, the models – Michele Safargy, Jeanette Elphick, Marie Roberts and Dorothy Dunkerley – paraded up and down the aisle and changed garments behind a curtained-off, cramped area at the rear of the plane. They then presented fashions for Myer's at the Melbourne Cup – the very first 'Fashions on the Field'. A Sydney-to-Cairns in-flight parade followed, during which I felt nauseous. When the queasiness continued on land, it occurred to me that I might be pregnant. My facial expression was so stunned that the lovable *Telegraph* columnist Jim Macdougall, who was covering the promotional event, guessed what I was thinking but kept my secret from the news pages.

Despite four months of morning sickness, I continued to work. As I grew in size, so did the business. We moved to the ninth floor of the Dymocks building on George Street in the city. When enrolments for the school bulged we ran extra classes in the corridor and across the road at Bisley House. I was approached to buy the Bisley House building for £85 000, but with a baby on the way it was just beyond my financial reach. How I regret that now. I was never a good business-woman as far as profit-making was concerned. I just worked hard and reaped some benefits as a result.

I loved the thought of becoming a mother and wanted to raise a family, particularly because I never had a sense of belonging to one. My mother, on the other hand, initially was not impressed by my pregnancy. To her way of thinking a baby would shrink her time with me.

However, Mother was happy to have me stay with her in the days before I was due to give birth since John was en route to Sydney from Melbourne with HMAS *Australia*. When I went into labour she deposited me at the hospital and left me to it, returning with John's sister, Judy Clifford, at midnight, when Carel was born. Typical of Mother's oscillating nature, as soon as she laid eyes on Carel she loved her. Of my four children – Carel, Timothy, Marc and Lisa – my first-born remained her favourite. As Carel grew older, Mother often remarked that she had the face of Princess Caroline of Monaco, and so she does. Marc looks very much like Prince Albert of Monaco. During the Sydney Olympic Games, Marc and the prince came face to face at the Regent Hotel. They stopped and stared at each other, as though they were looking into a mirror!

Within days of giving birth, I returned to work. It was the same when my other children were born. The day after each new member of the family arrived my secretary would visit me at the hospital so I could give her instructions about urgent work matters, and it was virtually business as usual. I remember doing a radio interview from my hospital bed not long after Lisa was born and being back at work ten days later. I breastfed all of my children, but not for long. When Carel was a baby, I hurried back and forth from the office to home to enable this. Then, at the end of each day, I relieved the babysitter, gave Carel another feed and got her ready for bed and for John to take over when I returned to the city to teach the deportment school students. Sometimes I would take Carel with me to my commitments in Sydney and Brisbane.

Not long after Carel's birth, John found a new career. With the help of Sid Albright, John secured a marketing job with Twentieth Century Fox's sixteen-millimetre film division. He was due home at 5.30 p.m., which meant I could get back to the city by 6 p.m. to teach the students. But often John would have a drink with the boys and arrive home around 6.15 p.m. In general, Australian men considered it their right to go to the pub after work before it closed at 6 p.m. – John included. Not only was this annoying and upsetting to me, it wasn't good for business. Yet if the class I taught ran fifteen minutes overtime and John had been waiting outside in the car to take me home he would be furious. I was so panicked about meeting John at the appointed hour that one night as I rushed out the door, I accidentally locked in two students who had been in the toilets. It took them some time to find my home phone number so they could request their release.

Comments from friends, family and the press about my working life must have made John feel awkward from time to time. From the beginning of our wedded life the press made note of my career in tones that verged on disapproval. In a short story about me for a Boans' spring fashion parade in the early 1950s, the *Western Mail* noted: 'Her husband, at present on HMAS *Australia* and far from home, does not mind her being so often away from their Sydney flat, as his duties require long absences from home.' The article never considered what I minded! By 1965 the attitude towards working wives and mothers had changed little. The *Sydney Morning Herald* noted that my children were 'well balanced, understanding of her career, and give no signs of being maladjusted,' inferring that the way they had turned out was something of a fluke. I always hoped that if children knew they were loved and they had a secure home life they would grow up well adjusted.

Throughout my marriage, I suspected that John and his mates felt he was hard done by because he didn't have a wife waiting with a hot meal on the table when he came from work. People would say to me, 'Poor John, why don't you give him more attention?' or 'You're neglecting your husband.' I'll concede that John had to compete for my attention what with the business, my mother and the children, but no one ever said, 'Poor June, you're working so hard.'

I found unexpected support from businessmen, and perhaps this is why I have maintained a great rapport and friendship with many of them. Women, however, generally were more critical. Their tut-tutting of disapproval was audible. I received abusive phone calls and letters at my office for being a terrible mother and wife and warnings that my children would end up delinquents if I continued to work. I was afraid they might. It began when Carel was born and continued into the late 1960s when Lisa was growing up. I was too tired and hurt to ever retaliate. I suspected the callers were ladies of leisure – possibly some were acquaintances from the eastern suburbs – because their calls always came in the afternoon, after a long lunch or tennis when the cocktail hour had begun.

How many other women who wanted to carve out a career were put down for their ambition and forced to give up their dreams? When I dared to pursue mine, I was made to feel a failure as a wife and mother, but I resolved to never give up the right to live my own life. Had I bowed to the status quo and stayed at home it would have destroyed me. Today I wouldn't be ostracised and criticised for being a working mother. Nowadays some mothers are made to feel guilty about not working and wanting to stay at home and raise children. But back then it was unusual to find a woman heading a business, let alone one who was married with children. The more I was made to feel guilty, the more I became determined to prove I was a good mother. I felt I had to demonstrate to the critics that they were wrong, so I tried to give my children the best opportunities and sought out the best home help I could.

Thus began trials and triumphs with housekeepers and nannies – a necessity for two working parents with four children. Sometimes I didn't make the best decisions when hiring. I was tired and desperate to find a quick solution. We took in a Spanish girl, sponsored by the nuns at Kincoppal-Rose Bay Convent, and explained as best I could that my family would like breakfast to be served at 7.30 a.m. The next morning there was no sign of our helper and I ended up cooking breakfast. Just as we sat down to eat, we heard a 'click, click' and the girl swept into the kitchen with castanets in her hands, twirling her full skirt and shouting, '*Olé*!' Her performance over, she promptly sat down to eat. I should have laughed, but at the time I needed someone capable. She couldn't speak English, couldn't boil an egg, and when I attempted to teach her how to make toast she buttered it on both sides. We sent her back to the nuns.

Then there was the girl from Germany, who shaved her head and seemed to believe in Gestapo methods of handling children. Timothy had his mouth sealed with masking tape so he wouldn't cry. When John and I found out, she was swiftly dismissed, but it didn't put an end to our testing times with housekeepers. We came home earlier than expected from an evening out to find our English housekeeper throwing a wild party. Her friends had stained the carpet with beer and let their cigarettes burn into the cedar sideboard. Another housekeeper and a nanny schemed to earn extra income and split it, with one of them taking an outside job and returning home only minutes before John or I were due to arrive. Then there was an Australian woman who came with excellent references, which she must have written herself. She checked in without luggage and left to collect it late in the day, promising to return in a short while. That was the last we saw of her and my gold jewellery.

Not all the hired help were disasters. The lovely Miss Elphick, who by coincidence shared the same surname as one of my most acclaimed models at that time, Jeanette Elphick, was our first nanny. When Miss Elphick accompanied me with Carel on an interstate business trip a large gathering of airport staff greeted us at the airport. They had obviously expected the model and were disappointed to meet her 50-something, heavyweight namesake. The airport staff flatteringly (or was it?) assumed I was Jeanette and Miss Elphick was me.

Timothy came home from St Margaret's Maternity Hospital to our new home – the bottom floor of a lovely old house in Fairfax Road, Bellevue Hill – and into the arms of a Karitane nurse. I continued to use these nurses for my next two babies, Marc and Lisa. My neighbour Sonia McMahon was another advocate for Karitane nurses. They came to us from New Zealand and it became a bit of a fashion statement in Sydney's eastern suburbs to have one.

Our first immigrant live-in housekeeper, Barbara, came from Germany, and we shared in the excitement of her fiancé Seigwarth's arrival and their wedding. I am godmother to their daughter, Sonia. Barbara's cooking was so wonderful that my family insist I make her potato-and-onion salad every Christmas. Yaap, a Dutch chef, was naturally a whiz in the kitchen, and I have kept in touch with him and his wife Toni. Mary Redfern was another blessing, despite her dubious Scottish wives' remedies. I've only suffered a couple of migraines in my life and for one of them Mary suggested I drink a mixture of castor oil and whisky. Mary thought our budgerigar was looking a little piqued, so she gave it some and the bird died. I thought I might too, but the concoction cured my migraine. Mary's broad Scottish accent rubbed off on Carel, who for a while also copied her kindergarten teacher's facial tick.

Any helpers I had at home had the weekends free, when I took over caring for the children. In effect, this meant I never stopped working. In those days husbands and fathers were not expected to help in domestic matters. It was also a time when men weren't allowed in to delivery rooms when their wives gave birth. They waited at home, played golf or had a beer with their mates. John washed the car while I was in labour with Lisa. In any case, I was happy not to have him with me because childbirth was hard work and I needed all the concentration I could muster to get through it. When I was in the first stages of labour with Lisa in October 1962, I was reading a new book on natural childbirth when Sister Ann (the nun in charge of St Margaret's where I gave birth to all my children) marched in, told me the book was 'a lot of rot', took it out of my hands and tossed it aside. There was no point in arguing with Sister Ann, who was an expert in childbirth and a stickler for doing things her way. I still had a troublesome labour because I wasn't fit physically and, deep down, knew the fractures that had appeared in my marriage would not be mended by the arrival of another baby.

Mother added stress to my marriage, often arriving on our doorstep unannounced and sometimes placing me in an awkward position. I was defensive when John spoke ill of her and just as protective of him when Mother took the same tack, particularly if she spoke poorly of John to the children.

Respite from my mother's mood swings came when she met Bill James, the musical director of the Australian Broadcasting Commission (later to become a corporation), at one of the Sydney Town Hall musical concerts that they each frequented. A kindly gentleman, Bill gave Mother a new focus and she began to visit our home less. For the first time in her life she began to reduce her workload. Now Mother had someone special to share her passion for music, particularly the piano. They were also both heavy smokers. I remember Bill playing the piano for hours – a cigarette permanently dangling from his lips. He died of cancer of the throat in 1997.

W.G. James was a noted composer, who made his debut as a concert pianist at a London Promenade concert. He later became the ABC's first Federal Director of Music. He composed the perennial Australian Christmas carols, including 'Christmas Bush for His Adoring' and 'Sing Gloria'. He adjudicated national concerts that uncovered the talents of Joan Sutherland and Richard Bonynge.

Bill impressed Mother and introduced her to the kind of lifestyle and people she had always dreamt about. Bill had worked with Sir Bernard Heinz (hailed as an influential figure in Australian music) and the ABC general manager Sir Charles Moses to establish Australian orchestras and concerts and bring them up to world standard. Sir Bernard and his wife Valerie attended their wedding. Charles Buttrose Senior was another ABC mate of Bill's, so Mother befriended Ita Buttrose's mother, Clare. They were great buddies. So began my long connection with the Buttrose family. As a teenager Charlie Junior courted Carel and even proposed to her and gave her a ring. They have remained good friends. And over the years there were several times Ita and I came together through mutual friends.

Bill's status ensured my mother's wedding at St Mark's Cathedral in Sydney in June 1960 made page one of the *Sunday Mirror*. Mother looked stylish in a cinnamon satin and lace suit, matching satin stilettos and hat. I was her matron of honour and hosted the wedding reception at my Bellevue Hill home. Tim and my housekeeper's son Archie somehow got into the champagne until we noticed they were much too wobbly on their feet, even for 5-year-olds. The ceremony didn't go off without a hitch either. The bride had arrived but the celebrant, a Reverend Goodwin, was nowhere to be seen until someone stirred him from a nap.

However, only a few years after her second marriage began, Mother and Bill separated. I wasn't surprised. Even before she and Bill married they'd had a period of separation. Mother never spoke about marital problems with Bill or what brought their relationship to an end, but I knew that Bill could be stubborn and my mother was certainly trying, so I didn't need to ask for details. In any case, Mother seemed untroubled by the split. Once again, she began to jostle for a prime position in my life.

Regardless of this, I was preoccupied with the business. As a workaholic, my energy was immense, but competing and constant demands stretched it to the limit. Mostly, my memory of being a young wife and mother was of complete exhaustion. By the end of a working day, even my eyelids were exhausted from the weight of wearing false eyelashes. The first thing I did when I came in the door from work was peel off the fake lashes. As a pre-schooler, Tim was so fascinated by this trick he tried to remove his own eyelashes, and thought I was ever so clever when he realised he couldn't.

Working set hours never occurred to me and wasn't possible when I was at the helm of my own business. I worked at the agency during the day and ran deportment classes on weeknights and Saturday mornings. During the week I'd be home at 8 p.m. or later if I had a dinner function to attend. Even when I was at home, I sometimes had to track down a particular model for a last-minute booking the next day or take their calls. Running a model agency required accommodating agencies and clients overseas – and their time zones. John didn't appreciate how demanding my work was and how fatigued it made me, but I couldn't entirely blame him because we never talked in detail about what it entailed. That couldn't have been good for our relationship. I was always running off somewhere for work: regional New South Wales, Queensland, Europe, the USA, the Philippines, Hong Kong, Singapore, Thailand, Korea, Japan. No wonder John got fed up. It was hard enough for me, let alone for John to keep track of my comings and goings.

I didn't deliberately avoid facing problems in my marriage by making work trips overseas and interstate, but my absences added to them. My disappearances also fed the eastern suburbs' rumour mill, churned by idle minds. John received a phone call from the wife of a naval dentist who suspected I was having an affair with her husband in Europe merely because we were both away at the same time. Another day, I received a call in the office from a woman who claimed John, who at the time was on a flight back from Melbourne to Sydney, was leaving me for a female flight attendant. These false stories were unsettling and put doubts in both our minds.

Increasingly, John stayed out at night with his mates. His naval background made him place great importance on mateship, which became another problem in our marriage. He was everyone's mate, charming and great company. Some of John's drinking buddies behaved like boys who didn't have any responsibilities. One night John had been out with his mates and didn't come home. The next day I was in a rage. I wanted to hit out at him, but instead tossed my wedding dress in the garbage bin. That would show him I was at the end of my tether, I thought. After all these years, I still regret throwing out that beautiful dress. John probably didn't even notice.

Our problems had set in long before that night. John and I had been married for fifteen years, during which time we had many arguments. Getting to really know, tolerate and accept your partner, and share a love that matures into respect must surely be the answer to a long and happy marriage. We couldn't achieve that. John and I didn't see eye to eye on anything, except eventually to separate for our children's sake. We decided that the children would be better off in a happy home with one parent to raise and discipline them, instead of two parents pulling against each other. I had learned from my childhood that an unhappy home could affect children all their lives. I believed a family home should be joyful, not full of anger and bitterness.

John and I agreed to part amicably, but I felt devastated the day he left. It was a Sunday, 26 May 1968. Carel burst into tears and Tim became quiet when their father told them he was going to live somewhere else. However, once they got over the shock of his news, they didn't seem really grief-stricken about his departure. John decided Marc and Lisa were too young to understand, so didn't try to explain the situation to them. Carel was 13, Tim, 11; Marc, 7; and Lisa, 5. Lisa has no memory of us ever being together. I sent the children outside to play with the neighbours' children so they wouldn't see their father leave the house. The children loved their daddy, but shared my sense of relief. The war between their parents was over. Everyone seemed happier and the home was brighter.

Mother gave me no sympathy over the breakdown of my marriage: 'Well, I'm not surprised. What did you expect?' Already emotionally weaker and feeling like a failure, my confidence was crushed by my mother's comments. This served to give her the upper hand in our relationship. Subconsciously, she was happy John was out of my life because it gave her the chance to recast her web of control over me. Not surprisingly, Mother never wanted another man to come into my life. Any man who showed interest in me was never good enough. 'You've already made one mistake,' she reminded me. Of course, it was to her advantage for me not to marry again, because it would have left her more alone.

In any case, I resolved never to remarry. My decision was perhaps influenced by my mother, but moreover because I didn't want the complications of involving my children with another family. Another husband would have been simply one more person to look after and I didn't need that burden when I already had so much responsibility. Unlike some women, I also didn't have a financial need to be married. I had always been the primary breadwinner in my marriage, earning four times as much as John. I have never had to depend on anyone. This was largely due to my dependent mother's determination that I should be a 'somebody'.

Where would we have been without what I earned? I paid for our car and by the time I was 30 I had bought my mother an ermine coat and myself a mink stole – every woman's fashion desire at the time – and my family a two-storey home in Bulkara Road, Bellevue Hill. It had a superb view overlooking Double Bay and to the Harbour Bridge and a self-contained apartment. I lived there for twenty years. Another owner sold it for several million in 2001 – a huge increase on its original purchase price of £12 150. Courtesy of my enterprise, I had also been able to provide overseas and typical Australian family holidays to the Gold Coast and Perisher ski fields.

In accordance with the law of the day, John and I had to be separated for three years before we could be divorced. Despite the time lapse, I felt emotional when I finally filed for a divorce. Some people seem surprised to know I had been married in the first place or that John and I had separated, because I had always been known publicly by my maiden name. When John remarried in the mid 1970s, the same pain resurfaced. I wasn't upset about John's second marriage, but as I watched my children prepare for his wedding I felt like I was giving them away. The children felt uncomfortable too. They only saw their father at weekends. Their relationship with their father wasn't as close as it could have been.

The cold war between John and I exacerbated the situation. It took about a decade for the frosted wall of silence to thaw between us. It began around 1980. John's second marriage hadn't worked out and he had been on his own for some time when we both happened to be in London over the Christmas period. Two people who are very dear, *Vogue* magazine boss Bernard Leser and his wife Barbara, had invited my family to use their delightful Chelsea apartment for the holiday period, and my children, John and I came together with friends for Christmas. Now John enjoys being with his children and grandchildren as much as possible. So we meet as a family for Christmas Day and birthdays. In 2001, we even shared a family holiday in Bali.

11 Travels with my children

Just as my mother and absent father had an impact on how I turned out, I have often wondered how John and I affected our children and the directions they took with their lives. We all pay a price for the choices we make in life, but I have no regrets about the decisions I have made. The business was my first baby and my children's oldest sibling. Rivalry between siblings is common and so it was between the business and my children. At the same time, the business fed and nurtured my children, educated and employed them, and indeed challenged them. In return, they have respected and loved it, have been jealous and resentful of it, and have fought for and against it.

The way the business ruled my life meant my children sometimes had to vie for the attention I gave to the business, industry associates, my mother, John, and anyone else who called out for help or friendship. The need to feel wanted has always dwelt strongly within me. As a result, I've been compelled to give my attention or help when anyone asked for it, and this must have been frustrating for my children. Looking back, there were definitely times when my children needed me more than the business or other people did. It upsets me to know that, once when I was away for work, Carel was missing me so much that she sat amongst the clothes in my wardrobe, comforted by my lingering scent.

When my marriage was over and I was through with unreliable housekeepers, all the children were installed in boarding schools. Soon after John left, Lisa then five, began boarding at Gibb Gate, the junior school of Frensham at Bowral. When Lisa was enrolled at Kincoppal-Rose Bay Convent, she and Carel were allocated sleeping quarters in the infirmary so they could room together. I thought she was in good care with the nuns and her sister to look after her. Carel mothered Lisa as well as her younger brothers, and there were times I relied on her to hold the fort. Even now, Lisa will phone Carel for advice before contacting me. This leaves me with mixed emotions: I'm pleased that they are close, but feel a little sad that they might lean on each other before me.

There were times the children weren't in boarding school, so Mother would stay with them. By the late 1960s she would not touch alcohol, thanks to a series of injections of some kind that made her body reject its taste. The treatment, administered by a psychiatrist, was so successful that she even detested the taste of vanilla essence. Comforted by the knowledge that Mother no longer drank, and blaming alcohol for her past erratic behaviour, I felt I could go away on work trips without worrying about her and her ability to care for my children. On my return, everything was in order and there were no complaints.

I can thank my mother for investing her time and money to encourage my children's musical talents. She imagined, perhaps too ambitiously, my children as future concert pianists, especially Carel whom she'd take to concerts at Sydney Town Hall. Once Mother hit on an idea, there was no way of reining in her enthusiasm to see it to fruition. She rented a piano for my children, but there were other activities to occupy their time. Growing up in a city, where there were many distractions to entertain them, a piano wasn't as important to them as it had been to break the boredom for my mother at Watson's Creek. To my mother's credit, Tim can play by ear, but chose the guitar over the piano as his preferred instrument. Lisa plays piano competently and, like Carel, was told at school that she had perfect pitch. Only Marc, along with his mother, isn't musical. I felt reassured that Mother's outrageous, self-deprecating sense of humour could make the children laugh. She could be great fun. Referring to her advancing years, Mother would sometimes say, 'I need a bit of an iron today.' I'm beginning to understand what she meant!

This arrangement seemed perfect until my mother's mental health took a turn for the worse in 1968. I've blocked out many memories of what she was like at that time. I don't know how my mother managed to keep working at my school and preparing meals for the children and me, while deep inside she must have been in agony as she tried to fend off irrational thoughts. Desperate to help herself and not wanting to hurt anyone else, she sought the help of the same eminent psychiatrist who had treated her drinking problem not long before.

The psychiatrist tried to address her problems by putting her through a radical treatment: deep-sleep therapy. Under this regimen, my mother and other patients were put into drug-induced sleeps. Deaths following deep-sleep therapy at the Chelmsford Private Hospital (Mother was hospitalised elsewhere) in Sydney in the 1960s and 1970s prompted a Royal Commission in the late 1980s. The inquiry heard that some patients were put to sleep for up to three weeks, during which time they received electric-shock treatment. Deep-sleep therapy has since been discredited and the Royal Australian and New Zealand College of Psychiatrists condemns the controversial therapy.

John and I had been separated only a couple of months when Carel suddenly came down with a life-threatening medical condition. One morning, when my daughter kissed me goodbye on her way to school, I noticed swelling around her nose that had ever so slightly raised one eye and eyebrow. I took her to the doctor and a rare tumour in her antrum was diagnosed. The same month that my mother was hospitalised, Carel underwent an operation to remove the tumour. Carel's tumor was unique in Australia. Her surgeon told us there were only four known cases in the world at that time, so he couldn't anticipate the future. I decided to take Carel to the Pak Institute in New York, stopping on the way in Honolulu for the opinion of Dr Walter Quisenberry. I had befriended Walter and his wife Evelyn during my visit to the island during the Mr and Miss Australian Surf tour. Walter was now head of cancer research for the Hawaiian Islands. He gave Carel a clean bill of health, so we travelled on to San Francisco and Los Angeles, where we visited Disneyland.

On our return, I became convinced that Mother's treatment had helped her. Conditioning myself to see only the good times Mother created, I blinkered my vision to her mood swings. Perhaps I had become immune to them. My children, on the other hand, weren't used to them. Just as I didn't know what state my mother would be in when I came home as a teenager, they sometimes didn't know how their grandmother would behave when they returned from school. They were unaware of the deep sadness she had experienced in life.

At least my children had enviable compensations for not having a stay-at-home mum: a privileged upbringing, a wonderful home, exclusive private school education, international travel, and as much love as I could give them. I wanted my children to become citizens of the world and in the spirit of 'grand tours of Europe' gain knowledge and sophistication through travel. The children were so used to travel that, after a stay at one of the Hyatt hotels in Asia, Marc placed numbers on our bedroom doors at home, assembled tables and chairs, wrote up menus, and made us register for dinner at the Clifford Hyatt Hotel. Marc was the family entrepreneur.

One of the best trips we had together was not long after John and

I separated. The children and I left on Christmas Day for a skiing holiday at Myoko Kogen in Japan, with a stopover in Manila. It was a wonderful time of togetherness and some unforgettable experiences. For starters, tempestuous weather untamed the cable car's journey to our lodge, causing Marc to lose hold of a toy poker machine we had been carrying around as a gift for my mother. He tried to grip the toy between his feet, and when the contraption plummeted into a snow-covered crevice I feared he'd go with it. Dressed glamorously, if inappropriately, in a mink coat, on arrival I tramped through thigh-high snow with the children to our accommodation. Keen to defrost, we ventured to the traditional Japanese bathhouse. Men and women bathed in separate facilities, but because my children were young the Japanese graciously offered us use of the women's large steam bath. I was drying myself when I heard water being sucked down a drain. One of the children had pulled the plug – perfectly normal at the completion of a western-style bath, but when the Japanese women arrived after a day on the slopes, there was no water ready for them. So rare were Western tourists in this area that a Japanese man who had heard an Australian woman was at the resort skied all day from his village to deliver a message. In broken English he told me, 'Thank you to the Australian troops for the kind way I was treated in the prisoner-of-war camp on Bougainville.' He bowed and left to make his long journey home. As bells rang throughout the land as part of New Year's Eve celebrations, I felt hopeful that the year ahead would bring happier times for me and my children.

  I was proud that through the business I could provide the best for my children, though it meant my time with them was sometimes sacrificed. Work commitments meant I sometimes missed being around on my children's birthdays, but then we did have many memorable ones: Lisa had her fifth birthday in Hawaii; Marc his seventh in London; Timothy his thirteenth flying over the Pacific Ocean en route to Los Angeles; and Carel her eighteenth in Switzerland. I thought those opportunities and material benefits, along with the love I gave them, would be enough to nurture and sustain them.

My business and commitment to work had both positive and negative outcomes for all my children. For Carel, my assessment of faces and bodies, physical flaws and fine features in the course of my work had helped to save her life. Another by-product of my business was that people expected my children to be impeccably mannered, well behaved, beautifully spoken, and groomed accordingly. If they did something socially out of sync with what I taught or they misbehaved at school, teachers would say: 'You should know better, you're June Dally-Watkins' child,' 'Is that how your mother teaches you to speak?' or 'Your mother wouldn't like to see you doing that.' Similar behaviour in other children would be considered as a minor aberration. Inadvertently, teachers and principals applied pressure on my children to be shining lights for other students to follow. Conversely, some people expected them to be snobbish spoilt brats or to rebel against my teachings. Either way, there were many times I felt I couldn't win.

Attaining anonymity was sometimes an uphill battle for my four children. As a result, they prefer not to be introduced as children of June Dally-Watkins. They are the children of June and John Clifford and that's how they like to be known. It is probably not an uncommon reaction for children of a well-known parent, who are keen to be seen and judged just as they are, and not as a cloned incarnation of their parent. For the most part, my children say they were unaware that a working mother who ran a large business and often travelled overseas was uncommon. Nor were they too bothered or sometimes even aware that outsiders had raised the bar of expectation for them. Maybe this was because I had not educated them as I would my students. There were no home lessons in etiquette, fine dining, speech and grooming; they simply learned by osmosis. I never lectured them about how to conduct their relationships, but instinctively they knew my views. I warned them to choose their friends carefully, but they were free to mix with whomever they wanted. I didn't impose curfews. When I was home I tried to give my children as normal a home life as possible. I cooked nutritious and exciting meals inspired from my travels overseas, and managed to make the children's lunches at night, drive them to school and parties, and attend their school functions. And if I made a promise to my children I never let them down. If I said I was going to return from overseas on a certain date or promised to go to a school event, I was there.

While my children withstood the pressure of being judged by others, I didn't. Every time they slipped up, I felt the smug scorn of critics pierce me and expose me as a failure. Although I didn't mind how my children dressed in their own time, if they came into my office dressed scruffily or spoke poorly, it represented a rejection of everything I taught at the school. It felt like a slap in the face. I couldn't tolerate this and had no qualms in telling them so. I had always been uncomfortable under the glare of others' judgment.

Determined not to be possessive of my children as my mother had been of me, I vowed to mother not smother them. This had an influence on their early independence as much as me being a working mother did. Before they reached their teens they could prepare their own snacks and iron their clothes. The international travel to which I had exposed them from a young age accelerated this independence. Consequently, the children left my nest to live and travel overseas while they were still in their teens.

Carel was due to begin her final year of high school at Kincoppal-Rose Bay Convent when I flew with her to Gstaad to install her at the Swiss finishing school, Institut Montesano, which had educated the likes of Christina Onassis. Carel trusted my judgment and didn't protest even though it meant leaving her friends. She completed her high school certificate at the Australian consulate based in Geneva. She had a wonderful year, learned to speak French fluently and to ski and shimmy down the school drainpipe with her roommate Gûl Inche ('the

Christina Onassis of Turkey'), and to dance the night away at the Palace Hotel disco – where royalty and the rich and famous partied. Educational pursuits ran a poor second to celebrity spotting. After a lunch in Montreaux with her 'Uncle' Bob O'Skea, a dear friend of mine from Philippine Airlines, she missed her train and consequently made a frantic road dash to catch up with it in Les Avants. It happened that David Niven was at the station, heading for Gstaad. He struck up a conversation with Carel and invited her to join him in first class to tell him about Australia. When they went their separate ways Niven blew her a kiss. After graduation, Carel worked as an *au pair* in Nice to perfect her French, then met up with Tim to travel around Europe. She came home to live in the self-contained apartment at my Bellevue Hill home, but returned to Europe before long.

The catalyst to Tim's departure for boarding school came when a neighbour complained that he had shot a pigeon and the street lights out with a BB gun. Fearing the I-told-you-so ridicule of critics who expected the worst of my children because I worked, and concerned that in the absence of his father he needed male guidance, I sent Tim to board at St Joseph's College. Joey's had a strong sporting and elite reputation and I thought it would provide the best environment for him.

Whilst there, he was caught smoking cigarettes and the Brothers caned him until blood blisters appeared on his hands. The beating didn't stop Tim from smoking, which he soon found out had no effect on his height. Growing to a height of six foot seven inches, he became the tallest boy at school. Tim resented being in an institution from which he could come home only once every three weeks. Meanwhile, his brother and sisters were able to enjoy more of a home life. Trying to make up for this, after teaching on Saturday mornings I'd race to watch Tim's Rugby games. On Sundays I packed a picnic basket for a visit with the children to the school. And when Tim and his mates occasionally sneaked out at night and arrived on my doorstep, I didn't rouse on him but cooked them sausages, bacon and eggs before sending them back to Joey's.

In hindsight, boarding school wasn't the ideal solution for my teenage son. Tim was a gentle soul – the kind who brought home stray animals, including a dog that ate the cork soles off of a pair of expensive shoes I had bought overseas. Tim never did anything the usual way. For example, when a friend drove him home and pulled up beside our car, he climbed over the bonnet of our car, then over our fence instead of taking the more conventional path to our front door. One weekend Tim was home from boarding school, I was heartened when he agreed to mow the lawn until I saw the result – a giant 'peace' sign shaped into the grass. Yes, I had a hippie on my hands, and it took me a while to accept it.

After Tim left school, he grew his hair long, and wore a beard and ripped jeans. He hitchhiked around Australia, rode a motorbike and worked odd jobs. His appearance and behaviour were anathema to everything I taught. It caused tension between us, but there were never any big blow-ups; I just worried privately and was relieved when he sold his motorcycle. I took his lifestyle as a rejection of me, instead of seeing him as simply a young man of the liberal 1970s, trying to find his own identity.

With my encouragement, Tim enrolled in a hospitality and hotel management course in London. I thought the European experience would expand his interest in the industry and encourage him to become a worldly person. I had the right industry contacts to help get him an important job, but Tim rejected my offer to open a few doors. It was hard to accept at the time, but now I understand why he needed to find his own path. I guess I can blame the teacher in me for trying to direct his path too much. Like his appearance, I took his refusal as a way to deny me as his mother, to show people he was his own person. Tim roamed in and out of the industry, but the five-star hotel culture didn't suit him. He enjoyed cooking, but on account of his height suffered back problems from working over low benches. After living five years in London and Europe he came home, and established and sold restaurants.

Marc was in a hurry to make his start in life. From a young age, he had shown ambition. First, he aspired to become Pope until his grandmother told him he wouldn't be allowed to marry and have children. His next career plan was to become Prime Minister. Our friendship with three of Australia's best-known Liberal Party families, the McMahons, the Peacocks and the Robinsons, obviously influenced Marc, who took it upon himself to sign up as a member of the New South Wales Young Liberal Party. Marc attended political functions in Canberra and skipped school for political events in Sydney until the Young Liberals discovered that their tall new member was only 12 – four years below the minimum age for members.

On leaving school, Marc worked as a storeman in a retail department store and within a year had saved enough money to buy his own airline ticket to Rome. Marc and I didn't argue about his plans, but he refused to allow me to come to the airport to say goodbye. The day he left I sat in my office and felt proud of him. For the next two-and-a-half years, he worked various jobs in London. I remember feeling concerned when I visited the modest bed-sit he rented in London. But I need not have worried about Marc. On returning to Australia and as a well-spoken and immaculately groomed young man, Marc was approached to be a New South Wales Liberal Party candidate in the 1984 State election. He was only 22 years old. The Labor member held the seat of Seven Hills, but Marc gained the largest swing of any Liberal in the State. Politics remained an interest, but eventually he followed his business instinct, entered the world of marketing and completed marketing studies at university.

Lisa was the last to leave home and travel overseas. Lisa and I felt that it was important for her to get away before she could complete her senior year at Kincoppal-Rose Bay Convent. My mother had fallen ill and come to live with us, making the home environment sad and not conducive to her studies. I needed to care for my mother, but was also swamped with business obligations. A solution presented itself when Carel, who was living in Milan, offered Lisa a place to stay. A year later, Carel was ready to return home, whereas Lisa decided to remain.

Despite dire predictions from detractors that my children would become delinquents, they didn't, and I'm proud of each of them. That all my children are wonderful parents and close, loving and supportive of one another is my great blessing.

12 Not just pretty faces

Some of the young women who walked through the doors of my business struck it rich, emigrated overseas, led glamorous lives, built flourishing careers, found their soul mates, and created families. Many married wealthy, powerful men (it was many a young woman's unspoken aim) and, whilst some of them married happily, others didn't make the right choice. As my business turned out some of the most striking women in the country, it drew men in swarms like bees to a honey pot. Well-known businessmen, politicians, sportsmen and other identities in public life regularly visited my agency to pursue my models or take them out on the town. When playboys and Svengalis prowled around my business and sometimes pestered me to know where a particular model was, I cautioned the girls and advised them how to behave. Some men thought the word 'model' was a euphemism for a good-time girl and deliberately sought out beautiful girls to help them impress others, boost their egos and ease their entrée into a social group. The fairytale life some models sought, and that other people generally assumed would be theirs solely because of their beauty, could turn nightmarish. Their looks became a curse. Wealth and marriage didn't always equate with happiness, and fate tragically intervened. It amazes me the sadness and illness that affected some of the most beautiful girls' lives. Whatever their destiny, these women have been unforgettable.

My agency had several dealings with Leonard Lawson, a commercial artist whose drawings of women for advertisements and cartoons were based on photographs he had taken of my models and other people. I had no reason to be suspicious of Lawson when he booked four models for a day's location shoot on a Friday in May 1954. One of the models brought along her younger sister for the outing to Terrey Hills, which was then isolated bushland. On arrival, Lawson produced some rope and said he wanted the girls to be tied up for the photographs, to which they naïvely agreed. Once bound, they were unable to fight Lawson as he raped them. With nowhere to run or hide, or anyone to hear them, the girls quietly returned to Lawson's car for the drive back to the city. On the way, Lawson gave in to one of the models' pleas to stop at a pharmacist. Coincidentally, the parents of my first employee, Yvonne Eastman, owned the pharmacy. The model told them what happened, the police were contacted and Lawson was arrested.

Two days later, John and I were hosting one of our lawn gatherings, when a friend phoned and asked if I had seen the papers. I hadn't, and she told me about Lawson's crimes. The case raised public and media speculation. 'How did he do it? The bloke should be given a medal' were the kind of insensitive comments that circulated. That Sunday John and his mates doubted Lawson's 'feat' too. Carel was only eight weeks old and I had a little postnatal depression, so this horrific news, compounded by the men's callous remarks left me even more distressed. Nothing bad had ever happened to my models. All our clients and contacts were people we knew; some were friends. The women Lawson attacked changed their names and tried to forget, but their lives were scarred forever. When one of them heard that I was

At the Edgewater Hotel, Honolulu, Hawaii, where I gave my one-woman fashion show in 1952.

OVERLEAF The one-woman fashion show moves on to Hollywood. Here I model a white mink Eisenhower jacket, poolside at the Roosevelt Hotel.

TOP My first television appearance was in July 1952 on 'The Marjorie Trimball Show' in San Francisco. I appeared in a Frank Mitchell gown.

LEFT With Tennessee Ernie Ford, a country and western singer, at the Marilyn Monroe party held at the Hollywood home of band leader Ray Anthony. On the surface of the swimming pool behind us, Marilyn's name was spelt out in flowers.

RIGHT Sydney photographer David Moore took this photo of me leaving the premises of the famous London fashion designer and Queen's dressmaker, Hartnell.

OPPOSITE I sat in Audrey Hepburn's chair between Billy Wilder and Gregory Peck at the end-of-filming dinner party for *Roman Holiday*. Hepburn had left Rome earlier, before filming was complete.

ABOVE My 'Roman holiday' with Gregory Peck in 1952. Here we are at Cinecitta film studios in Rome.

TOP Modelling in Rome for the House of Fontana.

ABOVE On my return from Europe in December 1952, I met Bing Crosby in Hollywood for the second time, having first met him in France. His wife, Dixie, was dying of cancer and there was sadness in his eyes.

LEFT 27 June 1953 was our wedding day. Helen Newham was my bridesmaid and Geoffrey Gillespie was John's best man. Here naval friends form a guard of honour outside St Mary's Cathedral.

RIGHT The bride wore a hat of massed white flowers with a white bow and a soft pink veil, a guipure lace top, a full tulle skirt with a pink satin underskirt and pink shoes dyed to match. (*Photo by John Hearder*)

ABOVE In my mother's Rushcutters Bay apartment practising how to curtsey for Queen Elizabeth's visit in 1954 with, from left to right: Marie Roberts, Jeanne Walsh and Jeanette Elphick (aka Victoria Shaw).

RIGHT June Dally-Watkins junior models take part in a fashion show in Sydney in 1953.

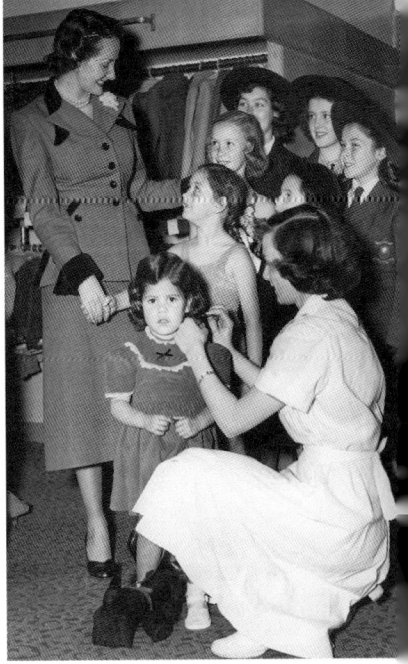

writing this book, her husband, a powerful and wealthy self-made Sydney businessman, threatened to sue me if I revealed his wife's identity, which I would never be so heartless as to do.

Lawson was given a life sentence for the crimes, but, by some cruel glitch in the law, he was set free after serving seven years and two months. Soon after Lawson's release, he persuaded a Sydney girl to come to his apartment so he could paint her portrait. She never returned home. When the girl's brother broke into Lawson's apartment, he found his sister dead – her throat had been cut and she had been raped. Lawson had fled and headed to an exclusive girls' boarding school, intent on taking a number of the students' hostage. As Lawson entered the chapel, where students were attending a morning service, a teacher noticed he was armed with a gun. She bravely tried to disarm him but the gun went off, killing a young girl and injuring others. Meanwhile, another teacher slipped away and alerted police, who arrived promptly and arrested Lawson. For a second time, Lawson received a life sentence, but it didn't stop his heinous behaviour. In 1972, he was part of a prison scheme to procure the early release of two prison inmates. The plan was that Lawson would attack one of the sixteen professional dancers brought in to entertain the prisoners, while the two seeking early release would 'rescue' Lawson's victim, with the expectation that their bravery would be rewarded. The plan failed when Lawson slashed dancer Sharon Hamilton's arm and neck with a knife. He is currently held in prison at Grafton as the longest-serving prisoner in New South Wales.

Only a few months after the Terrey Hills rapes, another model on my books became the centre of a controversial court case. Shirley Beiger presented at my office with her mother. She had inherited her mother's fine features and determination to succeed. However, Shirley's promising modelling career unravelled overnight. The story went that Arthur Griffith, a bookie's clerk, had two-timed Shirley – his live-in lover. On the evening of 9 August 1954, when Arthur said he had a dental appointment, Shirley doubted him. According to court evidence, Shirley enlisted the help of her mother, who suggested they confront Arthur with a rifle to frighten him. After they apparently spied Arthur entering Spellson's nightclub with a showgirl, Shirley asked the doorman to let Arthur know she would like him to come up from the basement nightspot to talk to her. When Arthur surfaced, Shirley aimed the rifle at him and it went off accidentally. Arthur was found dead outside the club, with Shirley nearby, sitting in the back of a black sedan cradling a .22 rifle. An all-male jury came down with a verdict of accidental death against the blonde and tearful beauty dressed mournfully in black. I never saw Shirley or her mother again. Alex Shand, son of the famous barrister who represented Shirley, was invited by his father to sit in court. He told me Shirley looked beautiful in court, sitting elegantly with legs crossed.

Of all the young models I have met, worked with and personally groomed in more than half a century, Jeanette Elphick remains probably the most beautiful – and among the most tragic. If only all the girls who envied her could have known her destiny. Jeanette was 15 years old when she came to my agency in 1951 with her handsome parents Neta and Frank Elphick. In those days parents accompanied their daughters to the agency. Today many girls contact a model agency by themselves. I prefer and respect the involvement of parents. I was struck by her exquisite facial features, up-tilted nose and perfectly proportioned body. So was the press who nicknamed her 'The Face'. Jeanette won a film role in *The Phantom Stockman* with Chips Rafferty in 1953 and became Australia's highest-paid model in 1954.

Jeanette was a natural choice when Bob Hope asked me to put together a parade of Australian clothes and models as part of his touring show in Australia the following year. I accompanied Bob on a flight from Sydney to Brisbane, during which he nursed my baby Carel. Over the years Bob and I corresponded and, having seen Carel's photos as a model in Milan, the comedian brazenly declared he would still like to nurse her on his knee! But during his visit in 1955, I noticed he was most taken by Jeanette. Although Bob's marriage to Delores has endured through the years, he had a reputation as a womaniser and over the years often had a starlet by his side. Jeanette wasn't a pushover, but Bob arranged for her to be screen-tested in Hollywood, where she was signed immediately with Columbia Pictures.

The studio bosses changed her name to 'Victoria Shaw' (coined from the name of a British queen and a British author to infer she was of English origin) and gave her speech classes to help her develop an English accent. Australian actors and their accents certainly were not in demand then. How times have changed! Now Hollywood clamours for Australian actors. Jeanette went straight to a starring role in *The Eddy Duchin Story*. On a promotional tour to Australia for the film in 1957, Jeanette had a car with the words 'Miss Victoria Shaw' emblazoned on its side and was feted by the media. I hosted a cocktail party at the Hotel Australia in her honour. It was heady stuff, but Jeanette already feared some people wanted to be around her only because she was beautiful and famous.

Jeanette began to retreat from the limelight as the career of her handsome husband, Roger Smith, the lead actor in the early hit television series '77 Sunset Strip', rocketed. Jeanette retired and had three children. He left Jeanette and later married actress Ann-Margret. Jeanette married Elliott Alexander, an ambitious career-climbing producer. By the time Jeanette left him, all her money had gone and so had her acting career, which had ended with roles in 'General Hospital' and television movies.

Jeanette moved into a large apartment block and made a living from managing it until ill health forced her to return to Australia. Jeanette had developed emphysema, which she blamed on working amongst chemical fumes used to stoke a fire for a movie she had appeared in years before. However, she was a heavy smoker and the Los Angeles smog had worsened her health. A near-death experience brought her back to Australia to recuperate at her sister's home in Taree. I had not seen her since she was a surprise guest when I was profiled on 'This Is Your Life' in 1976 and it was heartbreaking to see the transformation that had taken place. She had grown thin; her eyes stared out from deep sockets and her cheekbones protruded through tightly drawn skin. Jeanette could barely walk, but didn't give up smoking. For inner strength she turned to her religion, Catholicism, writing poetry and astrology. Drawing up detailed astrological charts, Jeanette was more interested in the stars than on being one.

Our friendship resumed easily. I was touched by a letter she wrote to 'Sixty Minutes' after it broadcast a story about me in 1986: 'You only scratched the surface! June Dally-Watkins gave us more than just the knowledge of outer beauty and the gracious manners to go anywhere and meet anyone with confidence. She gave us a sense of our own individual worth. She was ahead of the rest of the liberation movement. Dally is a rare and shining example of the fragile, gutsy, tender strength that typifies the best of our species. When women AND men come to realise that we are each a precious and unique jewel, we can stop all this nonsense about competing and get on with life.' She signed the letter 'Not just another pretty face'.

Australia Day in 1988 remains as one of the most precious times we spent together. We gathered at the Watson's Bay home of our mutual friends Helen Newham and Val Wolfenden for the festivities. I arrived with Carel and her son Christopher by yacht. I think Jeanette's own writing best recalls that time.

> You all know that June Dally-Watkins was my mentor and idol in my early modelling days in Australia. She now runs a successful model agency and school as well as a very ritzy finishing school for young ladies. She always was, and still is, the supreme lady. It was great to see her. We babbled on about our afternoon adventure as we sipped champagne and watched the sunset. June

and her family were also spending the night in order to see the First Fleet [re-enactment] arrive on the morrow. We ate a delicious barbecued dinner and watched the city lights compete with the gathering dusk.

Soon after dinner we discussed 'the plan'. It had been decided that the teenagers would sleep out in the park in order to reserve a good viewing spot for the morning . . . Now, the teens were having second thoughts about their proposed vigil. No one wanted to sleep out. June Dally said, 'Well, someone has to sleep out and, if no one else is willing, I will do it.' I heard myself saying, 'If you will, then I will too.' (Years of obeying June had undoubtedly caused this conditioned response.) You who know me well are no doubt shaking your heads in disbelief. Me camping out? Never!

It was dark when we arrived at the park laden with sleeping bags, air mattresses, blankets and pillows. Already there were people camping at various vantage points. We chose what seemed a good spot and Val, Helen, June and I settled down to sleep. It was quite breezy up there on the point and before too long Helen and Val, who had graciously given the sleeping bags to their illustrious guests, decided to spend the remainder of the night in their proper beds like normal folk.

And so it was that I spent the night sleeping with June Dally-Watkins in a public park. Well, *she* slept. I lay there, afraid to move lest I disturb her, wondering at what uncanny powers led to this moment. What strange and karmic events lead us along this circuitous path called Life? I looked up at the great canopy of stars overhead and then I began to giggle to myself – who would believe that Miss Dally would do such a crazy thing? I carefully turned to look at my companion. There she lay on her back with her hands folded across her breasts like a vision in an ethereal poem. How can she do it? She even sleeps like a lady! She snores.

Oh yes, she snores! Not like an ordinary mortal, with sniffles and grunts and snorts, but with the gentle, soft purr of a kitten. To this melody I finally fell asleep under the stars of the Southern Cross.

The following morning, Jeanette and I were up at dawn and came upon a bagpiper whom we invited to the house for a barbecue lunch. I don't know what the bagpiper made of our band of merry-makers, but he played on; we all did, until someone noticed flames from the barbecue licking a nearby tree!

Not long after, I was on the island of Hawaii conducting a personal development program for the Christian group, Youth With a Mission, when I received a fax saying that Jeanette had died on 17 August 1988, aged only 53. Helen Newham was by her side, holding her hand at the Hornsby Hospital Intensive Care Unit. Her funeral was the same day as Peter Hanlon's, the former husband of another beautiful woman, Jan Carmody. They both died too young. Mutual friends went to Jeanette's funeral in the morning and Peter's in the afternoon. I grieved alone.

Jan Carmody was with Pat Woodley's agency. To top up her earnings as a model she took a part-time job as a receptionist at Peter Hanlon's trendy hair salon at Kings Cross. Peter had the pizazz and talent that wooed Jan and impressed social ladies of Sydney's eastern suburbs: Mary, Lady Fairfax; Gretel Packer and Mary Hordern. He sometimes styled my hair too. At Peter's suggestion, Jan entered the Miss Australian Surf competition and won. The event organisers asked me to chaperone her and the newly crowned Mr Australian Surf, Colin Macfarlane, on their round-the-world, prize-winning trip in 1959, so, while I was away for six weeks, a housekeeper and a nurse took care of my two children, Carel and Tim, and husband John.

Our first stop was Honolulu, where the famous surfer Duke Kahanamuku and surfing officials presented us at the airport with so many leis around our necks that they piled up to our eyes. Colin took part in a surf competition at Punahou Beach, but the conditions were so rough that the women's competition was cancelled. This was a great relief to Jan who wasn't an accomplished surfer like the other muscular female competitors. Jan was really a country girl. To win the Miss Australian Surf competition she only had to swim around a buoy and back to the beach at Bondi.

In Los Angeles, Jan contacted Sammy Davis Junior whom she had met when he visited Australia. He arranged VIP seating for us at his show and afterwards invited us to his home. Immediately my antennae went up; I was aware of the wild goings-on of some celebrities, especially the 'rat pack' of which Sammy was a member. I thought, 'If this is a wild "rat pack" drinking party, I will insist we leave immediately.' However, there was no reason for concern. When we arrived at Sammy's home, which he shared with his parents and teenage sister, his mother was up waiting for us, his father was asleep in front of the television and a pretty blonde sat on Sammy's knee. We drank Coca Cola, ate a hot supper prepared by Sammy's mother and sat around watching old movies. Sammy showed us around his home, which had a television in every room. Most Australians didn't even own one at that time, so we were impressed. We were amused when Sammy showed us his bedroom, revealing that he would only sleep between black satin sheets.

Over the next few days, Hollywood opened its doors for us. Swimwear manufacturer Fred Cole of Cole of California (one of the competition sponsors) made his home available for Jan's swimsuit photo session around a V-shaped swimming pool, the point of which dramatically overhung a cliff above tinsel town. We visited the home of Bob and Delores Hope, a huge, rambling place with everything money could buy. At MGM, we were allowed to watch Jerry Lewis starring in *Visit to a Small Planet*, and met Charlton Heston and Gina Lollobrigida. Jeanette Elphick arranged for us to visit a movie set on which she was working, entertained us at her home, and hosted Jan's twenty-first birthday party at a restaurant. John Hayles, my darling friend who had become a fashion designer to the stars, drove us around Hollywood in his large convertible. Rod Taylor took us to lunch with some MGM publicity people. He had married one of my models, Peggy Williams, but left her when he became a star.

Several Paramount directors fancied Jan for the role of Daisy Mae in the film version of Al Capp's cartoon *L'il Abner*, but there wasn't enough time in our schedule for Jan to have a serious screen test. A casting director whisked Jan away from us into his office, claiming he wanted to make an appointment to view Jan in a swimsuit. I intervened and told him that Jan would send photos instead. I had previously cautioned Jan about how to handle advances from men and how to conduct herself: 'Sit up straight, smile and say little.' And I had tried to give Jan and Colin speech tips not to sound too Strine and to say Australia without dropping the 'l'. However, the studio bosses told Jan she would have to lose her accent and to keep in touch from Australia. In hindsight, Jan was fortunate to have escaped Hollywood. It would have eaten her up.

On the east coast, a chauffeur-driven limousine transported us to Arthur Loew's estate at Glen Cove, Long Island Sound. Unlike my first encounter with Arthur in 1952, this time he didn't make a pass at me but played the perfect host. His father Marcus Loew's castle-like mansion, Pembroke, was too big for Arthur's needs, so he had built a smaller modern home within its grounds. The grounds were also expansive, so we drove over to Pembroke in the evening to watch the yet-to-be-released Marilyn Monroe film *Some Like It Hot* in the old mansion's cinema. Before the weekend was over, we cruised around Long Island Sound in Arthur's luxury motorboat.

In London, Jan shivered in a swimsuit at Piccadilly to hand out oranges as part of a promotion of the Australian fruit. We made the rounds of the surf lifesaving clubs and were treated like surfing royalty in Bude, Cornwall. We kicked up our heels in Paris and Rome, and Jan and I visited the Isle of Capri. The final leg of the tour was a stopover in Singapore, which was like going back in history. We rode in rickshaws and had lunch on the verandah of the old Raffles Hotel – colonial Asia at its best. The Australian jockey Arthur Ward and his wife June entertained Helen Meehan, who married Mike Newham and was then living in Malaysia, Jan and I at their grand home. After indulging in too much champagne, all of us ended up in the swimming pool. Enthusiastically, I pulled one of the statues surrounding the pool into the water with me. We almost missed our flight. Such was the relaxed way of life then in Singapore that the airline held the flight for us; no one seemed concerned that we were late. Back in Sydney, John and others had been waiting at the airport but, after the delay, only Peter Hanlon stayed on. He welcomed a weary Jan with a star sapphire and diamond engagement ring. In marriage, Jan became Peter's unpaid receptionist and her photos were never sent to Paramount. They became the darlings of the eastern suburbs social set.

The mystery surrounding the death of a Sydney model and former employee continues to distress me. Caroline Byrne came to us in 1991 after graduating in Psychology at University of Sydney. She had been recommended by Gordon Charles model agency and fitted easily into the group of teachers at the school. My daughter Lisa taught her how to teach the Model course and they became close friends. As an employer, I couldn't have been happier with this vivacious young employee. We had a good rapport and the students adored her. A personal profile, which is completed by all staff, highlighted Caroline's strengths: 'respectful, considerate, loyal, faithful, sociable, positive, diplomatic, mixes easily, spirited, demonstrative, contented, animated, inoffensive, well balanced, optimistic and peaceful.'

The last time I saw Caroline she had the flu and was drinking camomile tea, but was in very good spirits. She had just been promoted to full-time sales representative and manager of the school on Saturday mornings, after persuading my daughter Carel, who was then managing director, she was ready for more responsibility. On Tuesday, 6 June 1995, Caroline waved goodbye to her colleagues when she left the Parklea Shopping Centre at 2.20 p.m., where she had been representing my Business Finishing College at a careers' market. It was thought that she was heading to her Potts Point apartment, which she shared with her partner Gordon Wood, who at the time of Caroline's death was the personal assistant to flamboyant share trader René Rivkin. At 5.30 p.m. she was booked to appear for a model shoot, but never arrived. Very un-Caroline. The following morning Carel played an answering-machine message from Gordon. He said that Caroline was sick and would not be returning to work. What happened to Caroline after leaving Parklea is a mystery. The coroner describes Gordon Wood's evidence as bizarre with a number of inconsistencies. On Thursday, 8 June 1995, Carel phoned Gordon to check on Caroline. Gordon informed her that Caroline was dead – run over by a car at Bondi Junction. My distressed daughter phoned me with this news. Within minutes, I received a call from a teacher to say Gordon had told her Caroline had been hit and killed by a car at Mosman. Soon after, Gordon phoned to say his girlfriend had been knocked down and killed by a car at a pedestrian crossing at Bondi Junction.

Shocked, emotional and concerned about these conflicting versions, I immediately took a taxi to the office. Unable to contact Caroline's family, we phoned the police, but they said they knew nothing of the accident we described. We enlisted the help of my daughter Lisa, then a television reporter at Channel TEN. It seemed no one could shed any light on a model being knocked down by a car and killed. Lisa then contacted the morgue. A body of Caroline's description was there. We learned that the Rose Bay police had been involved in the recovery of her body from the bottom of the cliffs at The Gap at Watson's Bay at 4 a.m. that day. We couldn't understand how someone who went to the gym and took care of her body would destroy it by throwing herself off a cliff.

According to Gordon Wood's statement to police, he had returned home at 1 p.m. on 7 June 1995 and Caroline was asleep. He said he returned to work and arrived back home at 6 p.m. Caroline was not home and he thought she was at her father's place. He sat down to watch the news on TV, intending to telephone Caroline's father after the news. He said he fell asleep in front of the television. Waking at 12.40 a.m. Thursday, he became concerned and claimed the spirit of Caroline had called him to The Gap. There, he saw her car. He phoned Caroline's father Tony and brother Peter, collected them and the three of them returned to The Gap. After borrowing a torch from two fishermen, Gordon thought he could see a pair of white shoes on the rocks that he believed could be Caroline's. After alerting authorities, the Rose Bay police shone their high-powered torches, but could see nothing. 'One glaring inconsistency is just how he [Gordon] managed to see a shoe below The Gap on a dark night with a barely operating torch,' the inquest report noted. The area where she fell was deserted and surrounded by bushes a long way from where her car was parked. The chief of the police rescue squad told the inquest that it was unusual for someone planning to end their life to go over headfirst in a dive unless they had a long run up to the cliff and there was a fence that would have prevented Caroline from doing this. The bodies of most people who had taken their lives at The Gap had been found three to four-and-a-half metres out from the cliff, not nine metres as Caroline's had.

'But by far the most telling inconsistency,' according to the report, was the evidence of two witnesses. They identified Caroline as the woman walking in Robertson Park with two men at 1 p.m. and at 3 p.m. on Wednesday, 7 June 1995. They identified the two men with Caroline as Gordon Wood and her agent Adam Lee. They also testified that, at 4 p.m. on the same day, they saw a green Bentley motorcar, which matched a description of the car Wood was driving that day, drive past The Gap restaurant. The inquest heard the witnesses had no ulterior motive to give this evidence and only went to the police in the first place because of a conversation with me and others at their restaurant several days after Caroline's death. The coroner thanked the two witnesses and said that their evidence was very strong and must be accepted. Evidence was also given that Caroline purchased petrol, milk and Freddo frogs that afternoon and at 3.50 p.m. withdrew $50 from her bank account at a Vaucluse automatic telling machine.

In the witness box, Gordon Wood denied claims that he was in Watson's Bay with Caroline and Adam Lee. His alibi for that day rested on him chauffeuring his boss René Rivkin and former politician Graham Richardson around town. Neither was called to give evidence at the inquest. Three-and-a-half years later, after having been interviewed by police, Graham Richardson, in an exclusive interview with the *Sun Herald* on 10 June 2000 said Woods' statement to the coroner was wrong. 'I did not think to look in my diary; I didn't, until police asked me last year. I believe I had lunch with Peter Moore on that day.' The inquest ended on Wednesday, 11 February 1998. The coroner handed down an open finding and said the police were still looking at the case. On Thursday, 30 April 1998, two homicide detectives from the State's top murder squad met with John Abernathy at the Glebe Coroner's Court. They told the coroner that a third witness had seen two men arguing with a woman at Watson's Bay on the night before Caroline's body was found on the rocks beneath The Gap on 8 June 1995. After hearing this and other new evidence, the coroner John Abernathy ordered the homicide squad to join the investigation into Caroline's death. The investigation is code-named 'Strike Force Irondale'. Because the first investigations into her death were inadequate, the inquest was also inadequate. Strike Force Irondale consists of a team of dedicated homicide detectives who have had to start from the beginning. They have interviewed over two hundred witnesses. The resources that have been ordered into this investigation are described as staggering and would not have been deployed unless a result was expected.

13   Rollcall

The 300 000 — and counting — students and models who have attended my school or joined my model agency have made for interesting and challenging work. The best of them have given me happy memories and lifelong friendships. Many of my early protégés and internationally successful models became great ambassadors for my business, and I owe them acknowledgement.

My business produced a number of women who won the most coveted national quest prize — the honour of being Miss Australia; among them Maureen Kistle (1955); Helen Wood (1957); Tania Verstak (1961); Jenny Coupland (1982); Maria Ridley (1985); and Caroline Lumley (1988). Pat Woodley and Maureen Duval each won Miss New South Wales in 1951 and 1952 respectively and travelled overseas as Miss Australia in the absence of a national titleholder in those years. Maureen Duval taught at my school and went on to host 'Good Morning Sydney' and raise four sons. Tania Verstak was a shy, highly intelligent and humble girl who came from a White Russian family. They had fled communism in their homeland and later in China and migrated to Australia. When she won Miss Australia, I remember her being showered with ticker tape during a streetcar parade in Sydney. She won Miss International only a year later. The global title was also bestowed on former student Kirsten Davison in 1992.

More kudos came to my business when model graduates Janette McLeod and her cousin Penny Plummer, respectively, won Miss Teen International in 1968 and Miss World in 1969. Both tall and blonde, Janette and Penny were in their last year at high school when they completed the Personal Development course together. I suggested that they consider modelling as a career. Janette signed up, quickly taking the Miss Teen International title. Penny returned to her family farm near Kempsey to finish high school and was nominated to enter the Quest of Quests. Winning that contest gave her the entry right to the Miss World quest, which she won in London at the age of 18. She fulfilled a hectic schedule, including visiting troops in Vietnam with Hollywood stars Bob Hope and Ann-Margret, but in the longer term she didn't pursue a life in the limelight.

Many young women who came through my doors became household names. From my Brisbane school, Delvene Delaney found fame on the 'Paul Hogan Show' and later on 'Sale of the Century'. Paula Duncan and the late Arkie Whiteley found their destinies as actors. Judy Done, the wife of artist Ken Done, worked as an in-house model for Grace Brothers and featured in some of her husband's early advertising campaigns. There was the 'Lithgow Flash' Marjorie Jackson who later became the Governor of South Australia. I remember telling Jan Stephenson on her graduation night: 'Your good looks combined with your golfing ability will one day make you a lot of money.' And they did. Jan became the pin-up girl of golf worldwide and settled in the USA. When 'This Is Your Life' profiled her life, she kindly credited my school with giving her the confidence she needed to become a celebrity. World-champion race walker Kerry Saxby was sent to us by her manager Frank Bates. He knew Kerry could reap more sponsorship and financial rewards if she polished her image. The biggest challenge proved to be teaching her to walk gracefully. Teenagers Jeannie Little and Maria Venuti enrolled too.

In more recent times in Sydney, talented siblings Roanne and Ana Donna Monte-Cumming attended my school. Donna has a spectacular voice that helped win her a coveted role in *Miss Saigon*, which I proudly watched with her mother Daisy in London. Roanne is now under the management of Elite in New York and is composing music. Daisy is an outstanding artist and has painted my portrait. Rani, Kamahl's daughter, is another singer to have graduated from my school and her parents are treasured friends.

I have always thought Queensland, particularly Townsville, produced the prettiest girls. In Brisbane, Billie North was the city's premier model for many years. She managed my school in Brisbane for quite some time before opening her own deportment and modelling school. I never resented Billie striking out on her own because she wasn't ruthless or mendacious in style. She cared for her students in a motherly fashion and, unlike some other competitors, never tried to put down the opposition or take anything, including models, directly from my business. Other Brisbane models and former teachers were fashion parades' producer Di Cant and Katy Edwards, who is best known for her naïve paintings, but in an earlier guise was Miss Teen Time. Another fine graduate was Meta Ransom, who married the businessman with the Midas touch, Keith Lloyd.

When I opened the agency in 1951, the foundation models were Jeanette Elphick, Jean Newington, Marie Roberts, Michele Safargy, Hazel Rogers and Janice Wakeley – they remain close to my heart. Janice Wakeley married the founder of Avis in Australia, Eric McIllree, and has a harbourside home in Sydney. In contrast, Hazel Rogers' life didn't turn out so well. Although she had a great sense of fun and the most outrageous humour, Hazel suffered depression, compounded by the death of her mother and later her husband, Keith Woods. She died after taking an overdose of sleeping pills.

Marie Roberts had been working in her school holidays as a dresser at David Jones. She helped me dress for a parade of fashions from the Texan department store Neiman Marcus. I encouraged Marie to visit my school, and she arrived wearing a pale-blue dress with a skirt filled out by petticoats that emphasised her small waist. Her long brown hair was pulled back into a ponytail and tied with a blue ribbon. I'll never forget it; she was a picture of wholesome beauty and had a soul to match. After completing my course, Marie modelled successfully and was much in demand by David Jones. Accepting my offer to manage my new school in Perth, Marie taught the ladies of the west how to curtsey to the Queen during her tour of Australia in 1954. After a ten-month stint there, she returned to Sydney. Every man desired Marie, but she married television entrepreneur John Collins, who went on to produce Don Lane's 'Sydney Tonight', among other things. After a few years of marriage, they separated. Marie raised their two children on her own and resumed working for me, judging country beauty quests and debutante balls and managing the deportment school in Sydney until 1972, when she married Ian Spies, the owner of several funeral parlours. A compassionate couple, I'm grateful for the support they gave me at the saddest time in my life, when my mother died.

The gorgeous Michele Safargy was born in Shanghai, where her father was a colonel in the French army. With World War II thwarting their plans to return to France, they moved to Sydney. Pat Firman spotted Michele, who lived across the street from her, and thought she would be suitable in a lipstick advertisement for one of my clients. With Pat's encouragement Michele came to see me. Michele always had that touch of French chic and had no trouble getting work. After Michele's first husband died, she married John Rogers who previously had been married to the doe-eyed model Diana Gregory. Michele and John have been together for over thirty years. The freckly, brown-eyed beauty Jean Newington became Model of the Year in 1955. This launched her international career in Paris and New York where she partied with Frank Sinatra, Marlene Dietrich and Rudolph Nureyev and modelled for Eileen Ford's agency in the USA.

Among other models from the early days was Lois Wherrit. I saw great potential in Lois, who turned down my offer to take her on an overseas trip to gain international modelling experience. 'No, June. I am going to marry Jim Fleming. Dad thinks it would be a mistake to leave him.' I thought this attitude was foolish but Jim became a wealthy businessman as head of Flemings Is Fabulous supermarkets and for many years was chairman of the Australian Jockey Club. Money, however, didn't bring them happiness and they separated.

Ingrid Gee came to me as Ingrid Grzonkowski. She had come to Australia with her parents from Poland aged 9, the first of many new Australian models and quest winners to follow. Justice Lionel Murphy, the Whitlam Government's Attorney-General, fell in love with Ingrid. Lionel was hailed as a reformer for introducing changes that made it easier to divorce. The law reforms also conveniently favoured his personal life, aiding him to swiftly divorce his wife and marry Ingrid. (Their son Cameron is now the spokesperson for Civil Liberties.) In 1973 Lionel encouraged a teacher at my school, Jill Ellen Fuller, to become the first civil celebrant in New South Wales. Along with Lionel, actor Rod Taylor, businessman Clyde Packer, the coffee-making Andronicus brothers, swimmer John Konrads, the aristocratic polo player Sinclair Hill, and entertainers like Col Joye and Johnny O'Keefe were among the men about town who took an interest in my models or dropped by the agency to court them.

Just as memorable were less-known models. One of my first models was Natalie McLeod, daughter of singer-songwriter Bobby McLeod. Meeting Natalie led to my long association with this fine family. Her great-grandfather, Robert Brown, was Australia's first Aboriginal stipendiary magistrate and her other great-grandfather, Jack McLeod, was given the Victoria Cross in World War I. Now cousin Peggy Carter is the first Aboriginal student at my Business College.

Deportment school students came from a variety of backgrounds and graduated into equally different careers and lives. As well as a growing corporate client list, from the late 1960s to the mid 1970s the Catholic Church in Sydney also became a client. The Church sent nuns who had removed their habits for the first time and found they needed wardrobe, make-up and hairstyling advice. Another unexpected client was the army. From 1971 to 1974, officer cadets at the Women's Royal Australian Army Corps were being groomed in deportment, etiquette and femininity. Around this time, the New South Wales Police Department also paid for some of its female officers on community duties, including escorting VIPs, to complete the Deportment course.

Charitable groups sent homeless and disadvantaged teenagers to my school where they received tuition free of charge. Some made the most of this opportunity, but for others it was just another welfare-style handout and not the leg-up I hoped it would be. When young people leave school, my business college and its range of courses help them to bridge the gap from school student to adult. I want to make them feel sufficiently confident and motivated to leave their unique mark on the world. When I think of all my former students and models, I am grateful to them all for enriching my memories.

14 An affair with Asia

My mother never ceased to be interested in my career or be on the lookout for opportunities that would catapult me to new heights. On her return from her around-the-world honeymoon with Bill, Mother excitedly told me that the who's who of Hong Kong wanted to meet her 'famous daughter'. Despite never praising me directly for my accomplishments, she must have boasted about me to others, because I don't think people in Hong Kong would have been aware of my name otherwise. Whatever the reality, her news spurred my business foray into Asia and led to some of the most exciting times in my life.

It began in 1961 with the first-ever parade of Australian models and fashions to be produced overseas. The Australian Department of Trade, Cathay Pacific Airlines and prominent Hong Kong gentleman Sir Sik-Nin Chau backed the concept, which aimed to stimulate trade with Australia and raise funds for Sir Chau's pet cause, the Hong Kong Anti-Tuberculosis Association. Hordern Brothers supplied the fashions and the Sydney *Sunday Telegraph* ran a competition to select four models for the parades.

The winners – Luce Carmagnola, Patricia Duffie, Lorraine

Knight and Judy Lindsay – were young women I had trained and each had won a Model of the Year award. They were unexpected discoveries from unpretentious backgrounds. Luce milked her family's cows each day on their farm at Camden before coming to my model school. I'll never forget the two bottles of homemade grappa Luce's father gave me as a gift. When all alcohol had been consumed at a dinner party I held at home, I produced the grappa. Before long everyone was sliding under the table, including advertising dynamo John Singleton. He still teases me about it. So potent was the drink that I still have the unfinished second bottle of it from that night in the 1960s. Pat was a chemist who made an elegant model. She later married a bank executive, who died tragically one evening when they were sitting in their spa at home. Lorraine was an A-grade tennis player and teacher at Sunday school, and Judy hailed from a cattle property at Narromine in far west New South Wales.

Overnight the models and I became quasi-ambassadors for Australia. The girls received tumultuous applause each time they took to the catwalk at the Miramar Hotel, then Hong Kong's only new hotel. I loved Hong Kong. At that time its hills were dotted with ugly clumps of shanties that spilled down to the water's edge and that over the years have been swallowed by multistoreyed buildings. I feel fortunate to have watched Hong Kong transform from an elegant, colonial territory to an adrenalin-fuelled mega-metropolis returned to Chinese sovereignty in 1997.

I compered the parade with the interpreting assistance of local television presenter Lily Leling before an audience of political and business leaders, including former Australian Prime Minister Sir Robert Menzies and his wife, Dame Patti. The Australian flavour was laid on thick with gum tips decorating the catwalk, the auction of a bleached kangaroo-fur coat donated by Cornelius Furs, and a menu of kangaroo-tail soup, fish à la Sydney, roast duckling with Hawkesbury orange, potatoes Tasmanian style, Yarra green peas and for dessert, peach Melba.

Despite French, Italian and American mannequin parades held in Hong Kong in the previous six months, the local press gave the Australian show the thumbs-up. *The China Mail* noted: 'It was a great performance of a great team of mannequins; they gladdened the hearts of fashion parade habitués and made the Australians living in Hong Kong proud as well as promoting the best relations for the country they obviously love so well.' We were a hit! We raised a significant amount of money to fight tuberculosis.

As guests of the Macau Government, we took the show to the then Portuguese colony, opening at the Don Pedro Theatre, a baroque opera house decked out in sumptuous red velvet curtains, golden pillars and a tiered dress circle. The cream of Macau's society assembled for the very first fashion show of foreign models. The models and I stood with the Macau governor for the Portuguese national anthem and with straight faces as they played 'Waltzing Matilda' for ours. The heat and humidity was unbelievable. I had to place my hands behind my back to collect, and then empty, the perspiration that was trickling down my arms to my cupped hands. With spirits inflated, we flew on to Japan for a brief holiday before returning home on 13 June, my birthday.

I was asked to return to Hong Kong to produce similar shows, but the demands of four young children, a husband and the business consumed my time, causing a hiatus between visits to Asia for about three years. However, the experience gave me the confidence to explore business opportunities further afield. By the mid-1960s I accepted an invitation from Philippine Airlines (PAL) to showcase Australian models and designs for Manila's elite. The show was well received. I could have taken orders for the Australian designs, but it was impossible to arrange for their importation. I knew nothing of the Philippines or the way this corrupt regime was run.

The visit was certainly a cultural revelation. Understandably I was alarmed to see hundreds of people had come to the airport just to see a handful of models arrive. After we were escorted through customs, I became separated from the models and was led back to the tarmac to a helicopter. This certainly wasn't part of the itinerary. Thoughts of a high-class kidnapping even danced across my mind. Thankfully, the pilot noticed my anxiety and explained, 'I am taking you to the Manila Hotel.' As the helicopter rose above the airport I had a bird's-eye view of a convoy of black stretch-limousines and six police motorcyclists that our hosts had arranged to convey the models to the old hotel. As my helicopter flew low over the limos, people lined Roxas Boulevard and waved and cheered as though we were royalty. Our VIP treatment continued. In honour of our arrival, Philippines Airlines' chairman Benny Toda and senior vice-president Bob O'Skea hosted a grand reception in the hotel's opulent ballroom. Ice carvings and flowers decorated the buffet tables and we dined on *lechon* (suckling pig) served with liver sauce, stuffed shrimp and *bagoong* (fermented salty fish with an overwhelming odour). Waiters, wearing white gloves, discreetly held an ashtray by the side of each smoker.

Although the old Manila Hotel was then the city's finest, it had been commandeered by the Japanese and then the Americans during the war and was showing its age. The rooms were basic and the air-conditioning worked in reverse with cold air flushing into the corridors and hot air blasting into our rooms – not a minor inconvenience in the stifling humidity of Manila. However, the hotel was the accommodation for celebrities and dignitaries. On a subsequent visit in early 1972, I stood with reporters as another hotel guest, United States President Richard Nixon, answered their questions before flying to China for the first time to hold historic talks that opened up the closed communist country to the West after forty years of isolation.

The models and I were shocked at the contrast between rich and poor. We had not been exposed to the kind of poverty that spewed from the shanties of tin and cardboard and onto the streets. Beggars seemed incongruous, considering all the privileges we were being given. My sensitivity hardened after I handed over a considerable amount of pesos to a mother with a young daughter on her shoulders. Without a smile or 'thank you' the mother walked away and the girl handed the money to a fat Filipino sitting in a large black limousine. Every building in Metro Manila had at least one armed guard. The mansions were situated in compounds with guard stations at the entrance.

In the tradition of the Spanish culture that prevailed amongst the upper echelons of society, our evenings continued into the morning, breaking my habit of getting sufficient beauty sleep. We were sustained by the excitement of being in an exotic city, not by drugs as some all-night partygoers are today. I didn't observe or hear any discussion of using drugs in those days. Our host for a given night would send a driver to collect us for a cocktail party that usually began around nine followed by a multi-course dinner at ten or eleven. Then it was on to a disco. The nightclub playboys always sought my permission before asking one of the girls to dance. Chaperoned girls were treated with respect; it was the Spanish culture. Even so, it was sometimes a challenge to keep these men in check. Some of the men declared their undying love for the models and threatened to kill themselves if they left. One of the models, Lesley Hutchinson, did return to marry a Filipino and their son, Jamie, is my godson. The Filipino connection continues.

Our opening charity show in Hong Kong was held at a palatial home at The Peak on Hong Kong Island for an audience of Tai Tai – the socialite wives of extremely wealthy Chinese businessmen. The models walked amongst tables set on a terrace that had an enviable view across the harbour to Kowloon and mainland China. The Mandarin Hotel sponsored a week of lunchtime fashion shows and a gala evening premiere in its grand ballroom. I choreographed the opening parade to taped didgeridoo music and arranged for the lighting to spotlight the models who were dressed in black leotards with Aboriginal designs in iridescent white paint. My compere's calm was tested when I noticed people leaving during the show. Only half the 400-strong audience remained when the show wound up after 11 p.m. I was convinced we had bombed. What I didn't know was that at that time of night transport back to Kowloon, on the other side of the harbour, was restricted to small hire boats called *wallah wallahs*, since the underground tunnel between Victoria Island and the mainland was not yet built. The newspapers gave us glowing reviews and subsequent shows were sell-outs to the Hong Kong Chinese, British and Australians. Our confidence returned and we began to enjoy the delights of Hong Kong. We sailed the harbour in luxury boats and exposed our tastebuds to exotic Asian cuisine.

At the invitation of Hong Kong's newly opened Hilton Hotel, I produced lunchtime shows at the aptly named Eagle's Nest restaurant on the hotel's twenty-third floor, where the models and I danced the night away. It was a time to party and we certainly looked the part. The hemlines of our dresses had crept ten centimetres above the knee – no wonder pantihose had become popular. Looking back, some of the wigs and hair extensions we wore were obvious fakes though in style. To complement our over-the-top hairdos, we wore false eyelashes, black eyeliner that extended past the corners of both eyes to give the eyes a heavy-lidded appearance and frosty pale lipsticks. By the late 1960s, I had launched Dally Lashes – semi-permanent eyelashes that were applied individually and with considerable patience. They usually stuck to the eyelid for weeks before replacements were needed.

The expatriate community made sure we lived it up. I caught up in Hong Kong with John Hayles who was spending a year surveying the fashion scene around the world. Glamour, gossip and good times prevailed whenever John was around. It was hard for the models to keep a straight face when he cheekily goaded them backstage with a 'tits up, tails under' command, just as they had to face an audience. I also became reunited with Kell Hutchence, who was working for a major liquor company in Hong Kong. Kell came to my lunch shows with his mates, and the models and I reciprocated by attending his wine-tasting functions. His wife, Patricia Glassop, took care of their two young sons, Michael and Rhett. Patricia worked as a talented make-up artist. I saw their rock-star son Michael just days before his tragic death alone in a hotel room in 1999. We had gathered in Double Bay for a visit with Pat, who was divorced from Kell and visiting from the Gold Coast. Michael was as sweet-natured as ever.

The Hilton extended an invitation to produce a show at its new hotel in Manila, the city's first modern high-rise. I grabbed the opportunity with both hands. I made sure there was time for the models, staff and me to swim and sunbake (no thoughts of skin cancer in those days), sip *kalamansi* juice and order pink papaya and mangosteen from the hotel's rooftop poolside bar. To keep up our energy for the evenings, we enjoyed the *merienda* – a Filipino late afternoon tea or early evening supper, a selection of delicious small eats, including my favourite, fresh *lumpia* with garlic sauce. We also indulged in spending sprees for inexpensive and exciting goodies at Rustans department store, manicures, and massages, the latter perfected by sought-after blind men and women who stood lightly on our backs and massaged us with their feet and hands. These trips were great ways to reward my staff and models, because we received first-class treatment all the way. The models valued the experience too.

My association with the Hilton and Philippine Airlines led to me becoming coordinator and a judge of the Miss Hilton Model Quests in Manila, Hong Kong, Seoul, Bangkok, Singapore and London. The winner's prize included a trip to Sydney where I had arranged modelling assignments and publicity for them. I chaperoned the girls around various cities for a series of East-Meets-West parades. All the girls had to be at least sixteen years old, and some were understandably naïve. I remember a judge asking a contestant in Hong Kong where she came from, to which she sweetly replied 'from my mother'. However, when Filipina Maita Gomez won the prize, this university student proved she was no pushover to the playboys who chased her.

During Maita's stay in Sydney she apparently poured the contents of a drink into the lap of promoter Harry Miller after he allegedly made a suggestive remark to her at a nightclub. She said that cooled him down. I later heard Maita became a political rebel.

In tandem with the Hilton quest, I took the winner of the Miss Roselands Beauty Quest, as part of their prize, with me on a two-week tour of the Philippines and Hong Kong to give them catwalk experience. Part of the arrangement meant that I had to judge the entrants who turned up at Roselands Shopping Centre in Sydney on Saturday mornings. Along with the overseas trip, the winner took home prize money, clothing and luggage, and a modelling scholarship at my school. Miss Teen International Janette McLeod and Judy Donaldson were among the winning contestants I handpicked for these shows. Janette married, had three beautiful daughters, and lives on the Gold Coast. Judy married cricketer Greg Chappell.

As an overseas tour approached, I gathered garments for the parades from new and established designers, including Brian Rochford swimwear, Trent Nathan and Carla Zampatti. It gave some designers the first and, at that time, only affordable and accessible avenue to showcase their work in Asia. I also worked out the models' order of appearance on the catwalk. In those days the choreography was simple – usually only one or two girls appeared on the catwalk at a time. The music was deliberately low-key and instrumental to ensure the models' gait remained fairly consistent throughout a show. This made the shows stylish and elegant. Producing and compering two parades a day, seven days a week, for a fortnight sapped more of my energy, but I wasn't completely a one-woman show. Staff and industry identities were eager to make these events a success.

After in-store parades in Hong Kong with the Shui Hing and Wing-on department stores, the Wing-on made orders to the Australian designers. The chairman of Shui Hing department store, Daniel Koo, OBE, became a lifelong friend. My Wing-on department friends were proud to show Australian clothes in their store, as they had a particular Australian connection. They welcomed me like a sister. The store, with multistoreyed branches on both sides of Hong Kong harbour and in mainland China, had its humble beginnings in Sydney at Paddy's Market where the great-grandfather had pulled barrows of vegetables, under the name 'Wing-on Produce', to make a modest living when arriving from mainland China. He scraped and saved and sent his family money, with which he opened a tiny shop Kowloon-side on the edge of the harbour. To negotiate payment for taking orders for these stores didn't occur to me. I was simply satisfied that my costs were covered. There was very little direct financial gain from these quests and trips to Asia, but the experience fed my insatiable hunger for travel and learning, and it was good publicity for my business in Australia. I was not driven by money alone, but motivated to seek out adventure, quality of life and style. I don't regret that focus, but I should have made considerably more money in many of my business ventures than I did.

My hotel and airline industry connections opened up new opportunities. When Hong Kong's Hilton manager and my friend Bryan Bryce defected to Hyatt Hotels, I moved my shows that way. Larry Tchou cared for us on subsequent visits. Each Hyatt in the region welcomed us with a large banner announcing 'The June Dally-Watkins Show' draped outside its entrance whenever the models and I were visiting on tour. Furthermore, my business's training of Qantas cabin attendants — before the airline set up its own in-house training run by one of my former teachers — led to my appointment as director of training for Philippine Airlines' cabin attendants. I flew to Paris to inspect the airline's newly ordered Pierre Cardin-designed orange uniforms so I could come up with suitably coordinated make-up and grooming for PAL staff. My teachers (Sue Smith, Jill Ellen Fuller and Wendy Poole, who also led classes in Port Moresby and Darwin) and I also conducted workshops to address issues of grooming and deportment. My PAL work delivered the bonus of travel benefits for my family and me. Courtesy of the airline, I began flying to the Philippines and various other countries in Asia.

Attending industry functions provided eye-openers to how business was really done in this complex country. One industry function was hosted by Philippines President Ferdinand Marcos and First Lady Imelda Marcos at their extravagant residence, Malacañan Palace. The dinner was long and lavish with entertainment, music and dancing. During the night at Malacañan Palace, I noticed the President had more than a wandering eye for pretty girls. When a model from another Australian agency became pregnant with a daughter to Marcos, the President paid her off with a handsome lifestyle and a Point Piper mansion. Marcos's love child lives in Sydney today.

Although I was unaware of the extent to which political corruption and injustice besieged the Philippines, a sense of danger was clear. Even judging a beauty quest could be risky. I was grateful not to be involved in a small quest in the provinces at which a police officer – and the boyfriend of an entrant who had failed to win – shot all the judges in retaliation for not voting for her. Shootings were a regular occurrence during Manila's pre-martial law regime. After a patron had been shot at a nightclub that the models and I frequented, the venue's security guards requested everyone leave their guns at the entrance. Sometimes an escort asked their date to hide his revolver in her bag. Guns were a way of life.

Despite the pervasive tension, I enjoyed the benefits of my influential contacts on the archipelago. Knox Booth, who managed Manila's polo club, and his wife, Josephine, became friends after I staged a fashion parade at the club. Model Ingrid Gee made a dramatic entrance in traditional riding gear upon a wooden horse that the club insisted I use. The Booths invited me to stay at their luxury house on Cebu Island. During my visits, Philippine Airlines' Benny Toda made available his green Mercedes and a driver who kept a pump-action rifle under the dashboard. On weekends, Benny and his wife invited the models and me to fly by private jet to their island, Hermana Mayor – a pristine environment of white sand, clean water and delectable food. Lumber-mill heir, Sonny Lim Junior, flew us to his parents' island, Fuga, off the northern tip of Luzon.

Being an intrepid traveller easily enticed to out-of-the-way places, I accepted an invitation to go to Jolo. Before the plane landed, goats were shepherded from the airstrip. I was jokingly warned by friends in Manila, 'You are fortunate it isn't a full moon. It is then the Muslims cut off the heads of Christians.' Their words came back to me at the airport as I saw the stern faces of bearded men dressed in turbans and flowing robes. The following dawn I was awakened by the sound of loudspeakers summoning the faithful to the mosque for prayer. In the evening there was a curfew. All those years ago unrest was stirring. Now, as I read about insurgency on those beautiful southern islands, terrorism and kidnapping, I shudder to think what is happening there and in other places of the world that have succumbed to this regime.

Thanks to my trips to Asia, particularly Hong Kong and the Philippines, I met many wonderful people. It hasn't been possible to keep in contact with everyone, but I treasure memories of those days and of the models and staff who made it all so enjoyable.

15 Quest for success

My business demanded much of me and in turn I demanded commitment and aptitude from the people who worked for it. I expected staff to adhere to the standards and style I had set, whether it was in their work dress or the way a student graduation was produced. If I thought the music a teacher selected for a graduation or fashion parade was inappropriate or too loud, I'd make sure it was changed to reflect the school's values. This wasn't about having everything my way, but a matter of preserving the business in the manner in which it had been set up. I also gathered astute staff to run it, including Janet Phillips; Diana Milford; much-loved Miriam Spring, my student consultant for fourteen years; and Trish Stafford, who was the agency's first manager and Tim's godmother. Busy lives have kept us apart, but I have fond and pleasant memories. Trish Fraser came to me as a beautiful young model (Patricia Sasse) when she was 16 years old. Now a mother of four grown children, she is still with me, giving the support I could not manage without.

For a long time I wasn't good at delegating duties. Dictating letters into a dictaphone was about as close as I came to letting go.

However, I was forced to rely on staff as my energies were pulled increasingly in new directions. Being a Gemini, I thrived when I had several competing focuses and challenges, so in effect I invited more work. Obviously, as my workload escalated there was a toll on my personal life and, eventually, the business itself. If I could pinpoint a recurring problem that came up, it was the rush of ideas for the business that I acted on without fully assessing the financial consequences. What I probably needed was a business partner who could have anchored me and transformed my ideas into worthwhile financial investments. Maybe the secretarial and bookkeeping course my mother wanted me to do when we first arrived in Sydney would have helped me after all. I had never been interested in the nitty gritty of company finances, so long as I could be a market leader and have a comfortable lifestyle. To be the best was always a firm resolve. The myriad expansionary ventures and for-the-fun-of-it forays made my business successful, but also stretched it, and me, to the limit.

Just as my first Asian tour approached, I was pressed to find a new home for the business in Sydney. I was faced with the threat of eviction from the ninth floor of the Dymocks building on George Street after tenants had complained that my students repeatedly left the non-automatic lift door open, after the lift driver went home, thus forcing them to take the stairs. I had no immediate alternative but to accept an offer to take over 4500 square feet in the building's lower ground floor where radio station 2KY was moving out to its new Orwel Street, Kings Cross building. I wondered how I'd ever fill it, but in time the school required the entire area. Its size, marble staircase entrance, decor in up-to-the-minute colours and walls adorned with glamorous shots of my top models impressed visitors. When pushed for space over the next couple of years, the model agency took over the building's fifth floor, and Femme, the hair and beauty salon I launched as an adjunct to the business, was allocated its own terrain on the first floor. All told, my business stayed in the Dymocks building for twenty-eight years.

Following the Asian tour and office relocation, I gave birth to Marc in January 1961. Lisa arrived not long after, in October 1962, so I really had my hands full. Despite this, the same year Lisa was born, I became one of three panelists on Channel Nine's 'Teenage Mailbag'. Roger Climpson hosted the question-and-answer program. During the half-hour program, we took on issues of teenage angst, from kissing on a first date to peer pressure. The topics were a far cry from the drug and sex issues that face teenagers today, but confronting enough for the program's afternoon timeslot. I found it challenging to come up with an appropriate answer on live television, but the camaraderie on set relaxed me. I was as comfortable talking to the television camera as I had been posing for a photographic one as a model. The experience led to my endorsement of beauty soap, cosmetics and wallpaper for television advertisements. Added to my workload at this time was an increasing demand for corporate training. Simultaneously David Jones, Grace Brothers and Waltons (although all in competition with each other) called for my school to train staff in deportment, grooming and presentation.

I spied another venture after I was the focus of a department store promotion in New Zealand and opened a branch of my business in Auckland in early 1965. Although I employed Elaine Hammond, a well-known local model and mannequin to manage it, I made several trips across the Tasman to conduct classes and undertake promotional work for my business. The branch thrived for a few years, but when Elaine resigned I couldn't find a suitably qualified replacement. Not having the time to invest further in this relatively minor market, I closed the operation, or so I thought.

Maisy Bestle Cohen had carved out a successful modelling career, and cashed in on this by opening a deportment school in Auckland. It was no accident that she called it the June Dally-Watkins School of Deportment. Maisy never asked permission to use my business name and took advantage of the fact that I had neglected to register it in New Zealand. My written plea to Maisy to desist with using my business name didn't have the desired effect and I was too tired to continue the fight. Four young children and ongoing demands had depleted my will and energy. A few years ago she was quoted in a New Zealand newspaper saying that she had 'more or less inherited' the business! Eventually Maisy pursued other business interests and sold the school in 1982. I thought that ended the matter, but I have recently discovered that my business name is still in use there. Fashion designer Babs Radon phoned me to say June Dally-Watkins New Zealand had reopened. Be assured that the model school and agency, June Dally-Watkins NZ Ltd, based in the trendy suburb of Parnell in Auckland, is in no way a product of mine.

By 1965 I had 100 full-time models in Sydney and booked up to 90 model jobs a day. I gathered men, grandmothers, children and babies on the agency books. Two years later, I had 300 students and 30 teachers. In Brisbane, business was just as hectic. After a stint in the Rex Arcade in Fortitude Valley, where we had room for a large deportment studio with a catwalk and a make-up studio with benches and backlit mirrors around the walls, it was time to move again. The eighth floor of Watkins Place in the heart of the city was better placed to cater for future growth. Moving in, I had the studios, model agency and Femme hair salon decked out in ultra-modern turquoise and white decor. The value of the building's name was not lost on me. When Ita Buttrose, then editor of *The Australian Women's Weekly*, visited my hair salon to have her hair styled, she alighted from a taxi, looked up at the large lettering on the twenty-eight-floor structure and exclaimed: 'Jesus Christ! She even owns the bloody building!'

Laraine Blades lived in Townsville and convinced me to start a school there, so I did just that. I employed her to manage it and kept it running for two years. The best graduates, including model Jay Tracey and television personality Alison Peters, made it from the far north to Brisbane, Sydney and even Paris. When Laraine moved to Brisbane, Wendy Short managed the Townsville concern the only way I wanted it – beyond reproach.

Dividing my time between these centres, I supervised parades and quests, hosted graduations, and presented models to the media, photographers, advertising agencies and manufacturers' agents. Within a year of opening the Auckland school, I was also offering the fourteen-lesson Deportment course at our new school in Wollongong. Classes also commenced in Miranda and Bankstown. Thankfully, staff and my mother came to my aid in running most of the satellite classes. In 1968, the school opened a branch at Parramatta. That year I was back and forth to Asia, dealing with the breakdown of my marriage, my mother's latest episode of depression, and my daughter Carel's potentially life-threatening tumour. I don't know how I managed to do it, but I remember being in a constant state of exhaustion.

I couldn't say 'no' when I was approached to produce charity shows, including events at St Margaret's hospital where I had given birth to my four children. There was an increasing demand on my time to address various schools, clubs and charities, covering everything from etiquette and deportment to 'will travel' and motivational subjects. After my marriage break-up, I lectured all over New South Wales and in parts of Queensland, not only to girls but also to boys' schools, as well as in the Philippines and Hong Kong. Exhausting as it was, I enjoyed reaching out to young people. There I go again, fulfilling my need to be needed.

In 1969, to mark the first landing on the moon, I organised and compered a lunar-inspired fashion parade to raise funds for a charity. Space-like clothes matched with what was considered out-of-this-world make-up and hairstyles were created for the event. For Christmas, I used a similar theme for a staff and client party I held in our large studio at Dymocks Building. The guests drank cocktails made with blue curaçao and the lighting was kept low. It was only when I bid goodnight to people as they left this artificial moonscape that I noticed their teeth and tongues had turned blue. That same year, *June Dally-Watkins: Manners for Moderns*, an etiquette guide edited by Christine Chaseling was released on the market.

My staff and I were busy taking classes in Canberra, Bathurst, Orange, Armidale and Tamworth. We worked from makeshift make-up studios. The conditions weren't ideal. The heat was trying and gnats would dive into containers of face powder and then fly away ghost-like. Despite this, the country students were most enthusiastic and it was a pleasure to host their graduation ceremonies. Alan Mortimer, who with the assistance of his wife, Shirley, photographed my school's graduation ceremonies for thirty years, travelled from Sydney to capture these moments. Going back to small country towns always made me feel at home and revived. I loved the relaxed pace of country quests and parades, and taking the time to chat at Kempsey fashion shows with the wonderful, old-fashioned gentleman Steve Keir, who created Australia's signature headwear, the Akubra. Whilst visiting Mount Isa to judge a quest I met a teenager, Richard Foster, who was desperate to talk about fashion and his plans to escape this mining town. Richard de Chazal, as Foster is now known, has stitched up a successful designing career.

In the early 1960s I spent time each year in regional New South Wales judging the White Rose Orchestra Beauty Queen for Frank Burke, the orchestra's founder. Burke's White Rose Ball and associated quests provided important social links between rural and regional communities. Dozens of beauties from remote properties and towns, such as Dirranbandi, Wee Waa and Gulgong, dreamt of claiming the title of White Rose Queen, for which the prizes included a modelling course at my school and a trip to the South Sea Islands. The entrants wore white gloves and traditional debutante gowns. The style of dancing and music at the balls where the Queen was announced were also more traditional – lots of waltzes and barn dances.

My quest commitments continued to steamroll. I accepted

dozens of invitations to judge model and beauty quests far and wide, including the Miss Showgirl at Mossman in Queensland's far north, Miss University quests, the Quest of Quests, and even debutantes at my daughters' school. No matter their size or importance, all the quests I judged were run in the most reputable way, and no one ever tried to influence my decision. It was a pleasure to judge several Miss Australia Quests at a time when the winner was draped in an ermine coat and crowned with a glittering tiara. Being Miss Australia meant instant celebrity status, an ambassadorial role travelling overseas, and perhaps meeting the Queen or receiving the key to a city. Entrants were judged according to 'beauty of face and figure', as well as poise, deportment, general knowledge and personality. Generally, girls who entered any quest were beautiful, fairly insecure, and trying to do their best for a good cause and for their town, State or country.

The Spastic Centre, which from 1954 sponsored the quest, increasingly received criticism for using a beauty quest to raise money for those with disabilities. In 1987, people protested outside the event. At the height of political correctness, men were allowed to enter and Brad Rogers became the first male to win the fundraising award in 1997. Despite raising more than $87 million for cerebral palsy over a forty-six-year period up to 2000, the quest was axed. I'm sad that era has gone.

I believe the quests I judged, and others I ran myself, gave young women the opportunity to shine, launch new careers, and change their lives for the better. I couldn't understand criticism of quests, which came under attack in the 1970s when the feminist movement gathered steam. Feminists would carry placards and protest outside hotels where the quests were being held. Once I was backstage at the Sydney Hilton getting ready for the big night when I heard a young woman on stage, giving her spiel about how wrong it was for women to flaunt themselves and be judged on their appearance. 'They must be brainless,' she said. How ignorant was this woman – an oaf wearing hobnail boots –

to talk to an empty room! Why couldn't women support each other and say something like, 'Good on you, girl, you go for it'? Men and women were allowed to idolise sportsmen as great Australians and expected to shun Miss Australia, who was not only exceedingly good looking, but also a well-mannered and well-spoken ambassador for the nation.

The feminists seemed to be embarrassed that they were women. They wanted to be like men, whilst at the same time patronising and condemning them. They urged women to burn their bras and not shave their legs, as if that would give them power over men. I never had to do anything like that for men to treat me as an equal or to become successful in business. Nor did I need a soapbox or to put men down to reach my goals. I simply went about achieving them in a hard-working, quiet way. I love being feminine. It's wonderful to have a man open the door for me or do something to help me, and it's great when I can say 'thank you' in appreciation. The feminist mood in the 1970s affected my business. Feminists condemned my school's teachings, leading to a slight downturn in student numbers. This came just as I faced attack from within the business. Despite the wonderful staff I had gathered around me to accomplish so many industry firsts and feats, I could not keep an eye on all of them.

After taking parades to Asia over a fourteen-year period, an ugly incident occurred that led me to stop these odysseys. One of my students was a good-looking 15-year-old when she came to my school, but had been too short to model, so I took her on as an employee in the agency. Proving trustworthy and competent when I had been overseas and taken leave to give birth to Lisa, I elevated her to the position of manager of the Sydney agency. I was friendly with her parents and had socialised with them. I thought Viv and I had a good level of respect and friendship, such that in 1963 I hosted a pre-wedding party for her at The Bistro, the then fashionable 'in' restaurant.

As a reward for Viv's hard work, I took her on one of the parade excursions to Asia. On our return, she resigned, saying she was going to have a baby. I wished her well and commented on several red blotches that had appeared on her neck during our conversation. 'It's nothing,' she assured and I believed her. No sooner had she left than I received a phone call from a friend telling me of Viv's plan to open a rival agency. During the Asian tour, she had apparently convinced each of the models to leave my agency, saying it was too big and that they would receive more attention under her personal care. I was dumbfounded and terribly hurt. She denied the plan when I phoned her, but soon after her agency opened. Why couldn't she have said, 'I'm sorry, June' and told me the truth? Then, I may not have felt so personally injured by her betrayal.

The wound to my business also wept. Many models with my agency followed the example set by the top models Vivien had lured on the Asian trip. Some of them didn't have the manners or decency to tell me they were leaving. I remember having a lovely chat with a model and her mother in my office, after which they left a note at the reception to say the model was defecting to another agency. I took these walkouts too personally; I shouldn't have. It is a commonplace practice in this fickle industry for models to agency-hop when the dollar signs and promises look more attractive elsewhere. As models walked from my agency, I began to believe that indeed my agency had grown too large. At its peak I had up to 400 models on my books. I lost heart instead of fighting back.

Viv's actions stung longer than when other employees left and set up rival businesses. In 1979, when I was consumed by my mother's ill health, I heard from a loyal model that the manager of my agency, Pamela Skelton, was setting up her own agency. Incensed by not being told directly by Pam, I sacked her. She then went to the press and claimed that my agency was too large. I reacted by issuing a defamation writ, but didn't go through with the legal action. Pamela's Model Management opened with a collection of models, some of whom had been working for me.

Ursula Hufnagl, a leader in the model-agency business in Sydney, became a model through my school and agency and participated in my Asian fashion tours. Some time had passed since she had left my agency when she opened her own, and now she runs Chic Model Management, so I never felt the carpet had been pulled from under me. My Brisbane agency has maintained a rapport with Ursula, and whenever we refer models to her agency, we receive a commission as the mother agency. This arrangement is repeated with Chadwicks, Cameron's and Gordon Charles in Sydney, and is common practice across the industry. Gordon Charles of Platform takes on much of the young talent from our Model course.

My Christian belief encouraged me to forgive Viv when she contacted me about ten years ago. She wanted to contract my models in Brisbane when she needed local talent. Tentatively, I accepted the exchange arrangement. A rollcall of all the Dally's models was arranged when she visited Brisbane, so she met them personally and took their contact details. Later I received a tip-off that she was about to open an agency in Brisbane. As we had no written agreement, I had no recourse. She set up in Brisbane and in due course some of the models who had been working for me were contacted, but very few joined her new agency. Nevertheless, my agency remains the leader in Queensland.

As a businesswoman, I was realistic enough to accept that models could switch agencies and former employees could open their own agencies and deportment schools. I never had an issue with my former employees and graduates, like Billie North and Ursula Hufnagl, when they branched out on their own because of the way they conducted themselves in this process. I can understand that when others see something special and profitable, they want it. However, there are ways to go about this.

Industry bitchiness and backstabbing reached an international level when my friendship with Eileen and Jerry Ford was severed in 1981. I had known the Fords, who then ruled the world's largest model agency, Ford Models, for more than twenty years. We respected each other's business territory and style, and became good friends. In 1965, when Eileen judged the Australian Fashion Awards as well as awards for the Model of the Year and Mannequin of the Year, I held a cocktail party in her honour at my Bellevue Hill home. Eileen reciprocated several times when I was in New York, insisting I stay at her home where actress Renee Russo, then a young model, was in their care. When many of my models headed overseas they signed up with Ford Models and I was proud of this association.

Such was the value of this relationship that I wasn't perturbed when Eileen thwarted an opportunity for me to open a branch of my model school in London. Hearing about the success of my school, April Ducksberry and Jose Fonseca, the founders behind the English agency Models One, suggested I set up a model school alongside their agency. The deal was almost sealed when, for reasons unknown to me, Eileen told them not to pursue the plan. Models One was dependent on Ford Models through a model exchange arrangement and heeded Eileen's advice. A few years later, during the model agency 'war' that was largely waged between Johnny Casablancas' agency, Elite, and Ford Models, Eileen tried to launch a model school, but the venture failed because Elite had cornered this market. In hindsight, I'm happy the London school didn't come to fruition, as it would have required me to spread my energy even thinner.

Despite each of our commitments, the Fords and I always had time for each other in Rome or Milan when we gathered for fashion shows, industry dinners and functions. I visited Europe three or four times a year to keep up with changes on the fashion scene and see my daughters in Italy. My last face-to-face contact with the Fords was in Rome in 1980, not long after the war between the model agencies had erupted. Part of Johnny Casablancas' strategy to topple the Fords from being the number one model agency in the world was to launch an international Look of the Year model contest. The Fords told me they would launch a model search, called 'Face of the 80s', in Monaco that year. (In the 1990s, the competition was renamed 'Supermodel of the World' and continues under this name.) It seemed that competition between agencies was becoming fiercer. Once an agent had worked hard to establish a model, other agencies would move in to poach her. These days there are dozens more agencies. They are of a more boutique nature, incorporate celebrities, and offer personal management services. Nothing stays the same.

The following year, Eileen asked me to look after her 24-year-old daughter, Lacy, who was visiting Australia to scout for talent. My daughter Carel was working for me, and we welcomed Lacy and held a party for her. Visiting various agencies to seek out new talent, Lacy also spent time with Vivien McDermott. After Lacy returned to the States, Ford Models struck a formal association with Vivien's and for one reason and another our friendship was severed. Consequently, in the absence of Ford Models establishing its quest in Australia, I launched my own local Face of the 80s quest in 1982. In comparison to Ford Models' global grand-scale quest of the same name, my national event was small-time. In no way did it rival Eileen's quest, nor did she react to its existence by contacting me. My Face of the 80s quest came about after the US-based organisers of the Miss Universe Pageant had asked me to take on the Australian franchise of its contest. To represent Australia in the Miss Universe pageant, the entrant was required to have won an existing quest, so Face of the 80s was born as a vehicle to find Miss Universe Australia. The winner simultaneously gained automatic entry to represent Australia in the Miss Asia Pacific quest. I had just received a telegram from the USA about taking on the franchise for Miss Universe Australia when I was due for drinks at the home of my friends, Sonia, Lady McMahon, and Sir Bill McMahon. Telling them my news I lamented, 'I can't do this. I don't have the time or energy.' Sonia offered to come on board as co-director and we staged the first Face of the 80s/Miss Universe Australia quest together.

For the next seven years while I kept the franchise, and with it the franchise for Miss Asia Pacific (Australia), I took sole responsibility for the event. My son Marc came on board as the event's director. However, it was never profitable – instead, it cost me money.

I gained satisfaction from running the quest. The inaugural Face of the 80s winner, Lou-Anne Ronchi of Perth, went on to become a James Bond Quest winner and play a part in one of the 007 spy-thriller films. Winners in subsequent years had their modelling careers rocket also. Face of the 80s was also a way to raise funds for cancer research and promote my new skin-care product Dallyence. And of course, I made sure I had fun while I worked. We gathered friends and industry contacts – including Susan, Lady Renouf; Sonia, Lady McMahon; Barbara, Lady Hickey; Gold Coast identity Thea Williams (wife of developer Keith); and Hollywood celebrity designer John Hayles – to help judge the entrants at gala events. Face of the 80s and my franchisee rights to Miss Universe Australia and Miss Asia Pacific (Australia) ended with the clicking over to the next decade.

16 Friends like these

Loyal friends, staff and appreciative students have restored my trust in people and picked me up at low points in my life. I have particularly treasured the friendship of some students long after they have graduated, as well as the ongoing contact I have with some of their parents. Over the years I collected a wealth of friends and acquaintances, some of them very influential and powerful, from all corners of the world. Having few friends in my youth, I thought I needed as many as possible and set about cultivating a wide network of contacts. An insightful comment made by my eldest grandson Christopher, when he was only 12 years old, revealed to me how insatiable was my need for an extensive network. Chris had declined to give his phone number to a Sydney boy with whom he had played during our holiday on the Gold Coast. I thought he was being unkind and asked why he had refused the boy's request. 'I have enough friends, Nonna,' he explained. Chris made me realise it was more important to nurture the relationships I had with my dearest friends. Now as a mature person, I don't want a social schedule. I have my family, my students and a loving group of friends to sustain me. My friends are a blessing.

Roma Blair deserves a special mention. A Rita Hayworth look-alike with auburn hair and full lips, Roma became a model at the age of 12. At 16, she met her future husband Leo Ossendryver. Leo was based in the Dutch East Indies and their nuptials were confirmed by telegram, making Roma the first Australian woman to be married by proxy. She had been reunited with Leo briefly and was seven months pregnant when the Japanese invaded and sent them to separate prisoner-of-war camps. After the war, in an effort to recover from camp-related health complaints, Roma took up yoga. We met in 1957, after Roma spotted me through the window of a city electrical store in Sydney during a 2KY broadcast of a program I co-hosted with Lyall Richardson. She introduced herself, and within days I employed her to teach deportment and yoga – long before this form of exercise became trendy in the West. By the late 1970s, she was teaching disco dance exercise classes at the school. I couldn't help but be charmed by Roma's sense of fun and her persuasion. I was a mother of four and found myself striking a yoga pose in a leotard for a magazine photo, learning meditation, and practising tai chi in a Hong Kong park when it was virtually unheard of in Australia. After seventeen years of working at the school in Sydney, Roma moved to the Gold Coast. At least distance hasn't broken the ties that bind us.

Colette Raynes managed our Brisbane, Sydney and Hong Kong offices for nineteen years, yet she still wonders how she secured a receptionist position in my Brisbane office in the first place. My accountant, the gruff but adorable Bill Stirling was preoccupied listening to the test cricket on a transistor radio when he interviewed Colette. Between cricket overs he barked questions at her: 'Do you type? Have you had any experience in this work?' The 19-year-old replied 'no' each time. However, being the tomboy sister of two sporty brothers, Colette knew a lot about the game and they discussed the form and techniques of the cricketers. It made an impression on Bill, who was fastidious about details, whether it was account keeping or cricket scores. Colette respected his meticulousness and loved him for his honesty and loyalty as much as I did. There were no surprises with Bill; you knew what to expect. In all the years I knew Bill, the frames of his spectacles were stuck together with a Band-Aid. He wore a beige lightweight suit, and on Wednesdays brought in his transistor radio to listen to the horse races. About one month after Colette came on board, we met at the 1967 staff Christmas party. Two years later she rose to office manager. But it wasn't until the 1970s, when she moved to Sydney and took over from our then manager Janet Phillips, that we became good friends. Colette is a perfect lady: feminine, intelligent and thoughtful. We have shared great times together, and I feel fortunate to have her as a big part of my life.

One of my most memorable times with Colette was on a holiday in 1984. At the invitation of Sonny Lim, a millionaire playboy whose family owns a lumber company in the Philippines, we flew in his private jet to his private island, Fuga, in the archipelago's north. Stopping for lunch along the way, we were driven through the jungle in the centre of Luzon to Sonny's isolated jungle home, fit for a movie set, and from there by jeep to an even more isolated area surrounded by bodyguards armed with Uzzis. Apparently there had been murders the week before. Guerrillas had captured, then decapitated, locals including the local school teacher. A gauze-sided safari-style tent had been erected for a sumptuous feast for the three of us. A whole baby pig was roasted on a spit and there was champagne. It was a surreal sight to behold. We continued our flight to Fuga, a speck of paradise fringed with coconut-coloured sand. Sonny had to return to Manila for a couple of days and installed us in his magnificent beach house. We were each allocated a bodyguard armed with a machine gun, who dutifully followed our every move, whether we were swimming in the sea or touring the island in a four-wheel-drive vehicle. Although each of us had been used to the attention of men over the years, it took a couple of days to become accustomed to this kind of gaze. Sonny returned and showed us a luxury bungalow about a kilometre from his beach house. It was fully staffed, just waiting for the Marcos family to arrive!

From Fuga we went to Mia Mia on the coast of Luzon. When a typhoon blew up Sonny wanted to carry us back to Manila by helicopter. Sonny flew out alone while Colette and I opted for a road trip south that turned hair-raising. My hotel industry friends arranged our stay at the Baguio Hyatt, subsequently destroyed by an earthquake. Luxury travel wasn't always available. Problems organising our transport back south to Manila forced us to take the local bus – a trip of several hours, with the locals, their chickens, roosters and a pig or two, and a blue video being shown to help while away the time!

While Colette was in Hong Kong she married Max Hunt, an Australian who was a significant figure in the duty-free business. They have since moved to Bali, where Max is semi-retired and Colette has set up a franchise for a fashion accessories business. They're parents to two gorgeous children, Pascale and Nicholas. Pascale and I have a very special friendship. When she was very small, we started watching the full moon together. Now it doesn't matter if we're in different countries when Pascale looks at the moon and tells Colette that she is 'praying to Aunty June'.

Brisbane's Di Cant is a mutual friend of Colette's and mine. Di Di, as I call her, has a spark that has never dimmed in the forty years I've known her. Di was five centimetres shy of the minimum model height requirement when she came to the school as a teenager. Nevertheless, her sassy look and effervescence won her some modelling jobs before she took on teaching Wardrobe and Social and Business Etiquette classes at the school over a seventeen-year period. Her association with Dally's Model Management in Brisbane continues today. Di is the fashion manager for Brisbane's RAQ Australian Fashion Design Awards. Dubbed the 'fashion empress' by the Brisbane press, she is clever, perfectly groomed and knows the fashion business backwards. The last time I returned to the catwalk was to support Di's efforts to stage Fifty Years of Catwalk in 2000, which raised funds for the Blood Cord Bank. I felt relaxed and happy to be on the catwalk to the tune 'As Time Goes By' for a cause close to Di's heart.

Helen Newham (née Meehan) and I are such old chums that we communicate at a unique level. We send 'thought messages' to each other. It works like this: I'll phone and she'll answer, 'I was just thinking of you' or vice versa. We have always understood and accepted each other for who we are and looked out for each other's interests. I can't count the number of times Helen was my rock during the ups and downs with my mother and during my marriage to John. It was great to have my confidante return to Australia after she had spent a few years in Malaysia working as a welfare officer attached to a British army hospital for the Red Cross. While she was in Malaysia she met her English husband, Mike Newham, who was managing a rubber plantation.

Helen and I are both ideas people, but some of her visions haven't quite sparked my enthusisasm – like the time, Helen tried to persuade me to go in with her to secure property at Lightning Ridge, in outback New South Wales. I drove up with my children to find an oversized tent-like shack with carpet covering a mud floor in the middle of nowhere. This was truly frontier territory. When we returned, Marc set up an 'opal shop' selling his treasures from a cotton wool-lined tray at our front gate or from the back of Lisa's tricycle as he door-knocked the neighbours. It was another hint that Marc was destined for a career in business and marketing. John and I had been living apart for some time when Helen and Mike separated. Helen came with her children to live in the self-contained apartment attached to my Bellevue Hill home for about nine months. It was great having so many children around. The Newhams' children (Greg, my god-daughter Susie and Nigel) are an extension of my family.

The McMahons were more than nearby neighbours; they became close friends. Every Christmas morning my family would join them for a drink and their three children came to our house to play. There were times when Sonia could not make every engagement, so once I stood in for her to accompany Bill to a function at Scone in regional New South Wales. Not long after Bill became Prime Minister in 1971, the diminutive leader arrived in his chauffeur-driven car and jokingly offered my lofty son Tim all his old suits. Despite being a dedicated administrator and hard worker during his term in power, Bill was devoted to his children and wife Sonia, who made a glamorous first lady. Sonia innocently created an international storm of publicity when she arrived for a White House dinner in a sexy white dress with a side split that showed off her shapely legs. She has always been the perfect lady.

The McMahon children have attracted media attention in their own right, too. Gorgeous Melinda graduated at 14 from my school and had a stint as a model when the first of the 'baby models' were in demand. However, as she grew older she wasn't tall enough to make a serious career of modelling. It seemed Julian was destined to become an actor and has held his own in the competitive environs of Hollywood. After a lunch at Bill and Sonia's, he and his sisters would perform an Abba song, using Bill's tennis and squash racquets for guitars. Bill always pulled back a curtain to introduce their skit. I had thought Julian's first marriage to singer Dannii Minogue would be a good match, but sensed that Sonia thought otherwise. Sonia didn't talk to the Minogue family at the reception and the media picked up on the tension. Sonia had a threatened miscarriage when she was pregnant with Debbie, the youngest, when we were all visiting mutual friends Eric and Narelle Robinson on the Gold Coast. As it turned out mother and daughter were to have difficulties in the years ahead. Bill was so proud of Debbie when she graduated from my modelling course with all the potential to become a fashion model. I'll never forget the expression on his face and Sonia squeezing his hand as Debbie accepted her diploma on stage at the Pacific Hotel at Manly.

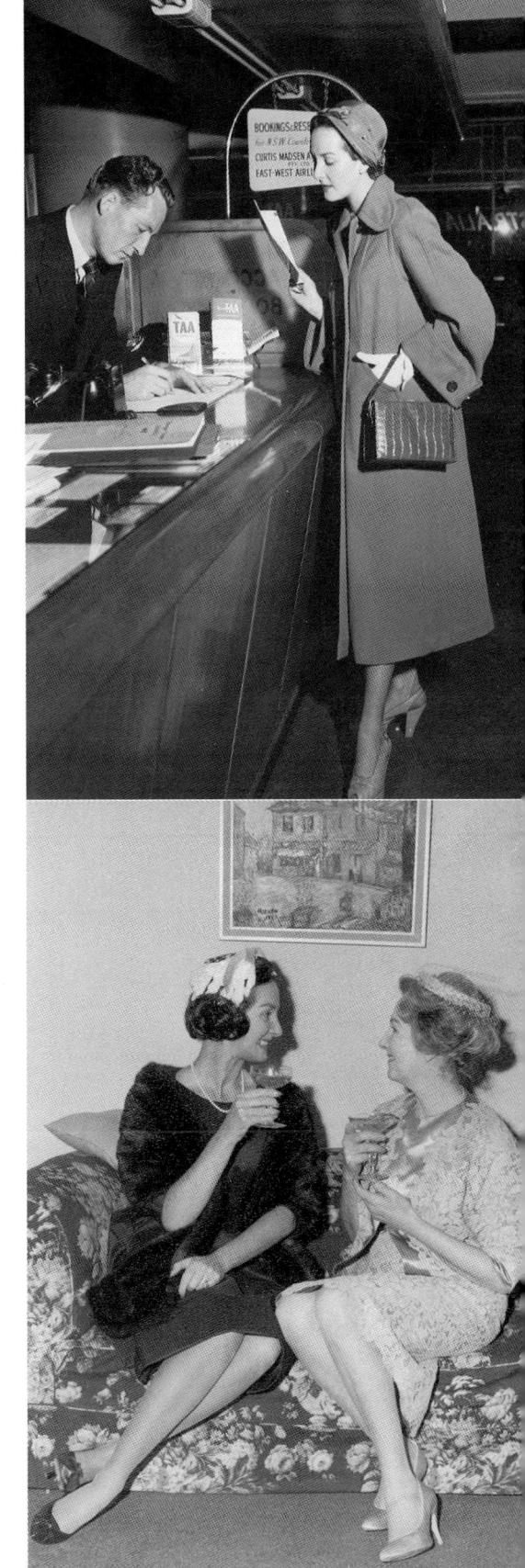

TOP About to embark on a TAA fashions-in-the-air tour in 1954.

RIGHT In June 1960 my mother and Bill James were married. Their wedding reception was held at my Bellevue Hill home.

ABOVE These top four models of 1961 took part in the first-ever parade of Australian models in Hong Kong. Left to right are Judy Lindsay (Narromine, NSW), Lorraine Knight (Sydney), Luce Carmagnola (Camden, NSW) and Patricia Duffie (Kandos, NSW).

OPPOSITE TOP Margaret Rose takes her turn in front of classmates from the Deportment class on the June Dally-Watkins catwalk in Dymocks' basement in 1961.

OPPOSITE BOTTOM In 1963, at the Baradine Memorial Hall, I was a judge of the White Rose Queen. The winner was Jenny Wilmott (Miss Spring Ridge).

ABOVE Class shots of June Dally-Watkins models taken in Dymocks' basement in the 1960s. The top shot is from the era of false hairpieces and false eyelashes. The girls in the bottom shot adopt a more natural look.

OPPOSITE TOP Compering a fashion show, circa 1964.

OPPOSITE MIDDLE At the school in 1966 with Mother, who for many years was our student consultant.

OPPOSITE BOTTOM One of my school brochures from the 1970s.

Let me help you look lovelier!

a message to women of all ages

from June Dally-Watkins

what my COURSE can do for you!

Every woman can be lovely to look at and lovely to know. Beauty and charm can be acquired. I have proved this by showing many young girls and women how to make themselves lovelier.

Suddenly they are glamorous — radiant in their new personality — because they have learned how to develop their own hidden loveliness.

During your Course with our School you will learn how to —

- Apply your make-up in the most attractive manner.
- Make your figure lovelier.
- Walk and sit gracefully.
- Wear your hair in a style that best suits you.
- Improve your personality and acquire poise and charm.
- Be sure your manners are perfect

CORRECT POSTURE

Most unsightly and life-less most learn to acquire grace of movement and good posture. The June Dally-Watkins Course will teach you to walk correctly, stand and sit gracefully, walk with poise up and down stairs.

MAKE-UP PERFECTION

Your face can look more radiant features more regular if you learn to apply make-up correctly . . . special tricks with foundation, powder, lipstick, eye make-up and rouge. Find the right colour to flatter your face.

EXERCISE AND YOGA

Exercise is necessary not only for taking off inches, but for improving posture and appearance. The June Dally-Watkins Course will show you how to correct exercises for your back, bustline, shoulders, bosom, waistline, thighs, legs.

An expert will instruct you in yoga.

DIET—WHAT FOODS TO EAT—WHAT TO AVOID

Concerning the food we eat! A diet will be suggested, whether it be to lose weight; to gain for those who are too thin; or a health-giving diet to improve your skin and give you the wonderful glow of good health.

STAR-BRIGHT HAIR

The secret of hair loveliness is included in the June Dally-Watkins Course. Learn the rules of shampooing, brushing and special care for special types of hair.

YOUR CLOTHES AND YOU

Once you've learned graceful posture, the correct skin care and make-up application, you give thought to your wardrobe. Attractive clothes depend on your figure type, height, skin, hair and eye colouring. Learn to select clothes that will make you look lovelier . . . colours which suit you, colours to avoid. Clothes to hide figure faults . . . with accessories and jewellery to complement your wardrobe.

HAND AND NAIL CARE

Cared-for hands complete the pretty picture of a well-groomed girl. Your hands are as pretty as you make them — said the June Dally-Watkins Course will show you how. Learn to give yourself a professional 'home' manicure. Also exercises to make your hands graceful. Hands can be slenderised and strengthened, made more flexible and expressive. GRACEFULNESS can be acquired for your hands, as well as your body.

ETIQUETTE — GOOD MANNERS — CHARM

To know the rules of etiquette is to feel quietly confident in yourself. CHARM IS A MAGNET—let the June Dally-Watkins Course suggest to you how to remember names, make introductions correctly, speak with a pleasing voice, listen attentively. You can become an attractive, well-groomed, charming unforgettable woman.

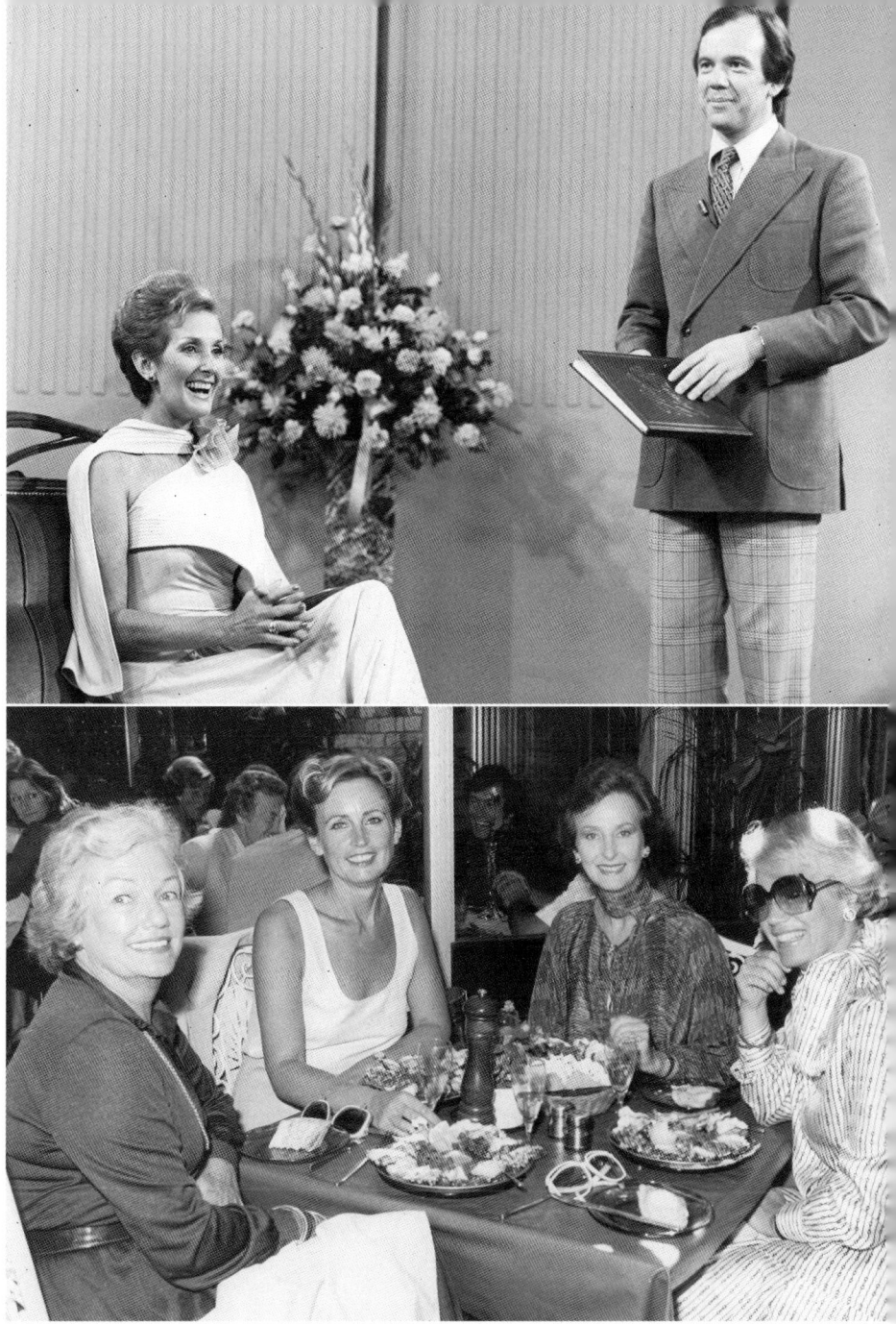

OPPOSITE At my Bellevue Hill home with my children in the year John and I parted, 1968. From left to right are Tim, 11; Carel, 13; Lisa, 5; and Marc, 7.

TOP On 18 January 1976, I wondered with excitement which of my friends Mike Willesee might bring out to surprise me on 'This Is Your Life'.

ABOVE Having lunch in Double Bay in 1979 with my mates. From left to right: Narelle Robinson, Sonia McMahon and Susie Renouf. (*Photo courtesy of The Fairfax Photo Library*)

In 2000 I visited war-devastated Bosnia and sat saddened among the remains of the elegant 16th-century Stari Most bridge, which had spanned the waters of the Neretva River in Mostar until it was destroyed by mortar and tank fire in November 1993.

I met Eric Robinson through his wife Narelle, the daughter of Stanley and Olga Jones. Eric became active in federal politics, rising to become Finance Minister in the Fraser Government and the Queensland Liberal Party's 'kingmaker' in the late 1960s. I have never been a member of any political party despite my connections with conservative politics. However, through the Robinsons, my circle of political acquaintances and friends grew. The Robinsons' beautiful Gold Coast residence became my home away from home and was the base for many Liberal Party fundraisers and social functions. For some of these events, I'd cook for one hundred guests. Like my mother, her mother and my aunts, I loved to cook and wasn't daunted by catering for such a crowd. Eric was still relatively young when he suffered a massive heart attack by the pool of his home in 1981. Sonia phoned at 1 a.m. to tell me he had died in hospital. Narelle lives at Mermaid Beach, but we have remained close. Visiting her with my grandson, Chris, about seven years ago, Don Chipp was there and asked Chris if he knew who he was. Chris didn't. He wasn't even born when Don was involved in the Liberal Party and founded the Australian Democrats – but Don jokingly threw a bucket of water over him to make sure he'd never forget. My grandson returned the treatment, so I'm sure Don, who has a great sense of fun, will always remember who Chris is too.

Through these connections, I judged several Queensland Miss Young Liberal quests. One year Susan Peacock was a fellow judge and we hit it off straight away. It seemed her husband Andrew Peacock was the heir-apparent to Bill McMahon. Not surprisingly, an aloof Malcolm Fraser, who was the next Liberal to take up residence in the Lodge, was also at the Robinsons' parties. One year I took up Susie and Andrew's invitation to stay at what we jokingly referred to as 'the Peacock Pool House at the foothills of the Dandenongs' to attend the Melbourne Cup. We arrived at Flemington with fanfare in a police-led cavalcade. Leilani, a filly the Peacocks had leased with another couple from the elderly New Zealand breeder Ian McRae, had already won the Caulfield Cup and was tipped to take the 1974 Melbourne Cup. She came second to Think Big and the celebrations never seemed to end. By Easter, when Leilani was due to race at Randwick in Sydney, we had organised a calendar of social events to keep us in a winning frame of mind.

I was with Susie at the Randwick Easter races the year she met her second husband, international bloodstock pioneer, Robert Sangster. Mother and I were with Susie in the members' stand when Robert was introduced to us. I noticed his white socks clashed with his beige suit and joked to Susie, 'I don't think he's very rich or very important.' Susie was smart; she wasn't taking notice of a minor fashion aberration! I watched their romance unfold from the moment they shook hands and when Susie accompanied me on a work trip to Hong Kong where she met up with Robert. Although her marriages to Andrew and Robert did not last, she has remained on good terms with both of them. Her late ex-husband, Sir Frank Renouf, on the other hand, is never mentioned.

When Susie and I are up for a chat it doesn't seem to matter the hour. I was staying in Melbourne with Susie when she knocked on my door at 1 a.m. 'Junie, may I come in? I have some champagne and good news.' Her daughter Anne Peacock had become engaged to Victorian Liberal Party president Michael Kroger. I adored Annie, and to celebrate this news, we sat on the edge of my bed and drank to the couple's happiness. Again, it was 1 a.m. when Susie contacted me to tell me she had become a grandmother to Annie and Michael's first baby. Oh yes, Susie and I can talk.

Susie is a dear and loving friend. She works at keeping her friendships; I believe in that. Friendships need, like all living things, to be nurtured. As the song made famous by musical actor Eddie Cantor goes, 'If You Knew Susie Like I Know Susie' then more people would know how she's been hurt in life. Most people see only the sunny persona she wears in public. In that way we are very alike. There may be some people who don't understand Susie, or are envious of her; they don't know her. She's intelligent and kind. All her homes – and there have been many – have been profitable and decorated with great taste. I know, having lived in her five-level mansion at Darling Point when I was in the midst of moving from Woollahra to a city apartment a few years ago. Susie went to London and I house-sat. When she returned I was to stay only a few weeks, but it became months.

Another friend I admire is Queenslander Alan Jones. You don't have to agree with everything he says on his radio show, but what he says is always thought-provoking. I can approach him about any subject and expect an intelligent answer. We also understand what it is like to grow up in the bush. Alan was raised on a dairy farm in the Darling Downs and had a four-kilometre horse-ride to school. His first ambition was to become an opera singer, but after attending Oxford University he taught at the King's School at Parramatta. He had not long left the elite school when we met at Quirindi, south of Tamworth. Alan was coaching the local team and for a time lived in a caravan in the garden of the beautiful property of Dr Geoff and Lois Abram. He was helping Geoff run his local airline, SKYWAYS. I was staying at the neighbouring property, Warrah Ridge, owned by the Melvilles. Surgeon Dr Bob would fly to Quirindi to help Geoff perform surgery in the region. Weekends were based around social gatherings at football, polo matches and tennis. Also regular visitors were William Van Otterloo, the world-famous conductor and his wife Carola, and Charles Buttrose Senior and his second wife, Margo.

I found many men less judgmental of me than women. I had more in common with male business leaders and they treated me as an equal. What's the purpose of being gender-neuter for the sake of political correctness? I have always appreciated it when a gentleman treated me as a lady and with respect. I've never understood why people assume that because you have a deep and meaningful relationship with a man it has to be sexual. Sex hasn't entered into the friendships I've had with many male friends, and their wives have become my friends.

John Hayles is a very close, long-time friend, who has come far from his birthplace Darwin, and Brisbane, where he was raised. John made clothes for Becky's Boutique at Potts Point, but Australia was too small for his considerable talent. In 1960, he packed his sewing machine and sailed to Los Angeles. Armed with my letter of introduction to Orry Kelly, he helped Orry assemble Marilyn Monroe's wardrobe for *Some Like It Hot*. He quickly became the darling of the silver-screen set. Pilar Wayne had praised him so much that her husband John Wayne, who was associated more with gun-slinging flicks than fashion, financed a ritzy salon in Beverly Hills for John Hayles. The A-list of Hollywood queued for John's designs, and still does. John has taken charge of the wardrobe department at Universal Studios. I still cherish the gowns he has made for me to wear on special occasions. They have made me shine, even if inside I wasn't feeling great. He instinctively knows what suits me. When John used to make clothes for Angela Lansbury's television program, 'Murder She Wrote', occasionally I spotted more than passing similarities between Lansbury's wardrobe and mine! Moreover, I treasure the nothing-but-the-best champagne times we've shared in Hong Kong and the Philippines and at Christmas-time in Australia.

One male friend remains close to my heart. Dr Bob Melville and his family lived across the road from my home at Bellevue Hill. When my daughter Lisa scrawled 'Doc' on Bob's Quirindi dust-covered car, the imprint remained for weeks; the name stuck even longer. He became affectionately called 'Docky'. Docky's son, Douglas was only a toddler when he accidentally nearly drowned my baby Lisa. She was outdoors in her pram when I saw her and the pillow on which she was lying rising gently as Douglas filled it with water from the hose. I'm glad I was around again when I heard little Marc screaming and saw

Douglas sitting on top of him, thumping his head against the pavement. They all survived and these are the memories that bind us as families. The Melville children and mine grew up together, as I laughingly refer to it, in the same gutter of Bulkara Road and the area was full of children. When the Melvilles moved, Ian and Shirley Norman of Harvey Norman fame bought their house. Their daughter Karen became one of Lisa's best friends, along with Janet Burns and Elizabeth Wadsworth, both of whom came from medical families – we were surrounded by doctors.

My children got up to some mischief also. Tim and his neighbourhood mate Mark Wadsworth used to climb a tree to peer across the street and spy on Fiona Melville who would tuck her school uniform into her underpants and perform cartwheels in the front garden. I could understand my son's attraction to Fiona. In appearance, she took after her beautiful mother Judy Gainford, who was crowned Miss Australia in 1947 and became a model.

After several break-ins in the area in the late 1970s, people began to lock their doors for the first time. Some of the neighbours sold up, including the Melvilles who were relocating to Double Bay. John had long gone, and Carel, Tim and Marc were overseas. Fearing Lisa and I could be attacked and robbed, I phoned the Melvilles for advice about moving. Docky answered the phone, sounding terribly low. I asked how Judy felt about their move. 'She's not with me any more,' he confided. She had left Docky for Peter Morrison, who lived nearby. Peter was the husband of one of Docky's patients, who was in hospital when he and Judy struck up a relationship. Judy and Peter are still together and run a publicity business. Docky adored Judy – I think he still does – but, when he told me about their separation, I invited him to dinner and he's been coming to dinner ever since. It turns out Tim wasn't the only one looking across the street. Docky confided that he used to watch me from his bathroom window as I raced out my front door laden with suitcases on my way to the airport or office. It would be early morning, he would be shaving before another day's operating, and the rest of the street was probably still in bed.

Many of our friends spent time at the Melville property at Quirindi and their beach house at Wagstaff on the New South Wales north coast, along with our children. For years, Docky has been my date for the theatre, dinner engagements, and other places. He phones me daily. My affection for Docky has been based on friendship and respect. No one has ever had a bad word to say about this giving and thoughtful man. Even Judy and he stayed on good terms. At one of his birthday parties, I was touched when Judy told me, 'I'm so pleased that he has you, June.' If I had decided to marry for a second time, I probably would have chosen Docky, however I vowed never to remarry. While his family and mine are great friends, I never wanted to take the risk of combining my family with someone else's.

Another factor stopping me from a deeper relationship with Docky has been my inability to share my innermost thoughts. Holding myself back from opening up and trusting people is part of my internal make-up – a make-up formed by my mother's experiences and my own broken marriage. To those outside my family, Mother and I appeared to have such a good relationship that it seemed too difficult to explain that for the most part it was not. So I never told Docky about the depth of my emotional disturbances with my mother. I did not manage to break through this barrier even after Docky had nursed my mother until her death.

17   A FINAL JOURNEY

Mother had not been well for some time, but it was not until Tim gave her a farewell hug before he left for England in August 1977 that I discovered the extent of her illness. My mother was convinced Timothy had broken some of her ribs, such was the pain she felt. I took her to the best – Dr Bob Melville, who was a founding member of the New South Wales Cancer Council. He was also responsible for introducing partial mastectomy to Australia and saving many lives. My mother could not have been in better hands.

Docky detected an aggressive cancer of the pancreas that had spread insidiously through my mother's body. After operating on Mother at the Prince of Wales Hospital, Docky could only close the opening. 'June, I can't do anything,' he told me. 'It's too late.' On my advice Docky told my mother, 'It doesn't look so good,' but didn't explain the nature of her illness. Now it's obligatory for a doctor to tell the patient their prognosis, but Docky knew that the word 'cancer' was unmentionable to my mother. Cancer was still something people didn't discuss, as if the very mention of it would lead to your demise.

I never told my mother she had cancer and she never asked

either Docky or me about it. Regardless of this, the weight of the unspoken between Mother and me always resounded more loudly. I'm certain she understood the nature of her condition. Maybe Mother didn't ask for details because she feared death and denial was a way she could hope for a miracle and try to defeat the inevitable. She also knew the signs. We had known many people who succumbed to cancer. The whites of her eyes had turned the colour of egg yolks, and her skin was jaundiced, itchy and she became very thin. Often she couldn't keep food down. My mother was dying.

By this stage I had sold my Bellevue Hill home and had bought a large apartment with a terrace and panoramic view of the harbour at Rosemont Gardens, which was part of the Lloyd Jones estate at Woollahra. I lived there for twenty-two years. No sooner did I move in than my children kept coming back to stay – in between romances, changing jobs and overseas trips. Then over a two-year period, Mother came to live with Lisa and me, sleeping in Marc's old room. When she felt a little robust she would return to the Elizabeth Bay apartment we had bought, but before long she was back at my place for more respite. In the last six months of her life, she moved into my home.

My mother recognised that she needed my care, but that didn't mean she resigned herself to the cancer. Some days, she would declare herself well, put on her full-length striped kaftan that hid her skeletal frame, apply make-up, paint her nails and announce that she was going shopping, swinging a basket as she walked down Ocean Street to Edgecliff Centre. By the afternoon, she'd be consumed by pain and bedridden. Our home gradually turned into a one-patient hospital. Her only relief was painkillers and a visit from Docky every afternoon. He would have a Scotch with Mother and hold her hand. He was her comfort blanket and mine too. It was a relief to have a trusted doctor and friend make house calls and save us from having to while away hours in medical waiting rooms and doing the rounds of doctors and hospitals.

Life had to go on. I was busy overseeing the school and agency and giving lectures at night. I tried to stay on top of everything, yet I could feel a strong undertow pulling me down. I recall vividly the feeling I had after working all day, racing home to prepare a meal for my mother, and then driving to Wollongong to give a night lecture. Returning home around midnight, a wave of exhaustion smacked me to the point of collapse. I was limp and numb. Docky convinced me to place Mother in hospital.

I was due to lead the inaugural and what transpired to be the only June Dally-Watkins Fashion and Beauty Tour of Europe when my mother's decline accelerated. A group of Sydney women had signed up for a tour that included attending runway shows at Valentino, Givenchy and Yves St Laurent, and the famous prêt-à-porter fashion events in Paris and London, and embarking on frenzied shopping expeditions in Paris, Florence, Venice and London. Torn between my duties to the tour group and my mother, and hoping Mother's health would pick up, I didn't tell the women that my mother was sick, let alone terminally ill. I waited until the eleventh hour – at the airport when they were all set to go – to tell them I wasn't going with them. Naturally they didn't take the news well and I don't think they believed that my mother was close to death. I called on Carel, who was based in Milan at the time, to escort them. Despite her best efforts, some women didn't want the daughter of June Dally-Watkins as their guide, and some complained during the trip, reducing Carel to tears on several occasions. Not long after, I sent Lisa to be with Carel, who was relieved to have her sister's company. For a brief time, Marc and Tim, who were living in London, met up with their sisters during the tour. It had been very traumatic for Lisa, aged 17, to live with her grandmother's declining health. She couldn't have friends over or listen to her music. Embroiled in business problems and looking after my mother, I didn't have enough time for Lisa. It didn't seem right to subject her to this lifestyle, so when Carel offered Lisa a place to stay with her in Italy, I thought it was the best way out of this situation. My youngest daughter wasn't enjoying school, so it didn't concern me that she had to leave in the middle of her senior year. When Lisa said goodbye to her grandmother she knew she'd never see her again.

Now it was just my mother and me – the two of us. The way it always had been. I knew my mother wouldn't want to die in hospital and I felt guilty about not bringing her home, but I couldn't manage her care any longer. The guilt I felt was complicated by the fact that after all these years it took the closeness of death for Mother's personality to soften. Her pain had overpowered any lingering bitterness against me. There were no harsh words between us any more. Shortly before Mother died, she gave me the sapphire ring that I had given her years before; I wear it often. As had been our habit, I followed her lead and didn't push her to confront her fate, but I wish she had said, 'June, I know I'm going to die, let's talk about it.' I wanted to say goodbye properly. After two years of fighting for her life, and about as long as Docky had expected Mother would be able to withstand the cancer, my mother slipped away. I was holding her hand and Docky was by my side when she died at the Prince of Wales Hospital. It was 1 a.m. on 6 October 1979. She was 75 years old.

All my children were together in Paris with the tour group when Mother died. I didn't ask or expect them to return for the funeral. Nor did I expect John to attend. Friends were supportive, but I couldn't share my true feelings about my mother's passing with them. It was a relief to have the sympathy of Helen, who knew what my relationship with Mother had been like. With Helen, I didn't have to articulate my thoughts. I'll never forget Sonia McMahon's warmth and loving care during the last months of my mother's life. One of my first students, Marie Spies and her husband Ian, a funeral director, took care of the funeral arrangements in the most sensitive and beautiful way. After the service, I stayed with my caring friends, while Docky went with the funeral cortege to have my mother cremated. I couldn't face it.

Just because my mother and I had a strained relationship at times didn't mean I wouldn't grieve or that I would miss her less. Not long after my mother's funeral I went to stay with Carel in Milan to come to terms with Mother's death. I had to get on with life, so tried to forget and move on. I couldn't really cry and grieve about my mother's passing until much later. Mother had suffered so much in her life and unintentionally caused unhappiness for my children and me, so that her release from her pain was also a sort of release for us. A sense of relief rolled over me and I removed the heavy cloak of responsibility that had weighed me down all my life. Like a claustrophobic finally let out of a closet, I could breathe more easily. Only a dull ache remained that in years to come would creep stealthily to the surface, making it a struggle to draw every breath.

Eighteen years and four months later, I dared to prise the lock I had fastened on finding out how my mother had really felt about me. During Mother's battle with cancer I had been aware that she had been writing about me in a 'giant jotter pad', but I had never dared ask about it or look at it. At her death, it lay near her bedside. 'I'll look at it tomorrow,' I told myself. As I packed up her belongings, I saw it again: 'I don't have time now. I'll read it another day.' It took fourteen years before I could flick through its foolscap blue-lined pages, then almost another four years before I read it in depth and released all my sorrow. Why it took me so long, I'm not quite sure. Was I afraid to discover that she hated me, that she loved me, who I was, who she was? It wouldn't necessarily matter what she had to say, I knew that looking at her pained handwriting and discovering her thoughts would open the floodgates on my emotions and force me to face a range of issues. It would break me, I feared. By not looking at the manuscript, I had been able to keep my emotions in check and a deadlock on the past.

When I finally read the manuscript in depth, it was about being in the right place at the right time. In 1998 – the first year I didn't teach at the school since it had opened – I decided to get away, not to celebrate my semi-retirement, but to visit friends in Hong Kong, travel to Florence when Lisa gave birth to her first child, and gather my thoughts for this book. To do this I needed isolation, away from Australia to allow memories to surface into my mind, or what I call my 'neck-top computer'.

Friends I had made through Carel when she was in Milan, Clare Littlewood and her former husband, Gianmaria Beretta, offered me their villa on the island of Filicudi – a speck of perfection in the Aeolian Islands, north of Sicily. Amongst these islands scattered in a crescent-moon formation, the moon could be my confidante again. It was perfect for my needs. However, there were many welcome distractions from the task of reading Mother's thoughts and considering my own writing. As the sun rose each day, it flooded my body with warmth. The villa overlooked Bronze Age excavations at Capo Graziano, a mountain on the extreme end of the island that rose out of the ink-blue Tyrrhenian Sea. On a clear day I could see Sicily's Mount Etna burp pillows of ash and steam. My friends Jan Carmody, the former Miss Australian Surf, and Maureen Daly, whose daughter won the first Miss Mossman Showgirl Quest I had judged years before, had come along to keep me company. Jan stayed only a short while and Maureen's planned two-week visit turned into a two-month sojourn.

The locals, who number about 250, made us feel like family, even though we could share only a few words of each other's language. They would say of me, 'she is writing her memories'. We quickly fitted into their simple and delightful lifestyle. We watched the locals sow their volcanic-rich fields, attending to their grape vines, capers, blackberries, figs, sage, fennel and olives. Long lunches were enjoyed by the sea, between swimming and visiting other islands to catch up with friends, even as far away as Regio Calabria on the tip of southern Italy's mainland. In the evenings, we danced with the locals on the terraces of their homes and trotted home by torchlight along a goat track and down the side of a mountain. Over summer the sleepy island was stirred by the annual invasion of visitors. To get away from the noise of the disco that opens only during summer and wait out the last few weeks until I was due in Florence, I stayed at a quietly located villa, on the opposite side of the island. The villa is owned by Australians, Joe and Carmel Moccora. When I eventually left the island to be with my daughter Lisa and her new baby, Natalia June, I had mixed emotions. Many of my new friends bid me farewell as I left by boat for Naples and watched the huge orange sun set beyond the mountainous island. I will treasure their friendship always.

Although I stayed on the island from April to August 1998, it was not until 23 June that I resisted the island's temptations and peeled open the pages of my mother's manuscript. I had deliberately taken it with me, intending to read it as part of my research for this book. This unfinished chronicle was one of the very reasons I thought I should write about my life in the first place. I intended to finish what Mother had started, but write my own version of my life in my own words. Always a team, my story was as much hers as mine. How could it not be? Even in death, it seemed Mother was there, urging me to go on, start a new venture, to blaze an unlit trail. How wonderful if she could know that this book had been written because her notepad of thoughts helped to make it happen.

When I read Mother's writing I finally shed the tears I could not cry when she had died. I wept more for her living and suffering than her dying. After many years quarrelling with each other, I realised I didn't know or fully understand her and there was much to comprehend about this complex woman and how she had truly felt about me. It's still very emotional for me to dwell on my mother's life.

What Mother had written appeared to be the workings of a biography about me. She had even given it the title *Portrait of a Lady*, so perhaps she had read the Henry James novel of the same name and thought it was an appropriate working title. She'd written fragments about my life: my youth in the bush, my first visits to Hong Kong and

Macau, my friends and four children. The detail that she remembered about my life surprised me. The thought that she spent the last painful months of her life writing about me was overwhelming. Her writing also issued sage advice, which she had given me over the years.

> Get some country education; don't be afraid to go there if any opportunity offers. The more rough and tumble the better.
> Modelling is a demanding career. You have to devote a great deal of time and energy. The name of the game in modelling is making money. A girl should model professionally with the aim of being as good as possible and to make as much money out of it as possible.
> Idleness is dangerous.
> If you're going to do a job, you should do it well or not at all.
> Don't always burden people with your problems.
> Above all brace yourself to give a cheerful smile.

Most surprising, however, was her expression of love for me. She used to say I was dreadful and other terrible things to me throughout my life, and yet reading this she had only good things to write about me. She had blamed me for her life, but none of that resentment or pain came through in her writing, so it was very special to read her innermost thoughts and feelings about me.

> I am so proud my daughter has done so much to put Australia on the map – in such a pretty and charming way.
> June has shown today that there is more to living than just breathing. Her gracious movements and every-ready smile have come from sheer hard work and drive of enlightened enthusiasm. I feel her application has been a source of inspiration for people concerned.
> [Writing about me at the school's graduation night] Never

a falter, never a mistake, smiling, and ready to hear and speak to each and every one.

I have been asked, 'Has June ever been hurt?' Ah yes! But June would always want to be the rose rather than the foot that crushed it.

She has a great admiration for working mothers. She thinks you have to work at being contented and, as for working mothers, children are happy if they see their mothers happy.

After thirty years of hard work, you couldn't say June Dally-Watkins has been lucky. Good things have come her way, but she has had the presence of mind to grasp them and make the most of them.

When I read these words a sadness overwhelms me and tears fill my eyes and my soul. I will always wish I could put my arms around her and say, 'I love you, Mum.'

18   THE SHADOW RETURNS

In the middle of teaching a class, suddenly he was standing there at the classroom door like an apparition. The memory of our last encounter quietly shuddered through me as I recognised the man hovering outside the classroom as my father. I remained composed in front of the students until I could wind up the lesson and see Bob alone. 'I had a strong premonition that I should see you,' he declared. I told him Mother had died only a few weeks earlier and he seemed surprised and remorseful. Surely he had seen the story, 'Model's mother dies' on page one of the *Daily Mirror*? My mind ticked over the 'coincidence' of Bob's appearance and my mother's death, but these thoughts were quickly dismissed with his outpouring of emotions. Bob declared he had really loved my mother, but her parents – my grandparents – had misjudged him and convinced her to reject him. He was sorry he hadn't been able to make amends to her. He didn't want to miss the opportunity to be a father to me and play a greater role in my life. 'I held you in my arms as a baby when you were born and fell in love with you, and I've loved you ever since.'

I wanted to banish memories of our encounters since I saw him at the David Jones parade in the late 1940s. Two other incidents involving my natural father had occurred before Mother died. They jolted my equilibrium and telling her would have been just as upsetting for both of us, so I kept these encounters to myself. When Carel and Tim were young, John and I had taken them, along with their nanny, Mary Redfern, on a holiday to the Gold Coast. It was trendy to stay at Surfers Paradise, which was then unscarred by the high-rise apartments that now shroud the beach in afternoon shade. Our stay was mentioned in a short newspaper article. The following morning a man phoned saying he was my father. I was silent and shocked. He then explained that he obtained our phone number from the journalist who wrote the story and proceeded to confirm his identity. He said he wanted to get to know me and for me to meet his family. 'This is it,' I thought. 'He really wants to know me. He must love me enough if he wants me to meet his family. I'll get to know them and be part of a family at last.' I saw something of myself in Bob's face when he turned up in his car to collect us for the visit to his home. On the way there, I had no trouble making conversation. Public speaking experience had made me adept at 'small talk' with strangers. So far so good, I thought. However, when we arrived, Bob introduced me to his wife and two young sons as his niece. The blood drained from my face and I felt faint. I didn't want to make a scene in front of his or my children and John, so I quickly made an excuse to leave. What purpose was there in introducing me as his niece? Did he only want to show me off as a celebrity? His wife has since told me Bob had talked to her about his famous daughter, but had not explained my existence to his sons.

By the time of our next encounter, John and I had separated. I was an established businesswoman and guest of honour at a dinner dance at the Sebel Townhouse in the early 1970s. A young woman came up to me and said nervously, 'My name is Patti. I'm your half-sister. We have the same father; he didn't marry my mother either.' I was in shock. Sitting at the head table in front of 300 guests, I tried to keep a calm demeanour and smile. Thankfully, people were making their way to the dance floor. I didn't think the woman looked like me and gave her the brush-off. Patti has since apologised for confronting me in such a public way. It was a spur-of-the-moment act of someone whose mother hadn't talked about her father either. She was desperately searching for the answers to riddles. Patti, who is only a few years older than me, had lived with Bob until she was five. He had since wandered in and out of her life when it suited him.

Some time had passed since the Sebel Townhouse night when Patti phoned and invited me to dinner at her home. 'I would like to get to know you, and our father is coming for dinner too. Would you like to come?' I wanted to believe my father was a good man who had been misunderstood by my mother's family. Perhaps it was the need to unlock my mother's secrets and to have more than an enigmatic idea of what a father might be that made me reach out to this stranger. I was curious about Bob and in need of family, so apprehensively I drove over alone to Patti's lovely house on the North Shore, leaving the children with a minder. I managed to remain calm and collected during the formal dinner with Bob, Patti and her family. Afterwards, my father announced that he wanted to spend time alone with me in another room. We adjourned to the study for our first real conversation. I don't know what I expected, but what followed left me confused and hurt. Bob showed no affection towards me, but talked a lot about himself, bragging that he had been a sea captain in the merchant navy. He had travelled regularly to the USA where his investments had proved bountiful. One day this fortune would be mine, he promised. This outlandish story sounded too good to be true, and it was. I never heard another word about my inheritance from him.

Fast-forward a few years and, with the flourish of a few sympathetic words from Bob, I forgot those painful memories. He plugged the abyss in my life. With my mother gone, no husband and four children living overseas, I reached out to Bob to fill the void and provide a sense of family. My mother's passing also meant I felt free to embrace him as a father. Accepting another invitation to his home at Surfers Paradise, this visit gave me reason to believe his words were sincere. Bob openly acknowledged me as his daughter. I learned one of his sons had been electrocuted in an engine room-accident on a merchant navy ship, so I felt even more sympathetic towards him. His wife was warm and welcoming, and I accepted her as my stepmother. Bob and his wife took me shopping and bought me a dress, and gave me a black opal brooch set in gold and diamonds that came from their gem shop. To me, these gifts were signs that my father was trying to show his love for me and made me willing to return that affection. Here I was a grown woman, yet needy like a child for the fatherly love I'd never experienced and whose trust and love could be bought with gifts.

Gradually, however, the fantasy I built of my father crumbled. I had joined my four children for a month's holiday at a villa in Lucignano in Tuscany in June 1980. Carel was about to head back to Australia, Lisa was immersing herself in the Italian lifestyle and the boys came over from London. The days were punctuated by the long, pleasurable drive across a landscape of vineyards, yellow wild rape flowers and terracotta farmhouses to Arezzo to meet the train bringing new houseguests – English and Australian, the children's friends and latest love interests. One day I arrived home with mail from Australia and gathered the children together so I could read them a letter from Bob, the grandfather they hadn't met.

> Dear June, I am bubbling with good cheer . . .
> I have reached the top of the moon,
> Because I'm completely in tune
> With that lovely girl called June,
> To improve I should not try,
> I'm so happy I could almost cry,
> Because I'm meeting June in July.

Dearest love and a parental kiss to all the nice Cliffords. A journalist called at our home and explained that she had had an interview with you and Lisa. She said that you were a lovely dignified lady and that Lisa was very refreshing, like a youthful breath of spring [that got me in]. She asked for photos . . . I gave her some snapshots taken in our garden. The article enclosed has several small inaccurate details, but I suppose you could call them acceptable journalistic variables.
I am your loving relation,
The Ancient Mariner and his mate.

Enclosed was an article cut out from *The Gold Coast Bulletin* about the 'ancient mariner's' two famous daughters – an attractive half-sister Jan, who had appeared on 'The Graham Kennedy Show' and myself.

This letter was a swift uppercut to my dignity. Only Helen and Shirley Wakefield knew of the recent reunion with my father. They had been surprised when I told them who had given me the opal brooch I had been wearing incessantly; I had been telling people for years that my father had died when I was a baby. News of his 'resurrection' wasn't something to drop lightly into conversation. I had planned to tell people close to me in my own good time – not on Bob's time and in such a public way. What would people who had thought my father had died think of me? I felt exposed, ashamed and angry. Bob must have thought I was a fool to tell me that the journalist had somehow stumbled upon him when I hadn't even mentioned him to her. I figured Bob must have approached the woman and made a boastful declaration about his famous daughters. How dare he take such liberties without consulting me first? I knew about Patti, but the article didn't mention her, only his other 'famous' daughter, of whom I had been unaware until then. His tack was thoughtless and cruel and his letter sapped the warmth from the Tuscan sun.

My children knew Bob had come into my life, but they hadn't met their grandfather. They knew I had grown up at Watson's Creek with my grandparents and mother and had put the jigsaw pieces together, but I hadn't really talked to them about how my illegitimacy had affected me. So eager was I to have a father and believe that he was the aggrieved one, that I gave him another chance. I bundled up my hurt and embarrassment and tried to forget about the newspaper article. It was the only way I knew how to cope with thorny situations. I had been doing that all my life. In any case, I had already arranged to meet up with Bob and his wife in Hong Kong where I was staging a fashion show. Carel was there too. I introduced them to my friends who extended their homes, Rolls Royces and boats to us. Bob was trying hard to please me and it seemed easier not to rock the boat and confront him with my questions and concerns.

When I returned to Sydney, Bob and his wife continued on to London. I had told him Tim was living there and about his work. Without any warning, Bob walked up to the bar of the restaurant where Tim was working and announced, 'I'm your grandfather'. Unsure how to react to this stranger, Tim told him to take a seat and he'd talk to him when he could. The place was crowded, the opportunity passed, and Bob left without even saying goodbye to Tim. It was typical of the insensitive manner in which Bob tried to railroad his way into our lives. During the same European trip, Bob and his wife stopped in Florence where they sought out Lisa. Bob found her behind the counter of a leather goods shop and without identifying himself asked if the shop sold horse saddlery. 'No,' Lisa told him, 'but I know who you are.' From the moment his green eyes had fixed on her in the shop, she had seen the resemblance with me. Grandfather and grand-daughter hugged and cried. That night Bob and his wife had dinner with Lisa and her boyfriend Paolo. It was the only time they spent together. Marc and Carel met Bob back in Australia, but didn't feel any closeness to him.

Soon I would feel the same way. As guest speaker at a function at Conrad Jupiters on the Gold Coast, I proceeded to tell the audience about growing up at Watson's Creek and how my mother had been the driving force behind my success. I told them how we had little money when we arrived in Sydney and no financial help to start the school. Bob's wife had been my guest at the function and was distressed by my words. 'I find it hard to understand why you give so much credit to your mother for helping you get started and none to your father who gave you the money to open your school,' she said on the drive back to their home. 'Why don't you say wonderful things about your father? He's done so much for you.' What lies had Bob been feeding her, I wondered? The only funds I had when I started the business were my meagre savings from modelling.

As troubled as I was by this during my stay with Bob and his wife, it was my father who delivered the coup de grace. We were sitting down for breakfast when he fired what was probably a payback for not acknowledging him in my speech: 'June, I'm not sure you're my daughter.' Shaken, I somehow rose from the table. 'I can't stand this any more,' I cried. 'I've tried, but it's beyond me. You're a cruel, cruel man.' There have been times when I've been so hurt that I've lost my temper and become hysterical, but not this time. I fought back the tears, packed my bags and hurriedly left for the airport the day before I was due to leave. I never saw Bob again and never tried to make contact. Nor did he.

Some time later, one of the women's magazines had a story on me, referring to my upbringing and Lisa's recent return from Italy. It made no mention of my father. Showing a lack of understanding of how the media works, Bob seemed to think that Lisa, with whom he felt he'd established a strong connection during their Italian one-off meeting, had some influence over what had appeared in the article. Incensed by the article's failure to acknowledge him, he posted to Lisa a copy of his last will and testament, which he had deliberately and dramatically singed at the edges. It was such odd behaviour. Attached was a copy of the magazine article and an angry letter stating that, as a result of the article, he had disinherited the children and me. It was a substantial amount of money, but by this time I didn't want anything to do with Bob. I was also doubtful that it was a legitimate document anyway.

I began to doubt Bob's other grandiose stories. I realised Bob had told me so many lies that I couldn't tell truth from fiction any more. Bob had convinced me he was anything but a loving father and everything my grandparents knew him to be: an egocentric man whose scam was to lure me into believing he was more noble than he was. A handsome man, he had a tremendous ability to charm people, but I was no longer under his spell. I could see that he suffered from delusions of grandeur.

He had told his wife that people had kept him from being a father to his two other daughters as well as me. When she quizzed him about it, he'd gloss over details, change the subject or accuse people of maliciousness. He believed he was right and insisted everyone else was wrong. His wife wanted to believe him. After all, she had fallen in love with him at first sight, possibly like the other women he seduced, including my mother. So she stood by him to his death from cancer on Good Friday in 1990. I didn't go to the funeral, though his two other estranged daughters attended. I saw no reason to break ties with his wife, who had become a dear friend, of whom I am very fond.

She recently gave me a file that Bob had compiled of press clippings about me and my mother, who had appeared a couple of times in the newspapers. Perhaps I should have felt flattered or touched that he had followed my life with such interest, but I believe he was motivated by my status as a public figure. What if I had amounted to nothing? What if I had not turned out to be the 'somebody' my mother and I had worked so hard for me to become? Would he have wanted to claim me then? The article in *The Gold Coast Bulletin* had tellingly only mentioned his two well-known daughters and not the third, who was anonymous to the public. There's no way to know the whole story about my father and his relationship with my mother and grandparents. Perhaps it's unwise to keep secrets for so long because then it's too late to make sense of them. They can only fester into sores that won't heal.

19 Dynastic dreams

So intertwined was my business with my identity that to get my attention in the office Carel gave up calling me 'Mum', because I responded more quickly when someone addressed me as 'Miss Dally'. My work was an unavoidable part of my children's life. They had grown up around the deportment school, model agency, beautiful people, quests and parades. The industry was second nature to them. Over the years all my children came into the business: when they were curious to learn about the industry; in between jobs and overseas travel, when they were unsure what path to take in life; and to help sort out their oldest sibling's woes and need to grow. There was always some position they could step into whenever it suited their needs. Having them on board often suited my purposes. However, I was also anxious that giving such comfortable lifestyles and career paths on a platter might deter them from chasing dreams of their own creation. Could there ever be a win-win situation for mother, children and business?

With my mother departed and a handful of disloyal staff having turned rivals, naturally I was keen for my children to come into the business. I thought each was capable of playing an important role and hoped at least one of them would take the reins when the time came for me to let go. Just as my mother had nurtured dreams for me, I had all kinds of plans for my children. I imagined them achieving whatever they wanted, assuming high-profile professional positions or wanting to work with me. In hindsight, perhaps, my expectations and aspirations were unrealistic.

Tim's stint working with me was the briefest of my children's employment in the business. After his time in London and the cessation of a partnership in a Sydney bistro, Tim came to work for me. A talented photographer, he offered to take my students' test shots and graduation photos for half the price that other photographers were quoting. It was a deal I couldn't refuse, but working for his mother didn't appeal to Tim in the longer term. He bought a landscape gardening business, then moved to northern New South Wales and ran a tropical fruit farm. Marriage and fatherhood settled Tim. He put his hospitality and business training to good use, running a pizzeria in the Blue Mountains and a café at Maitland with his capable wife, Vicki. They have two sons, the serious Jack and the mischievous Brody, both of whom I love dearly. Tim has since moved into a marketing job for a training organisation. As fate would have it, his line of work is not too far removed from my field. But perhaps he wouldn't be where he is today if he hadn't cut his own circuitous route.

As a toddler, Carel sometimes sat on my knee while I ran the agency. Carel's finishing school experience and the fashion industry choices she made independently of me primed her to excel in my business. Every career step she took was like advancing in another training module towards corporate leadership of the school and agency. On her return from finishing school in Switzerland and travelling through Europe, Carel worked as a sales representative for Revlon. However, she decided to pursue the love of music she inherited from her grandmother and train her beautiful singing voice for opera by taking private singing lessons. She came to work at the agency, through which she secured part-time modelling work, with the intention of saving enough money to return to Italy. There she planned to improve her understanding of Italian opera and the language. Carel took a job as a nanny with a family at Lake Como, near Milan, but fate brought her back to the modelling industry.

During one of my regular jaunts to Milan to attend the various fashion shows and network with other agency bosses, I brought Carel along as my translator to a lunch with Giorgio Piazzi, who headed one of the major agencies of the time, Fashion Model. Giorgio ran a reputable agency, which had close ties to Ford Models. It happened that he needed an experienced English-speaking booker who could liaise with models arriving in Milan from England, the USA and, in smaller numbers, Australia. Carel fitted the requirements perfectly. For the next four years she booked models, honed her knowledge of the industry and worked part-time as a catalogue model for fuller-figure fashions. She booked for Sharon Stone and Greta Scacchi before they became famous as actresses. Green-eyed, dark-haired and with perfect skin and a wonderful smile, Carel made it to the pages of Italian *Vogue*, and flew to Germany, Switzerland and France for photographic shoots. However, she worked at the coalface of the industry primarily as a way to make money and travel.

Preferring to work out of the spotlight and missing Australia and her family, she returned home at the age of 22. Armed with international industry contacts, Carel approached me with the concept of starting a niche agency that would deal only in elite models working the global fashion circuit: Paris, London, Milan, New York and Tokyo. I embraced the idea – the agency wouldn't compete with Dally's, but run in tandem with it. Models Worldwide was incorporated into the June Dally-Watkins Group of Companies and opened in the same building as my agency in September 1980. It quickly established a strong reputation, and within three years Carel had met her targets of launching talent and placing top models on magazine covers around the world. Having done this, she became restless for a change, dissolved the business, placed the models with other agencies, and entered the real-estate industry. I was disappointed that she let go of a dream, but couldn't dissuade her from quitting the industry. Looking back, I didn't take her decision as well as I should have.

Carel's foray into real estate lasted five years and she became a licensed agent. However, the work hours did not suit her when she became a sole parent. This was a time when feminists were telling young women that they didn't need male partners, except to conceive a child, and that they could do it all alone. Carel had been in a serious relationship, but made the choice to raise her baby alone. A loving, supportive family is important to get through single parenthood and Carel had that. Knowing I would give her the freedom to work more flexible hours, she returned to manage our Bankstown school. I was concerned that growing violence in the area was deterring parents from enrolling their daughters at the school. After evening classes students had to be escorted to their cars or arrange for someone to collect them. We eventually closed the branch.

Following its closure, Carel came into the city office and stepped in to fill Colette Rayne's management shoes. She found herself running the entire group of companies, which stretched from Sydney to Townsville. Although Carel hadn't set out to take on this responsibility, she was very capable and oversaw the business according to my unwritten code. That didn't mean we agreed on everything, including the potential of a skin-care range I put my name to – Dallyence. I sought to develop the product line after one of my male models in Brisbane told me about a biochemist who had discovered an extract from the devil's apple fruit could successfully treat skin cancer. Given the number of people I had known who had died of cancer and eager to fulfil a long-held desire to produce a skin-care range that would protect Australians' skin, I arranged to meet the brains behind this breakthrough – Doctor Bill Cham. Bill was originally from the

Caribbean island of Aruba where the locals smeared themselves with the juice of the aloe vera plant for protection against the harshness of the wind and sun, so I had every confidence in his suggestion of developing a skin-care range based on an extract of the soothing plant. A deal was struck whereby Bill produced the Dallyence range, which included a cleanser, eye cream, acne cream, and day and night face cream, and I took responsibility for its marketing.

Bill mixed the first batch of Dallyence at home. Its market debut in 1985 was less modest, with Sonia McMahon and publicist Max Markson launching Dallyence at the Sydney Hilton, followed up by promotion through my Face of the 80s quests. Both effective and affordable, the products had enormous promise. They were initially sold through my schools and agencies. Carel felt that the business had become too diversified and wasn't as passionate as I was about having yet more products to sell. After some reflection, I came to agree that the business had grown limbs that were distracting our attention from its core focus. Despite the demise of Dallyence, such is my faith in it and Bill Cham's work that I still order the product for my personal use under its current name, Curacel.

When one door closed in my personal and business life, another usually opened. I had been holidaying with Colette in the Philippines and afterwards in Hong Kong, where we had met up with John Hayles and another friend, multimillionaire property developer Cecil Chao. I had met Cecil through influential hotel industry contacts I had made in the 1960s during my Asian parade tours. Whenever I had taken fashion shows to Hong Kong, Cecil arranged for a driver and his gold Rolls Royce, one of many cars in his garage, to greet us at the airport. His harbourside mansion, Happy Lodge, which has a helicopter-landing pad on the roof, became a party venue for the models and me. We held swimming races in his pool. The Aussies always won.

The treats Cecil had in store for us on this trip were just as impressive. Over dinner at the Eagle's Nest restaurant at the Hilton,

Cecil suggested I open a school in Hong Kong. 'I have built two buildings. You can take your pick of the space and I will help you in every way I can.' It seemed too good an offer to pass up. The plan was for Colette to return to conduct a feasibility study on launching the school. I chose a space on the nineteenth floor of the Wah Kwong building at 88 Queens Road, Hong Kong Island, and launched my deportment and model school in November 1984, with Colette as its business manager.

I also recruited my daughter Lisa for the Hong Kong school. She had been living in Italy where she had worked full-time as a catwalk model for the past year. When Lisa first arrived in Italy as a teenager she became an au pair and studied Italian at the University of Perugia. At 17, whilst working part time as a drinks waitress to supplement her income, she met the love of her life, Paolo Consumi, a medical student who is now specialising in medical dentistry. His family took Lisa into their home as their daughter and Paolo's mother, Gemma, taught Lisa the kind of hearty Tuscan cooking that makes you salivate just thinking about it. Lisa and Paolo were almost ready to make a commitment to each other but, being a young, independent Australian, Lisa baulked at the traditional lifestyle of an Italian wife. Although Lisa loved Paolo, I think some of my mistrust of men had rubbed off onto her. From that time onwards she flitted between her homeland and Florence.

The Hong Kong job offer came at a time when Lisa wasn't ready to leave Paolo, but I wrote him a personal letter that explained the venture and included the feasibility study. Together they were convinced the Hong Kong school would be a success and a tremendous opportunity for them both.

Born into the business, she had an intimate understanding of my expectations from staff and students. She knew how I wanted my business to run and there was little I needed to explain to her that she didn't know intuitively, so this, together with her modelling experience in Italy made me feel that Lisa was qualified to assume the top Hong Kong teaching position.

I saw Hong Kong as an opportunity for Lisa to build on her skills and commence training to perhaps one day take the helm of my deportment and modelling schools. Also in my dreams, I saw Carel becoming chief executive of the business. Carel was more business-minded than Lisa, good at dotting i's and crossing t's. I thought she would be more at ease being in charge of backroom operations. Lisa was more a people person, a communicator ideal for front-of-house operations, so the two of them would make a formidable team. When I told Lisa of my grand plan she was flattered that I had thought she was capable of assuming leadership. With this plan in mind, I flew Lisa to New York to attend an international model convention, arranged for her to act as official chaperone for the Australian representative in the international Miss Universe quest, and gave her rein to choreograph fashion shows in Asia.

During Lisa's year in Hong Kong she came to realise that the model industry was not for her. Perhaps she felt that teaching her mother's principles and guidelines left no room for her own creativity. She needed to break free from my shadow and express her own self, make it on her own terms, not mine. The process of breaking away from the security of working for her mother involved much soul-searching and so it was that one Saturday afternoon Lisa was at a dance studio in Kowloon to rehearse some of our models for a fashion show. She had choreographed many parades in Hong Kong and the region. At the studio she noticed some young men and women practising dance routines. One of them, a tall, striking young man introduced himself as Jimmy Stewart. He and his friends had noticed her and he asked if she'd join them for some tea after the rehearsal. They were training to become missionaries with Youth With a Mission, a non-denominational Christian group. Lisa joined them for dinner at their base in Borrett Road at The Peak and stayed on for a prayer meeting and singing.

When she phoned me sounding at peace I asked, 'Have you had a beautiful experience?' She wondered how I could tell, but a mother – even if she is on the other side of the world – knows her child. Lisa told me about her Youth With a Mission friends and asked if I would be upset if she was baptised as a symbolic gesture of being reborn as a Christian. Recognising the positive impact this group had on Lisa, I gladly gave her my blessing, grateful she had even asked. Becoming a born-again Christian gave Lisa the confidence and strength to find her own path in life, leave my business and Paolo, and pursue a career as a journalist. Lisa vowed not to work in my business again and, with the exception of stepping in briefly to help Carel and teach students a few years later, has kept her promise to herself. Knowing that she had been unhappy in Hong Kong and that she now had a definite career goal in mind, I accepted her resignation better than I had Carel's previous departure from the business.

So Lisa returned to Australia. Having been told she had a good voice for radio, Lisa won a Macquarie News Network scholarship to study journalism at the Australian Film, Television and Radio School at Ryde in Sydney. After graduation she worked as a radio journalist in Bendigo and Sydney. However, missing Paolo, she returned to Florence. Theirs was to be a long romance put on hold and reignited over many years. During one of their rendezvous, I visited them in Florence before continuing on to Rome and Hong Kong. When I returned to Sydney, Lisa had beaten me home, having left Paolo again.

After much deliberation, Lisa determined to marry Paolo. A wedding in Italy was planned; Lisa's dress was designed, 150 invitations posted, and my friends Susan Renouf and Sonia McMahon were looking forward to attending a Tuscan wedding. My airline ticket had been purchased and I was excited at the thought of a happy family event. Then Lisa phoned, saying she was unable to go through with it.

She returned to Sydney and for five-and-a-half years she had no contact with Paolo, while I sent cards for his birthdays, holding onto some hope that their situation would change. In the interim, Lisa joined Channel TEN as a reporter and then became a producer of its late-night news bulletin. Feeling financially secure, she turned to freelance writing and co-authored a popular guide, *Walking Sydney*. When a newspaper sponsored Lisa to cover various stories in Italy, she phoned Paolo from Milan to let him know she would be visiting Florence. 'I will drive up and collect you,' Paolo offered, adding, 'Your engagement ring is still in my safe-deposit box.' Three months later, Lisa returned to Sydney wearing the ring. They married in Florence in 1998 (nearly nineteen years after having met) and now have two adorable children, Natalia and Leo. To them I am Nonna Junie. Lisa and her family live in the wing of an ancient villa that belonged for many years to the Florentine nobility. It is surrounded by huge gardens and is only ten minutes from the centre of Florence, just outside the historical city wall.

20 More to life than champagne

Lisa wasn't the only one who had a revelation in Hong Kong. Colette had been caught up in the heady lifestyle of Hong Kong. As Lisa left Hong Kong in 1987, Colette resigned. Naturally I raced to this jewel of capitalism to try to pick up the pieces. During my plane trip over, I read and re-read a book that Lisa had given me about Youth With a Mission – the Christian group responsible for her spiritual awakening. The slim manifesto *Is That Really You God?* rekindled thoughts and feelings I had suppressed for years. The group's founder, Loren Cunningham, wrote about his own conversion to Christianity and how he had begun to fulfil his dream of recruiting young 'missionaries' of all denominations to work in their communities as disciples to teach about the Bible and the Lord. It stirred long-suppressed thoughts. I had always believed that a guardian angel of sorts had protected me throughout my life. I liked to think that 'angel' was my grandfather, but it didn't explain the presence I had sensed when I was a child and the feeling that he was still about. Who was the presence I felt then? Who shared my solitude? Who was soothing me, assuring me it would be all right? I intended to meet Lisa's Christian friends to try to answer these questions, but Hong

Kong was demanding; it took over and swept me along its merchandise-cluttered streets. After three weeks I had not made contact, when fate intervened. One afternoon I felt a voice was urging me to buy an expensive gold evening bag I didn't really need and couldn't afford. As I was walking along Pedder Street to buy the bag and arguing with myself over this indulgence, someone took hold of my arm. I turned to see Norma Young, a former fashion adviser for Grace Brothers and the Katies fashion chain. Norma was usually based in Sydney, so I was surprised to see her. I was more amazed when this businesswoman who lived life in the fast lane revealed that the fashion world had lost its appeal and she had become a missionary for Youth With a Mission. I had mistakenly thought only young people were members of this group. Norma assured me it was inclusive of people of all ages and backgrounds. I had also wrongly assumed that born-again Christians didn't wear make-up, dressed plainly and only mixed with church-going people. Norma didn't look less stylish or different as a born-again Christian, just happier.

I believed our encounter was a sign that it was my destiny to seek out Youth With a Mission, so tentatively I began to attend the group's prayer meetings and church services, meditate and learn more about the Lord and myself. Youth With a Mission was a spiritual oasis I never knew existed on previous visits to Hong Kong. The territory was an unusual place to find the Lord. It was seemingly a godless place, if the number of Rolls Royces, gambling dens and illegal activities of triads were taken into account. Indeed, it appeared that the Lord had abandoned thousands of its inhabitants – old women hauling heavy barrows, rickety men sweeping streets, families living crammed into high-rise apartment blocks. Before and after the British handover to the Chinese Government, Hong Kong's relentless pursuit of financial wealth had sidled up incongruously against the resigned acceptance of having little or nothing.

I have often wondered why it was in Hong Kong, with most

of my life already consumed, that I accepted the Lord fully into my life. One guess is I had been so busy and preoccupied trying to lead others for years that it had taken this long to manoeuvre me into a situation where I would surrender and allow the Lord to lead me. My religious reawakening came at a time when I needed spiritual muscle to understand why Lisa and Colette had to leave the business, as well as the inner strength to go on fighting for it. Having faith was also to give me succour during some personally challenging times I was yet to face, so perhaps it needed to be sown within me then, in readiness for the future.

I used to scream out loud, of course, only when I was alone, 'Lord, why are you punishing me? You're cruel. I hate you, I hate you.' I blamed the Lord for my mother's acidic personality, for my marriage breakdown, for bad luck, for whatever was askew in my life. Occasionally, and only at low points in my life, I would pray, but more often I denied the existence of any god. All the while there were signs that I was being called to lead a more spiritual life. Although religion hadn't been a part of my childhood, as a young girl, I sought out religion, attending various churches in Tamworth. My isolated childhood made me yearn to belong to a group, to be an insider instead of an outcast. The shades my grandparents had drawn on Catholicism were lifted when I married a Catholic, albeit a lapsed one, but I didn't turn to it as a religion until after Lisa was born and my marriage was becoming precarious. My friend Helen Newham was a Catholic and helped to arrange my conversion. Perfectionism being both a blessing and a curse for me, I set out to be the best Catholic I could be. I became devout. No matter how exhausted I was from work, every weekend I dressed my four children in their best clothes and took them to Saint Mary Magdalene Church at Rose Bay. The parish priest, Father Michael Harfield, was young, handsome and outgoing. He injected a fresh and participative approach to these masses and the congregation began to swell. Carel played guitar and sang in a youth group at masses on Saturday evenings, and Marc served as an altar boy. Father Mick joined the children and me surfing at Bondi Beach and smiled proudly when the children called out 'Come on, Mum. Come on, Father.' People would comment to us, 'You have lovely children.' After fifteen years at Rose Bay, he was suddenly transferred. Father Mick eventually left the priesthood to marry a former Miss Australia, Kerri Doyle, and become Mick, the father. After his departure, a traditional, less friendly style of mass was introduced at Rose Bay. Consequently, the children stopped going to Mass, and gradually I did too. I couldn't come to grips with some of the dogma and rules and didn't feel accepted amongst the traditionalists in the Church. I may be wrong, but their tone seemed to infer, 'But you were never brought up a Catholic, were you?' Often I felt I did or said something offensive to Catholics, but perhaps this was more a reflection of my own self-doubt as a Catholic. Despite turning away from Catholicism, I respect the religion and find it reassuring that my Italian-born grandchildren are being raised as Catholics, because it is the dominant religion of their homeland as well as their father's religion. I also have the highest regard for many people I've met who have entered a religious order.

Nevertheless, Youth With a Mission replenished my soul and gave me an inner happiness I had never experienced by visiting other churches. I learned to let go, stop trying to control everything and trust in the Lord. I began to open up and for the first time face the fears I'd had as a parent. So I asked Jimmy Stewart, 'How can I best handle my relationship with my children?' His advice was simple: 'Just love them unconditionally.' With those words, my perception of my relationship with my children changed forever. It had never occurred to me to love them this way. I loved them dearly – with all my heart – but I did put conditions on this love by trying to direct the way they should live their lives. I had always believed that it was a parent's responsibility to guide their children. I felt I had missed out on this guidance in my youth and, partly because of this, lacked the skills to give my children the guidance they needed. Had I been at home more, I might have had the time to explain in depth my views and how I came to them through different experiences, instead of merely saying, 'Do this, do that.' It was a revelation to suddenly understand that my children had a right to find their own identities and paths in life, even if it was the hard way. Sometimes this would be despite and in spite of my dreams. I had to accept that rebellion and breaking away from me was necessary to their growing up and, if it caused me heartache, resign myself to it. I learned that all a parent really had the power to do was advise their children and hope they made the right choices in their lives.

As a symbol of being reborn, I was baptised in the South China Sea near Lama Island, not far from Hong Kong. My newfound friends dunked me under the water, prayed with me, sang and played guitar. Having been involved in such a glamorous industry, it was refreshing to let the glitter fall away and explore my true self through this simple ceremony. This experience was an epiphany for me. I used to think that if I had champagne for the rest of my life, I had made it. I realised for the first time there was more to life.

Although I found the Lord within three weeks of arriving back in Hong Kong, it didn't mean I had to lose sight of the reason for my being there. For the next five months I worked hard to keep the Hong Kong business going. I worked day and night, attending business functions to network and promote my business. However, I didn't understand the acuity of the Chinese business mind and was taken aback when they haggled over the cost of my courses. I didn't know how to do business this way. I also realised that my choice of location on Hong Kong Island was not ideal for capturing my target market. I had chosen the more prestigious address, but the Chinese I was targeting as potential students lived Kowloon-side. Maybe a business finishing school would have attracted more students, perhaps I should have delayed the school's opening, or possibly I should have stuck it out a little longer. It is easy to hypothesise about what could have been, but business decisions require swift action informed by the current financial situation and a level head. I had to act. Reluctantly, after six months of trying to turn the business around, I closed the school. The experience didn't leave me empty-handed or regretful. Many new and continuing friendships were made in Hong Kong. One staff member, Colleen Fong, runs our Saturday School in Sydney. I also returned to Australia with a sense that I had been destined to set up the business there, if only to find the Lord.

Back in secular Australia, it was difficult to discuss religion for fear of being labelled a zealous nut who had blindly fallen into a cult. Friends commented that I looked different and, when I explained the change within me, I saw their eyes narrow to see how crazy I had become. What my friends had really seen was a previously highly charged, uptight person who had found inner peace. I looked happier. It was hard to explain to them that I was no longer empty inside, alone or lonely. The Lord had become an ever-present source of companionship.

Now I commune with the Lord at any time or in any place. I am never lonely. To me it doesn't matter what church I visit. I don't believe in denominations or even call myself a born-again Christian, but I address Christian groups who invite me to speak to them and share the story of my life and my beliefs. I simply believe in Christian ethics and that all religions should be tolerant of each other. As I go about my work, I remember that the Lord is my guide and the inspiration who uplifts, sustains and strengthens me. Embracing the Lord finally revealed the hidden purpose in some of the turns my life had taken and I could reason why suffering was sometimes to be found on the path to self-discovery. The secrets and pain I had known suddenly had meaning. My life assumed a new meaning. I could see everyday miracles, even in some of the unhappy times that had led me to this point in my life. The miracles were about to keep happening. What I didn't know then was that I had to experience greater suffering to see them unfold and change me.

21 Dissolution and retreat

I returned from Hong Kong to Sydney just in time. After twenty-eight years in the Dymocks Building, the rent was raised in the mid-1980s so Dymocks could take over the entire space for themselves. I took over other city premises in Hunter Street. The economy was in recession, so I was forced to overhaul the business and abandon its less profitable activities. The school was exceptional in the educational market, so it was protected from the restructuring process. Furthermore, I was passionate about the school and the need for Personal Development courses. Whatever was going on in my private life, my devotion to the students had never wavered. I enjoyed a sense of achievement in motivating them to succeed and improve themselves.

The model agency had become the most demanding and heartrending part of my business. Although Dally's Model Management in Brisbane was a leader in the local market, its Sydney twin began to face tough competition. The industry became increasingly cutthroat. It became obvious to me that the Sydney agency would require a lot of my effort. I resolved to close it and save the heart and soul of my business – the school. I had also tired of dealing with the whims of models. Models tended to be dependent and demanding.

In the early days of being a model agent, I had gained satisfaction from discovering so many beauties. Indeed, I basked in the reflected warmth of their success. I was proud that some people could pick a June Dally-Watkins model before he or she even set foot on a catwalk ramp. As I polished young men and women to become models, I was concerned with their reputations, manners and grooming as much as their physical appearances. Nevertheless, even then many of the models didn't fully appreciate the work I did for them: the late-night or early-morning phone calls I made to secure them work overseas, as well as fielding phone calls for them from their mothers and their boyfriends about all sorts of personal and business matters. Models fresh from the country or interstate sometimes lived in the self-contained apartment at my Bellevue Hill home – free of charge – until they could find their own lodgings. Many didn't say 'thank you'. They didn't understand the personal strain I was under in my private life, nor did I share my troubles with them. My family protested at having models stay, so gradually I stopped these intrusions into our domestic life.

Having a live-in arrangement for some models might seem odd in any other industry, but that's what it took to be a successful model agent. In fact, I had emulated Eileen and Jerry Ford's practice of accommodating in their home models who were new to their agency. Nowadays Ford Models has a string of apartments for its models, complete with live-in chaperones for minors. Despite the Fords' generous overtures to models, Eileen also felt the strain of catering to their demands. I'll never forget her sage advice to me: 'Models want your blood and when you give it to them, they want your bones and your skin too.' It's a generalisation but not a gross one, I think, to say models tend to be self-involved takers who, due to their beauty, are accustomed to people giving them what they want. When they don't get their way, they seek someone else more likely to oblige. It would be wrong of me, however, not to acknowledge that there are many wonderful exceptions. In my experience, the ones who remained on top in the industry and kept their reputations intact weren't always the most beautiful, but the ones who worked hard, were genuine, and of good character.

Just as my energy to mould and launch models had waned, so had my enthusiasm for the industry. The model world had changed significantly from the one I had pioneered in Australia. From what I had observed and heard, the models' world seemed like a nest of vipers and I felt reticent about remaining an active part of it. The advertising world's increasing demand for models had spurred competition between model agencies and saw a proliferation of new ones. Agencies seeking to keep and poach talent raised models' fees. By the late 1970s, many agencies in Europe were taking 50 per cent of a model's fee, yet models were still raking in enviable earnings from working illegally on the Continent and beyond. I heard stories of models flying out of Rome with money hidden in their clothes or in their luggage. This was before X-ray cameras at airports. Some girls working in Milan drove across the border to Switzerland to deposit money into Swiss bank accounts.

The business of wooing clients and models was done over long wine-soaked lunches and dinners at trendy upmarket restaurants in the fashion capitals of Milan, Paris, London and New York. The Fords had a standing reservation for a suite at the Parco de Principe Hotel in Rome, where every day they entertained on the terrace over three-hour lunches. I attended these lunches and other industry dinners, mostly during the years Carel was working as a models' booker at Fashion Model in Milan. Carel and Lisa didn't like the necessary networking that is pervasive in the industry and the need to entertain models and feed their egos. I loved these social occasions and dancing at Nepenta disco, but gradually noticed the scene changing for the worse. Hired playboys began to come along to industry dinners, after which everyone would go to a disco. Some partied through the night, many fuelled by drugs.

With all that money around, it was inevitable there would be spilling of blood to bring the situation under control and force some players out of the market. Elite's Johnny Casablancas went after the Fords with the intention of taking their crown as the world's leading model agent. Among the major agents I had met, Johnny was charming, but he was also ruthless in his campaign to take control of the model-agency market. Many smaller agencies became embroiled in the contest, were swallowed by predators, and switched allegiances between Ford and Elite.

Some agents began to use unorthodox methods, depending on their scruples or lack of them, to lure models into their stable. They played on models' vanities and insecurities, lavished them with luxury, and some even went so far as to get them addicted to drugs and pleasure. Many of the supermodels of the past few decades and those of today have met their demons through their work. Naomi Campbell, Kate Moss and Karen Mulder are among the current generation of models to have confessed to drug and alcohol abuse. There were even handsome playboys who took lonely, young and homesick girls under their wings and sometimes seduced them, in order to receive payment for introducing the girl to a new agency. The playboys became essential conduits between naïve young models and some agents. Some sleazy agents paid the playboys commissions for luring models to their agency, where they would entice prospective talent on hedonistic weekends when drugs were freely supplied. Karen Mulder has claimed that former members of one of the world's leading modelling agencies raped her and forced her to sleep with people against her will in order to get better contracts. Not all the models were unwilling or naïve – many enjoyed the attention, the jetset whirl and supposed glamour that came with drug-taking and wild parties. However, entrapment of some inexperienced and unworldly models was achieved with the help of alcohol, other drugs, sex and money.

A well-known Sydney model told me she had accepted an

invitation to spend a weekend at a country villa near Cannes in France, only to discover, after being there a short while, that she was expected to take part in lesbian orgies. As the night progressed, she climbed out a window, walked to the nearest road and hitched a ride back to Cannes. The result of other models' experiences included unexpected and unwanted pregnancies. Carel was aware that some agents arranged abortions for teenage models, so the girls could keep working and their parents would be none the wiser. This kind of situation gave some agents more power over models.

Carel and I heard stories about drugs, but didn't see them – only a lot of champagne. Sometimes, if champagne had not already been supplied at a photo shoot, models would insist it be delivered to the set. At 1 a.m. in Rome, at the request of some overworked models, I went with Eileen Ford (before our falling out) to deliver the requisite bubbly to keep the models working throughout the night. Girls who took part in catwalk presentations of new collections at the beginning of each season worked hard. Some were booked for several shows a day, as well as night-time photographic shoots of the fashions they had worn in the shows that day. The next day they'd do it all again. Behind the scenes, champagne flowed from 10 a.m., when the first show started. Some would drink, do a hit of cocaine, and go on the runway, facing the world's fashion celebrities and a pack of photographers. Drugs kept them arrow-thin, fuelled for work and parties, and willing to do anything to maintain their habit. These young women thought they could handle it, but their looks and minds faded. With the mastery of clever make-up artists and hairstylists, and possessing a strong bone structure that drug-slimming habits exaggerated, they remained employable. This new regime shocked me. Models never had to be plied with drugs or alcohol to perform when I worked as a mannequin. I made my money and name from sheer grit and hard work.

I had also heard stories about industry fringe-dwellers and sham photographers who took advantage of young models in Australia and overseas. These were men who fooled girls into believing that they were professional fashion photographers with the power to make them successful models. They didn't even have film in their cameras when they took photos of the girls; they just wanted to seduce them. There were even a few legitimate male photographers who, once equipped with a camera, felt god-like and able to make any girl desire him. Since the recommendation of a leading fashion photographer could make or break a model's career, the model could become beholden to the whims of a photographer. The situation hasn't changed much today. Although a few supermodels hold the upper hand in these working relationships, there are thousands of ambitious girls who will do anything to break into modelling. In general, photographers are not my favourite human beings. I don't like the way many of them exercise power once they have a camera in their hands. It makes some rude and arrogant.

Photographers increasingly photographed prepubescent or 'baby' models, who grew in demand because their young faces didn't require lighting tricks to conceal wrinkles. The use of clever make-up and styling, and adult clothing disguised the age of these young models, but their hands – generally unmarked and childlike – betrayed their sophisticated and sexy gazes. The market's demand for baby models made me uncomfortable. Baby models risked exploitation. I knew of some parents who had handed their children over to agents on the promise of supervised care and more money than they could ever dream of making, only to be let down and have their child's innocence taken away.

My daughters' perceptions of the modelling industry further influenced my distaste for it. Carel had also been struggling to stay in the industry. She had been carrying the burden of trying to make the agency work to my standards in a field where many of the main players didn't have any. I knew that it had been personally draining for Carel to run the agency. I realised that neither of us could commit the blood, sweat and tears required to lift the agency above the competition. After nearly forty years, I closed the Sydney agency.

The Brisbane agency, along with the school, prospers. Their current home is the June Dally-Watkins Centre in Edward Street, under the competent directorship of Jodie Bache-McLean. Model agencies from the fashion capitals of the world approach the Brisbane agency when they want to book local talent or seek out new faces to join their agency; at one time they refused to venture beyond Sydney. Thanks to Jodie, I am confident the school's values are upheld and models are in the best of care. She has the stamina and passionate drive needed to survive in the industry. After graduating from my school as a teenager, she worked successfully as a model before taking up a teaching role at my school. In fact, most of my teachers have been former students and models.

I wouldn't fit into the modelling world today, either as a mannequin or as a model agent. Models in some of today's haute couture shows are encouraged to saunter onto catwalks with arms dropping from hunched shoulders and heads falling forward and a strange gait called 'the pony walk'. They wear little else besides a vacant expression. Looking deliberately bored or out of it, in some segments they make obscene gestures to the audience, and their hair hangs in greasy, spaghetti-like strands over their faces or in outrageous styles. Full lips and skinny adolescent girls are ubiquitous. Some model agencies say they do not encourage models to be thin, yet skinny models get the bookings so, of course, their agents are not telling the models to fatten up. Many of the clothes that models wear on the catwalks are over-the-top, impractical and indecent to many people. They seem to be created almost entirely to shock and therefore attract media attention. The 'heroin chic' look that became popular in the 1990s has become passé. In fact, there are few elements of any fashion parades that I admire today. The exceptional designers Akira Isogawa and Collette Dinnigan inject elegance into the industry, as does Elle Macpherson, but overall the elegance I strove to achieve, both as a model and for my models, seems to have gone forever.

In any case, when I closed the Sydney agency I was focused on my next endeavour: to launch the first business finishing school in the southern hemisphere. In Carel's absence, Marc's wife, Trish, an astute businesswoman, quit her job to work full-time. A business school had been in my mind for some time. Years before, I had dreamed of one that would be exciting and up-to-the-minute; one I would have been happy to attend. The catalyst was the departure of my receptionist, who resigned to travel overseas. The search for a suitable replacement uncovered sloppy candidates. I gave the best of them a trial run and was appalled to find they lacked the professional finesse required in the workplace. Some chewed gum whilst working at the front desk, and others had poor spelling and grammar. I noticed that many of the candidates were willing to work, but needed to polish their skills and manners before they could secure a good job or conduct themselves with confidence and grace in social and work situations. I decided that it would be easier to train a candidate to my standards than find one ready-made. Surely other employers faced the same predicament? There was only one solution: start the June Dally-Watkins Business Finishing School (now College) to turn out the kind of graduates I would want to employ.

The term 'finishing' is an appropriate one because students are given training in Finishing Image, which includes corporate grooming and presentation. The course aims to open students' eyes to the world, so they can cope in any social or work situation. It gives them a broad overview of different industries to help them work out their future. Classes are diverse, including: Stress Management, Goal Setting, Fine Wine and Food Appreciation, Function Management, Human Relations, Assertiveness, Body Image and Language, Word Power, Microphone Use, Sales, Wardrobe, Colour Analysis, Grooming and Make-up. Business Communications classes aim to improve students' written, verbal and non-verbal communication. Administration classes focus on work ethics, banking, reception, telephone skills and records management. Students also learn time management, computer keyboard, information technology and English. Through the course they are introduced to various industries – real estate, travel, accountancy, hospitality (including conference and function management), marketing, market research, advertising, public relations and legal. Armed with Executive Business Diplomas, when the students complete the course they find jobs in these fields mostly as personal assistants, secretaries, receptionists, office managers, bookkeepers and public relations officers.

It is compulsory for business finishing students to wear a uniform. My friend and former neighbour at Rosemont Gardens, Mel Clifford, designed a maroon suit with a white shirt. I believe it gives both the students and the college dignity. It also prevents students competing with each other on the basis of what they wear. I don't want students – some of whom have enough money to turn up each day with a different Prada handbag – to rely on clothes and brand names to make them who they are. I want them to grow within themselves to build character and style, not rely on designer labels to make a statement for them. In Term 2, students wear corporate dress on Fridays when personal development and self-improvement classes are held. During these classes, the requirements of appropriate work clothes are discussed. By wearing corporate dress the students have assembled a working wardrobe by the time they undertake work experience, which forms a part of the course.

After realistically assessing where my future energies should be directed, I withdrew from the costly exercise of running beauty quests. I had already surrendered my Australian franchises for Miss Universe, Miss Asia Pacific, Miss Young Teen and Face of the 80s, when I took up the franchise for Miss International Australia. The global beauty pageant, Miss International, had begun in 1961 in

California, and three of my students won the coveted title: Tania Verstak (1963), Jenny Annette Derek (1981), and Kirsten Davison (1992). For three years I had been on a panel of judges for the international final of Miss International, which was traditionally held in Japan.

I began to realise that I had never really enjoyed judging others. It meant rating and comparing people, knowing that my decision, along with that of other judges, would make only one person a winner and render the other entrants – all of whom would have tried just as hard – losers. For years I had withstood the cold-shoulder treatment from disappointed entrants and their supporters, and I no longer wanted to feel responsible for their happiness. I was also tired of fighting the knockers who criticised quest entrants as bimbos and didn't see these events as a way to open doors of opportunity for them. It was time to move on.

By now it was 1992. Carel agreed to come back into the business. Carel and I decided I should leave her to run the office – it was time for me to cut back on work. I knew it was the right thing to do. In 1997, I stopped teaching, but continued to visit the school as its figurehead, to host a lunch as one of the students' cultural excursions, to lead the annual grand tour of Europe, and to deliver the opening address to students on their first day of classes and another at their graduation. It seemed I was now free to redirect my life, but, seriously, how could I, as a mother, stop taking care of all my children, the business included?

22   Miracles

One person, one small act or moment can change someone's life forever. Call these intervening forces coincidence or fate, to me they are small miracles. On the morning of 30 June 1997 – the day of the historic handover of Hong Kong from Britain to China – I made a phone call that gave my life a new direction. In Sydney some months earlier – after a Christian luncheon where I'd been a speaker and indicated my plans to conduct two small group tours to Hong Kong in the days before the handover, an occasion Colette and I had promised each other years earlier we would share no matter what – a lady from the audience asked if I'd contact her friends while I was there. I phoned Jane Henderson's friends – Sally and Malcolm Begbie – to pass on her best wishes and love. Sal explained by mobile phone that they were huddled under umbrellas in the rain near the harbour, so they could secure a good view of the evening's ceremony. Feeling at ease with Sal, I invited them to use my hotel room, which offered great harbour views, and arranged to meet Sal and Mal at the hotel for lunch the next day. In the meantime, I headed to Colette and Max Hunt's apartment at Mid Levels, halfway up Victoria Peak, to celebrate this momentous occasion. On this special night, we stood on the terrace of their apartment overlooking the harbour and watched the amazing fireworks.

Over brunch the next day with Sal and Mal, I was transported to another world. I learned that they had come to Hong Kong in 1986. Malcolm had worked as an accountant and Sal in public relations, each undertaking charity work in their spare time, until they came to a crossroad in their lives. In the wake of devastating floods in China in 1995, they had been providing aid, and were begged for more, after which they gave up jobs and, with their sons David and Joshua, established a registered charity – Crossroads International. Since then Crossroads has distributed donated goods of all kinds, locally and around the world. They have been almost flooded with high-quality donations from manufacturers, hotels, hospitals, schools and the private sector. They ship these off to places where there is need, particularly to help broken people reconstruct their lives in the wake of war, natural disaster, medical and educational need, and poverty. They ship to many destinations in Asia, Africa, Europe and South America. The government of the Hong Kong SAR has given Crossroads rent-free storage for its warehouse in the old passenger terminal at the former Kai Tak airport. The Crossroads team lives in a block of old holiday flats on Lantau Island. The Begbies exist there at subsistence level, grateful for donations that come their way. Dozens of volunteers come from around the globe to stay there. Australians are increasingly among Crossroads volunteers, who work as packers, office workers, drivers and gophers during their tours of duty. The volunteers pay a small amount for their accommodation and board.

Admiring the Begbies and their charitable work, I called on them during a stopover after my visit to Florence for the birth of my grand-daughter Natalia. I was on my way to Manila to revive memories of my times there for retelling in this book. However, my plans were thwarted. When I was due to leave Hong Kong, I read that Philippine Airlines had cancelled all flights and ceased to operate –

ultimately only temporarily. Over breakfast with Mal and Sal, I pondered my next move. I had two weeks before my return flight to Sydney. Sal and Mal invited me to stay in a vacant building that Crossroads had taken over. Despite Mal's warning that the accommodation was basic, it felt right to accept the Begbies' offer.

For the next two weeks, I slept in a single bed that used to belong to Pascale Hunt. Colette and Max had donated to Crossroads many of their children's belongings, including Pascale's old bed. In the spirit of the communal lifestyle at Crossroads' base, I mastered the trick of cooking in a cramped share-kitchen and, using very basic cooking utensils, made Filicudi-style pasta for the volunteers. It felt good to be useful and needed. Noticing that I was keen to assist the volunteers during my stay, Sal asked if I would become Ambassador-at-large for Crossroads. The charity needed someone with a range of contacts worldwide who could be called on as an experienced public speaker to help spread news of Crossroads and procure the support of others. Although flattered to be asked and willing to take on the responsibility, I had no idea how to assume this role. I felt undeserving of such a grand title and agreed to have Crossroads business cards printed only after I had proved myself worthy of the honour.

My test came soon enough. Flooding in northern China had left thousands of people homeless and without possessions. As winter approached, many only had the clothes they stood in. Crossroads wanted to provide aid, but the safe delivery of it was problematic. Max Hunt was well connected in Hong Kong, so he was the first person I called for advice. Max suggested I contact Ronnie Chan at Dragon Air, which ran flights daily from Hong Kong to many cities in China. For two days I tried unsuccessfully to make contact with Ronnie. Half an hour before leaving to return to Sydney, I tried again. This time Ronnie answered the phone and I explained why I was calling. He told me to contact an Australian colleague, Laura Crampton, for confirmation on whether the airline could help. Minutes before my departure, Dragon Air came to Crossroads' rescue. It promised to provide seats each month for two Crossroads representatives, plus their bags bulging with life's necessities for the flood victims. After the flooding subsided, Dragon Air's generosity continued. This chain of events proves every action has a reaction and sometimes major chain reactions. Call it the ripple effect, you can never tell where the ripples will go. The important thing is to throw the pebble.

Sal phoned me in Sydney to say I had earned my business card. I felt ready to accept the honour. I promised myself to live out this ambassadorial role and not wear the title as a mere accessory. After trimming back my work hours at the office, I needed a new outlet for my energy and this role was one way of keeping negative thoughts at bay. A feeling of lethargy about life in general had been hovering ever since I had pulled back on my work commitments. I wasn't used to idleness, so the Crossroads work came at the right time.

Despite my eagerness to live up to my new title, I rose hesitantly to Sal's next challenge. She had already suggested I join David and her in the Balkans in September 1999 to visit recipients of Crossroads' humanitarian aid. Colette had given me some magazines that Sal and I had browsed through during my stay at Lantau. One story greatly moved Sal. A 1998 issue of *Hello* reported the Duchess of Kent's visit to Bitola in Macedonia, where many acutely disabled babies abandoned at birth were doomed to live unloved in poorly resourced institutions. After reading the story, Sal demonstrated that she was a woman of action. Writing to Buckingham Palace, she heard back from the Duchess's secretary and committed Crossroads to helping the orphans. Crossroads volunteers rallied at the storage warehouse to select and pack goods for the orphans. Several shipping companies offered a huge container for transportation and Sal made arrangements to be in Bitola when the shipment arrived to see first-hand that the cartons were unloaded and their contents distributed to those in need. Armed with still and video cameras, she and David decided to record the receipt of these gifts to show donors and Crossroads helpers that their efforts had been worthwhile.

Having planned to visit Lisa and her family in Italy around the same time and then visit Moscow, I had no reason to refuse Sal's invitation until I broke my leg. Lisa, Paolo and Natalia were visiting with Paolo's mother, Gemma, and aunt, Maria, for Christmas 1998. When Gemma and Maria set off to Gosford, my grandson, Ben, and I escorted them to Sydney's Central Railway Station. As I entered the rail carriage to show them where to sit to take in the views on the journey, I slipped on something greasy – a fried potato chip. As I lay on the floor of the carriage, I spied the chip squashed and protruding at the end of my shoe, and another on the floor. The left side of my body took the impact of landing and the doctor told me my leg would never fully recover from the trauma. Apparently an operation was unnecessary, but I had to wear a leg brace for about six weeks. It wasn't until I could put weight on my foot that I realised I had also sprained my ankle. Several months later, a searing pain in my neck and shoulder was also attributed to my accident. The incident was reported in the press as a 'joke' – imagine, Australia's queen of deportment falling over and needing lessons on how to walk!

Eight months later, hoping I had recovered, I set out on my European tour as planned, but soon found the pain had only been in abeyance. Travelling revived a throbbing ache in my left arm and swelling in my leg. It seemed I had a good reason not to join Sal and David on their trip. Deep down, I was relieved. I had been concerned about how safe it would be in the region. The Balkans was only ever mentioned in the news in the context of war, death and destruction. My family in Australia thought it was too dangerous a journey to undertake. 'You shouldn't do it. You might be shot,' they warned. By this time I had missed the first part of Sal and David's journey to visit the orphans in Bitola, but Sal wasn't about to give up on me. 'June, after Bosnia and Macedonia, David and I will be going to Rijeka in Croatia and you could meet us there. I think it would be easy to take a boat or plane from Italy,' she e-mailed. Doubting it would be 'easy', I phoned a travel agent and was relieved to learn that boat travel had not resumed since the war; flying was complicated, an alternative mix of train, aircraft and bus transport sounded more difficult. I had forgotten that miracles, however small, can happen every day. Just when I was about to give up on the mission, Paolo suggested an alternative route – taking the train from Florence to Trieste on the northern border of Italy, then a bus to Rijeka, which was perched on the edge of the Adriatic Sea. Paolo convinced me it would be a scenic trip. Sal assured me it was safe to travel, so we arranged to meet in the lobby of the Hotel Bonavia, the main hotel in Rijeka, and then find cheaper accommodation for the night.

I set out alone to take the train to Trieste. En route, I stopped in Milan and visited David Brown, an Australian family friend. He now runs his own agency, but was then head of Ricardo Gay Model Management. The young and the beautiful wandered in and out of the agency with their model portfolios, seemingly carefree. David and I discussed the model business. He managed all the supermodels – Elle McPherson, Naomi Campbell, Claudia Schiffer and Kate Moss – when they were in Milan. The next morning I was transported to a very different world – only a day's journey away.

From Trieste, I took a bus that made its way over the mountainous terrain. I looked down at the Adriatic Sea and over to Italy and wondered what I was doing with my life. At the Slovenian–Croatian border, guards ordered some people off the bus, questioned passengers, checked passports twice and searched everyone's baggage. An hour later, I was unable to contain my concern any longer, 'What is happening?' I said out loud, hoping someone would understand me. To my surprise, an American voice informed me that the guards were searching for drugs, as further down the coast was Split, the drug capital of Croatia. As we neared Rijeka, I told the American: 'I am meeting my friends at the Hotel Bonavia.' Another voice on the bus spoke up, 'That hotel has been pulled down and is being rebuilt.' I held my breath and wondered what I had gotten myself into. By the time the bus pulled into Rijeka, darkness had descended and I glued my tired and frightened face to the bus window searching for an answer. To my relief, I saw Sal's big smile; it was as warm as the hug she gave me.

My fear subsided and hunger bit sharply. I hadn't eaten since 11 a.m. and it was now 8.15 p.m. 'I am starving and very thirsty. I hear they have great beer in Croatia,' I said hopefully. Sal delivered the next blow, 'June, it is too late to eat. Croatians have one big meal, usually at 3 p.m. or 4 p.m. and that's it for the day. I have some cheese, olives and bread in my backpack. We won't get to eat anything else until much later.' On hearing this news, I felt like turning around and going home. Frazzled by the journey so far and thirsting for a drink, I protested to Sal: 'I haven't had anything to drink for hours. Could David get me a beer, a cold beer? Otherwise, I may just die.' After some cans of cold Croatian beer were stashed into David's backpack, we approached the car that would take us to our accommodation. Had I known that I was about to meet a truly special person, perhaps my thirst would have abated. The driver of our car was Stevo Dereta, who gave his time and care to the Christian organisation, *Moj Bliznji*, which translates to 'my neighbour'. Through *Moj Bliznji*, Stevo had strived to set up refugee camps and bring peace to the people of Bosnia and Herzegovina.

We travelled south for over an hour until we reached Crikvenica – a popular seaside resort for Europeans – now a mere shell of its former self. We checked into the Peace Centre, a building that *Moj Bliznji* volunteers had reconstructed to give children respite from their grim world of violence, death, rape and starvation. There were no children staying when we arrived, but usually parents from various war-torn towns in the north sent their children by bus to the centre for a three-week break. Members of *Moj Bliznji* gave the children a glimpse of a different, peaceful life.

Finding our way to the centre's communal kitchen, a gracious lady smiled warmly, embraced us, and offered us fruit tea, cheese, sliced cold ham and black bread. Her offering was gratefully received, but its meagre size did nothing to sate my hunger. The woman didn't speak English, but her smile was constant and welcoming. Sal's contact, Srecko Ilisinovic, a member of *Moj Bliznji*, arrived and explained that the woman was a Croatian refugee. She and her husband, who had been mayor of a town in northern Croatia, near the Serbian border, had lost everything during the war and had no alternative but to live in hiding. They were victims of Croatian retaliation. Confused as to why the Croatians would punish one of their own, Srecko explained it was punishment for her marrying a Serb. Now I understood why the woman's husband had not surfaced during daylight. At night he stood in the shadows and acted as a guard for the children's refuge. The refuge could only shelter the couple for six weeks, after which they had to find somewhere more permanent. With no money, no pension, no possessions, and their home destroyed, how would they exist? Thankfully, the future of these people, whose names I never knew, lay in the helping hands of Srecko, Stevo and Teo Secen.

It was about 11 p.m. when David, Sal and I settled into our rooms. Before going to bed, David and I devoured the snacks that Sal had in her pack and the beer. No beer had ever tasted better. Sleep came quickly. I took a double-bunk in a bedroom adorned with images of cartoon characters like Winnie the Pooh and Donald Duck. They seemed as out of place as I was.

When Stevo and Srecko were asked how Crossroads could help refugees in the area, they suggested we could help furnish *Moj Bliznji's* refuges. The next day they took us to another centre; this one was called Life Centre International. With the help of financial donations from the USA and the UK, workers were donating their time and expertise to rebuild a neglected holiday guesthouse that overlooked the Adriatic Sea. The centre was to offer humanitarian and psychological aid to those devastated by war. Continuing north, we drove to the village of Fuzine in the Dinaric Alps to visit a third refuge, the Hope Centre – a large three-storeyed building that the *Moj Bliznji* members were also repairing.

It was now 3 p.m. on Sunday and over forty hours since I had eaten a decent meal. Just as I was wondering if people ever ate in Croatia, Stevo said, 'Let's eat.' It was just warm enough to sit outdoors and take advantage of the lakeside view from the Bitoraj Ristoran. We tucked into delicious mountain fare of venison goulash, wild boar, smoked pork shanks, sauerkraut, mushrooms, *sarma* (stuffed cabbage rolls), frankfurters, prosciutto, cheese and *burek* – a tasty pancake. As we watched the local Croatians sing and dance, it was good to see some people who had the money to buy a meal and enjoy life. Afterwards, we met a group of refugees at a nearby centre. A mix of emotions – guilt, despair and hope – stirred through me. They weren't singing, dancing, eating – they were sad-eyed, sick and living in very poor conditions. Some looked years older than their age. The stone dwelling they shared had broken windows, which needed urgent repair before the onset of winter, and the weather was already cool. They had barely enough blankets and no money to buy oil to keep the furnaces going. There was no money for dental or medical help; many people were unemployed; some families had had their homes taken from them.

So depressed was the blind father of several children – all of whom shared a cell-like room – that he refused to leave his bed. A non-medicated, epileptic man in his thirties was troubled by seizures and couldn't leave the room he shared with his wife and two children. His wife embroidered doilies, hoping to sell them to visitors. An elderly woman, Magdalena, had lived in the centre for many years on the dream of being reunited with her son, daughter-in-law and grand-daughter. The Serbs had destroyed her home near Vukovar.

'God brought us here and said good night,' she told me through an interpreter. Another refugee told me: 'We haven't come here to start a new life, but to die a slow death.' These people touched our hearts and I longed to show Magdalena and her friends that God had brought us there to help them. We promised to return and make their lives more comfortable and give them hope.

It was late when we returned to the Peace Centre. The smiling woman in the kitchen was ready to wait on us. She dished out two boiled frankfurters each, black bread, and a packet of mushroom soup to feed Sal, David and me, even then I suspect she had probably deprived herself and her husband of paltry rations. Using Srecko as our interpreter, we asked her why she seemed so happy under those difficult circumstances. 'I am the happiest I have ever been in my life because the Lord has come into my life. Now my husband and I have no possessions, we don't know what our future holds, but we have the love of the Lord, and we have faith he will care for us.'

Physically and emotionally exhausted, we slept for five hours before leaving at 4 a.m. to drive to Rijeka. David and Sal took a train to Frankfurt while I returned by bus to Milan. I arrived at the Marriott Hotel in Milan in the early evening. Exhausted, I took a long bath and wondered how long it would take to find me were I to die. The next day, ignoring fatigue and a creeping pain in my left arm, I began another mission. My destination was Moscow and my purpose there was to speak to the International Christian Women's Club. I had never dreamed of going to Moscow until a graduate of my Personal Development course, who had gone to Moscow with her husband to become missionaries, mentioned me to this club. I had been bedridden by my broken leg and met this woman only once on the last day of the course in Sydney, but whatever she told the group about me as a public speaker led to me receiving a formal invitation to address them. My sponsor for the trip was an American, Jill Phillips, who was a member of the club and devoted her time to helping the needy.

On arrival, Jill's driver deposited me at the Ismailovskovy Delta – a monolithic multistoreyed hotel where each floor was run independently. For instance, reception staff on the ground floor held my passport, but I had to check in on the twenty-third floor, where an imposing woman demanded cash for my overnight stay. There was no record of my credit card details having been phoned through from Italy. Reluctant to take on the big woman, I paid twice. The room was basic, and I felt apprehensive being alone so far from home. I became more nervous when I answered the phone at 11 p.m. to a heavy Russian male voice. 'Are you lonely? I would like to come to your room and keep you company.' Shocked and frightened, I slammed the handset on the receiver.

The following morning, I transferred to Jill and Jerry's apartment. Jill helps those in need in Moscow and throughout Russia, so she has her work cut out for her. Poverty, crime, alcoholism and desperation are rife. Though much of the land is blanketed by poverty, it is also embroidered with opulence, history and glory. The courtesy of the people, their love of song, their courage and their endurance moved me. Jill's Christian friends had set up soup kitchens and were visiting wayward teenagers in the ghettos in an attempt to rescue them from becoming criminals. They had also set up informal educational groups and were trying to source computers to teach the teenagers about the latest information technology. Sal and David stopped in Moscow on their way back to Hong Kong and, after meeting Jill's friends, they committed Crossroads to sending goods to an orphanage and to teenagers in educational need. I stayed on to address a meeting of the International Christian Women's Club. With the help of a translator, I spoke to about eighty Russian and American women. The Americans were in Moscow either as missionaries or accompanying their husbands posted there for work. In honour of my visit, the club had organised a fashion parade featuring the garments of a leading Russian designer Elena Pelevina. Elena's mother was working busily behind the scenes, organising the clothes in order of appearance for the parade, tidying up, and packing up after the show. As she proudly and lovingly watched her daughter, I was reminded of my mother and how she toiled for my success.

It was time to go home. Deeply exhausted and enduring unrelenting pain in my left shoulder and arm, the journey home seemed endless, drawn out by hours of waiting at airports. I broke the trip with a visit to my Crossroads family in Hong Kong. Sal's and my focus returned to talk of the refugees we had met and how we could deliver more goods to them. However, getting my health in order was a priority before I could contemplate another journey to Croatia.

Back in Sydney, I sought medical attention for my left arm and shoulder, but various treatments failed to ease my pain. At night I lay in bed, crying in agony. It turned out the ache in my arm and shoulder was in fact caused by a neck injury from the train accident. Finally, a specialist at the Royal Prince Alfred Hospital administered cortisone injections that gave me immediate relief. After much physiotherapy on my leg and arm, I was on the mend. (Now my knee only swells if I've been on my feet and travelling long distances.) However, my health was still not perfect. After detecting a suspicious-looking lump in my left breast, I quietly went into Prince of Wales Hospital and had the lump removed. Thankfully, it was benign. With Carel's care, I recovered.

The medical care I received, compared to the lack of basic medical supplies and facilities in Croatia, certainly reminded me that I lived in the lucky country. I was now impatient with Australians who complained. Some didn't want to hear of the suffering elsewhere, fearing it would impinge on their comfort. How difficult it must be for immigrants who lose everything, including their own country, to come here and face new customs and a different language. I listened to critics who said I should stay at home – Australia had enough problems and should take priority – instead of helping people in faraway countries. Although I am concerned for troubled people in Australia, a welfare safety net exists in this country and there are many wonderfully generous and hard-working Australians already helping the needy. The refugees I met, particularly in Fuzine, didn't have pensions, prospects of employment, basic living conditions, or even hope.

23   Smiling through

With Carel running the business in Sydney, the rest of my family getting on with their own lives and Jodie taking the reins in Brisbane, I returned to Croatia in May 2000. For the previous eleven years I had hosted the business finishing students' annual cultural tour to Europe. I enjoyed taking small-group tours and sharing my love of Europe, so I was pleased to be able to link the tour with my journey to Croatia to deliver aid to my refugee friends. Leaving the group in Florence, I would have three days to make the delivery and rejoin the group in Venice. It was a mammoth task, so I was grateful when two Business College students were eager to accompany me. Ruth Margetic had already delivered humanitarian aid with her secondary school to Cambodia and John Hannaford was a dedicated Christian. Two former business school graduates who had signed up for the European tour also decided to come to Croatia.

In the lead-up to my trip, I raised $3000 as a guest speaker to various groups. My family begged me not to carry such a large amount of cash, but the Fuzine refuge centre desperately needed it to buy supplies. They feared I would be arrested for smuggling money or at least interrogated at one of the border checkpoints. I thought the risk was worth it. On the journey to Croatia, I had the cash in a money belt that I strapped around my waist. It never left my person, except when I bathed. I had also collected donations in the form of goods from various retailers and friends. Harvey Norman gave me much-needed blankets for the winter in Fuzine. Discount shops donated T-shirts, toys and large plastic bags in which to carry everything. Helen and Val handed over Amway vitamins and cosmetics. My hairdresser Joe donated smart designer clothes he no longer wore and my son Marc gave some of his clothes. The Saturday school students from the Corporate Grooming classes brought in clothes and helped to pack the bags. The bags were too many and heavy for the students or me to carry on the tour, so I headed off two days before the tour group to offload four enormous bags of blankets to Crossroads in Hong Kong. It was only through the generosity and help of various people along the way that all the goods reached Croatia.

When I met up in Hong Kong with my charges, they were laden with ten other large checked plastic bags of goods for the refugees, plus their own luggage. We stayed at the newly rebuilt Miramar Hotel, where forty years earlier I'd put on my first overseas fashion show. Knowing Hong Kong intimately, I didn't waste a moment of our one-day stopover. That night, as we assembled our mountain of luggage outside the hotel, its concierge insisted I pay an exorbitant sum for each piece of luggage to be loaded onto an airport transit bus. I objected strongly to his demand with a defiant 'no'. Seeing that I was prepared to dig in my heels, the concierge disappeared. Eventually an empty bus came from where I do not know – another miracle. It took us at no charge to the airport train terminal.

Mysteriously, at the train station that takes commuters to the airport, a ground hostess approached me: 'I have been instructed to check all your luggage through to Rome.' Sal had contacted the Hong Kong manager of Lufthansa Airlines to explain why our group was travelling with so much luggage. He knew all about the troubles in Croatia, and, from that day forward, Lufthansa has helped Crossroads International when and wherever possible.

The students' expressions as they arrive for the first time in Europe always give me great joy. In Rome, memories of Gregory Peck flooded back as I showed the students some of this ancient city's sights. I gave the students a map of Rome, typed instructions, and left them to discover its delights. This gave them freedom, self-assurance and responsibility. I had always developed a friendly relationship with the students, but was aware that due to our age difference they had more fun without me. Before I gave them free rein, I always cautioned them about the prevalence of pickpockets and the kind of man who deliberately preyed on female tourists intent on taking their innocence and sometimes their money too. He would tell a girl that she was beautiful, that he loved her – anything for a one-night stand. The next night he would parrot the same words to a different girl. Whenever I saw playboys chatting up my students, I introduced myself as their chaperone and noticed how quickly the young men became more polite to, and respectful of, the girls.

Arriving in Florence, Paolo had hired a truck to take the luggage to our *pensione*. The excitement of being in Florence with Lisa and her family masked my anxiety about the journey ahead. When it was time for the five of us to take the train to Trieste, we were weighed down with eleven bags, plus hand luggage. Thankfully, Srecko collected us at Trieste in a mini-van to continue the journey to Fuzine in Croatia. When we arrived at the Hope Centre in Fuzine, which had been a rundown shell of a building only a year earlier, I was heartened to see groups from the UK and USA had made progress towards rebuilding and refurnishing the facility. The three-storeyed building was habitable and could accommodate a large number. No one was staying there yet, so it became our lodgings for the night. It was freezing, so we kept on our coats, gloves and headgear to stay warm.

The following day we visited the refugee centre nearby and I found that big improvements had been made there also. The refugee centre had not received government aid for many months. Corruption was rife in government, depriving the most needy of access to medical and dental services. Sadly, dear Magdalena was not there. Medical attention had been hard to come by to treat her high-blood pressure, so she had been hospitalised in Rijeka. Srecko and other Christians had stepped in to try to redress the situation. Sewage still flowed into unhygienic open drains, but some windows had been replaced, cooking facilities had improved and the cell-like dormitories had been made more homely by the appearance of a few more donations. There were signs of a fledgling cottage industry in embroidered doilies and knitted socks made by the refugee women. However, the major difference was the heartwarming sight of children playing and the smiling faces among the centre's fifty or so residents. I caught up with some of them. The epileptic father, who could not leave his room the previous year, now ventured outdoors – thanks to donations of medication and protective headgear.

American air-force personnel and their families had driven in a convoy from the Aviano air base near Venice to help the refugees. They told me that their bombing campaigns against Milosevic had led to homelessness and devastation in Croatia, and their visit was a chance to give something back to the people. It was the weekend before Easter, so they came bearing gifts and food: ham, turkey, corn on the cob, beans, peas, sweet potato, bread rolls and Italian cakes. Turning the day into a greater celebration, we divided the gifts into balanced amounts and distributed them to each family living at the centre. The children's joy at receiving toys brought tears to our eyes. It was immensely touching to meet people whose only possessions were the things we had sent from Hong Kong. To show their gratitude, the women at the refuge waited on the Americans and us at long trestle tables, serving us their favourite food – *burek*.

Our mission accomplished, we drove the next day to the seaside resort town, Opatija Riviera, a former playground for wealthy Europeans. It had been deserted during the war, but its stylish, grand nineteenth-century hotels remained intact. It was heartening to see this resort town slowly waking to a new era of peace and tourism. We left before dawn the next morning for Trieste, where we took the train to Venice.

Safely reunited with our tour group, we took the train that evening to Milan, since accommodation wasn't available in Venice. Realising the depth of my exhaustion, I deliberately chose to share a carriage with John, who had been a calming strength during the trip to Croatia, and Karen, a gentle student. I needed tranquillity and rest. I had always found a talkative person a vexation to the spirit, especially when one is exhausted, and there was an enthusiastic talker amongst the group, so I planned to have a sleep. The younger girls were in one compartment and the older group in another. I gave one of the younger students the name and address of our *pensione* in Milan and told her to pass it on to the older group, as we would need three taxis once we arrived to take us to our accommodation.

When the train arrived at Milan, five policemen suddenly confronted us. Two Italian women were pointing accusingly at the older women in our tour group. When the police demanded to see our passports, one of them said, 'Don't give it to them.' This was a big mistake, serving only to irritate the police. They told the women in the older group to 'come to our office now.' I feared they were being arrested. Not wanting to escalate the policemen's anger, I didn't question them. In hindsight, I should have accompanied the older group. Instead, I elected to stay with the students who were unfamiliar with Milan, and at 9.30 on a rainy night, I felt it would have been irresponsible to send them unaccompanied to the hotel. After the police had taken the women in the older group away, I was informed that the student I'd entrusted with passing on the name and address of the *pensione* hadn't been able to do so. She'd failed to whilst on the train, because, when she'd tried, the older students had indicated there had been a problem in their carriage and so asked her to go, since they didn't want to risk implicating her. 'Don't tell Miss Dally,' they added. Hearing this information made me livid. After all, I was the tour leader. Whatever happened on tour, I was ultimately responsible. Had I been made aware of the problem, with my understanding of some of the Italian language and culture, I might have been able to diffuse the situation. To this day, I do not know what happened in that carriage.

Believing the women with the police would not know where to find us when released, I reluctantly sent the other students by taxi to the *pensione* and remained at the station, watching every exit for my missing charges. I couldn't observe every exit from a seated waiting area, so I stood on the platform for almost two hours. Exhausted and hungry, it was about 11 p.m. when, in the distance, I saw the older group coming out of a restaurant, laughing happily. My reaction was like that of a parent who is reunited with their missing child. The parent is so relieved by their child's appearance that their anxiety boils over into rage. I don't think I have ever been so cross. I demanded to know why the police had questioned them. They refused to tell me. I told the talker of the group to 'shut up'. Sadly, long friendships were severed irreparably.

Were they leagued in mockery against me? Were they cackling about me? Self-doubt began to gnaw insidiously. Over the years I had been parodied and had my fair share of personal put-downs – it's part of being a public person and I accept that. Often I have loved the way people characterised me. In the mid 1960s, Gordon Chater would regularly send me up on the satirical 'Mavis Bramston Show'. In his skit, he would appear as an ocker, uncouth man wearing a floppy hat and singlet stained with spills from a meat pie, and sound off about Jane Dilly Popkins – alias me. I couldn't wait for the show to come on every Wednesday night and roll around on the floor with laughter.

When lesbians marching in the 1993 Mardi Gras mocked me, I laughed just as hard. Donning beauty pageant sashes imprinted with the words, 'June Dally-Watkins Rejects', they wore hats in the shape of stacked books and carried pictures of my face scribbled in with a moustache. This behaviour on my tour, however, I felt displayed a disregard for me, as well as for the other students. It hurt like the verbal sticks and stones that people flung at me as a child in Watson's Creek. It cut me to the quick and churned up the past. Try as I did, my past rose up again to haunt me.

Back at the *pensione*, I heard students phoning their parents, saying five policemen had taken away the older group. The next morning the students did a quick walking tour of Milan. My heart wasn't in it; it had died and my spirit with it. The train incident awoke dormant anxieties about myself. I felt suddenly insecure, old and foolish – negative thoughts that had crept into my mind after my accident at the train station in Sydney crowded in once more. Depression began to take me prisoner. I pretended I wasn't depressed, but knew I was falling further into its clutches.

We journeyed to Paris by train and, once the students had their bearings from an introductory tour, they were free to explore alone. Refusing to share a room with one of the women in the older group, I opted to bunk with some of the students. They complained that I snored. I joked that, if they mentioned my snoring to anyone, I would refuse to issue their diplomas at the end of the year. I hadn't quite lost my sense of humour, but I felt dazed. A threatening voice inside my head began to speak to me and distracted me from the goings-on. 'You must suffer. If you don't your grandchildren will be hurt,' it bellowed. It was as though I could really hear a person's voice. 'The more you suffer, the safer your family will be.' I don't know why I kept hearing the voice tell me this, but it drove me further towards introspection and self-criticism. Was I smiling too much, grimly? Was anyone aware of my condition? Thankfully, the students were too busy having a good time to notice. I didn't know what else to do but smile as the jaws of the black hole opened wider.

We arrived in London. Language wasn't a barrier and its culture was familiar, so the students could safely visit various tourist sights without me as their chaperone. Grateful for the opportunity to stay in my room, I buried my head under the covers. I dragged myself out of bed to keep only one appointment – my annual long lunch with former model Dorn Fraser. We met at the Grosvenor Thistle Hotel at Victoria Station to enjoy traditional English fare – roast beef and Yorkshire pudding. We laughed a lot and Dorn didn't notice anything strange about me. I put her on the train and went back to bed and to the brink of the abyss. It was the end of the tour and whilst I may have seemed tired to the group, I had convincingly concealed my self-destructive thoughts and emotions. When the students returned to Sydney, there were no complaints from them or their parents about the police incident in Milan or any other aspect of the trip.

With the students gone back home, I returned to Florence to stay with Lisa. By the time I arrived at my daughter's apartment, I had no emotional or physical strength in reserve. All I could do was sit and watch Lisa as she busily cared for Natalia. Naturally, all her attention was devoted to her little daughter, so she didn't have time to notice or understand the cause of my lethargy. Frustrated at seeing me doing so little to help her, the tension between us grew. Children like their mothers to play the maternal role when they need to be comforted and helped. They enjoy us as a friend when the time is right. It is a wise mother who can tell when her child wants her to be a friend or a parent. Children don't really want their parents' problems; they have enough of their own. The most parents can do is help their children to become independent; be there when their children want or need them; and get on with their own lives.

Depression finally took me hostage following what otherwise would have been a trifling incident. Lisa had given me a book that she suggested I read and set about preparing a meal. Some time had passed and then I heard her say, 'Mum, why haven't you set the table?' That set me off. I can't remember what I said, but I became hysterical. I felt out of control. Lisa couldn't calm me as I stormed off to the room I was sleeping in and began repeatedly hitting my head hard with my fists. Looking back, this behaviour was frighteningly similar to how my mother had beaten sticks against her head when she fled to the bush at Springvale more than sixty years earlier. Lisa's words had summoned dark memories of me reading a book and my grandmother saying, 'You lazy thing. You're here in my house and I'm looking after you, feeding you and clothing you. Put down that book and go out and bring in some wood.' Gran made sure my mother and I never forgot that we were in debt to her and Grandfather. The sadness of my early years at Watson's Creek flooded over me. I had buried those feelings of being unwelcome until Lisa's words, and a feeling that my presence was more of a nuisance than a help to her, dug them up. Until then I had thought the boil of my past had been lanced. It was a shock to discover the wound had not healed cleanly. I had been staying with Lisa for two weeks and was due to leave the following day. Now I refused to stay a minute longer. Lisa and Paolo could not console me. I packed my belongings and Paolo drove me to a hotel where I spent a sleepless night. I left Florence the next day without explaining my behaviour or saying goodbye to my daughter.

The next day, with a sad heart, I boarded the train for another journey into the unknown – this time to Zagreb, the capital of Croatia, and on to Mostar, the capital of Bosnia Herzegovina, where I would meet Sal. Being nervous about travelling overnight alone, my prayers were answered when I secured a sleeping compartment to myself. I was the only passenger in the train carriage, so I still felt nervous. Sleep did not come easily. After midnight, a loud banging on the compartment door awoke me, and a male voice shouting foreign words I could not understand. I heard a key unlock the door and it burst open as far as the safety chain would permit. I was now terrified. The police demanded my passport, which I handed through the gap of the door. To my relief, they studied it and handed it back, closed the door and I heard the door lock turn. I was shaking and couldn't sleep. Arriving in Zagreb early that morning, I was relieved that war had not touched this city. I wandered peacefully for a couple of hours until I met Sal and Crossroads worker Leighton Joyce, who recorded our visit on camera. After a day in Zagreb, we took a long overnight journey to Mostar. I covered up that I felt I was sliding into a black pit of depression. I don't know whether Sal noticed I was troubled – if she did, she never mentioned it. If she had, it could easily have been put down to two nights and three days without sleep and the exposure to much devastation. However, she did notice a large bruise on my forehead. I was too embarrassed to tell her I had caused it myself.

Never will I forget the awe-inspiring drive down the mountains to the Neretva Valley (not long ago dubbed the 'Valley of Death') and Mostar. This area had been embroiled in violence over the past decade: Kosovars, Croats, Serbs, Bosnians, Albanians, Macedonians – one way or the other, all had been caught in the crossfire. In Mostar, we met two wonderful Christians, Ivon and Karmelo Kresonja, who took us to a war-devastated ten-storey apartment block. Shelling had pockmarked every facade, windows were missing and there were gaping holes where once families had lived. All the apartments had been deserted, except one, where we were to stay. A soccer player who owned the apartment offered it to AGAPE, a humanitarian agency, which distributed aid throughout Croatia and Bosnia. Following Sal and David's earlier trip to the city, Crossroads had sent donated furniture to outfit the apartment and AGAPE had restored it. It was surreal to be sitting there at a dining table surrounded by furniture from exclusive Hong Kong hotels.

The main street in Mostar resembled an archaeological dig. The magnificent four-hundred-year-old Stari Most Bridge, the heart of Mostar, had been destroyed. Opposing ethnic groups had fought from each side and some victims of war had been trapped on the wrong side of the road when war erupted. 'I was at the dentist on the other side of the road the day war broke out,' one woman recounted. 'The road was blocked so I couldn't get home for four-and-a-half years. When I made it home, I found my house destroyed and had to search until I found my family.' Our host told us: 'My grandmother was also on the wrong side of town. She could not get back to our home again. She died alone, six months later. We never even knew until years after that.' Such life-and-death division across a road seemed unbelievable. The street itself was no wider than William Street in Sydney, with a nature strip down the centre. *Miracle in Mostar* (Lion, Oxford, 1995), edited by Gerard Kelly and Lowell Sheppard, quotes Stevo Dereta:

> The racial war was fought before a single shot was fired. It was a war of words and hatred, fought through daily press and television. It took just months for people who had lived in peace for forty years to hate each other. They had no defence against the lies raining down on them. Such a force of mistrust and hate had been released that nothing could contain it. The guns are evil, but the hatred is more evil.

By the time I arrived back in Australia I had sunk so far into a state of depression that I thought life wasn't worth living. I drew a circle around myself and didn't let anyone in. I couldn't express my feelings to anyone and shut people out of my life. I looked in the mirror and saw a woman who looked more and more like my mother. I considered myself as someone with fresh ideas. Now, no matter what I said I thought it was considered wrong and old-fashioned, so I began to speak my mind less. My poor children didn't know what to make of my state of mind. I needed reassurance from my children that they loved me, but the more I withdrew from them, the less chance there was for them to give me this message. I felt I was receiving love only from my grandchildren who were too young to understand what a terrible person I was. Keeping my children at a distance only exacerbated my fear that they didn't love me. It fed my sense of inadequacy and insecurity. I felt that they didn't care enough to see through my silence.

Carel suggested I get medical help, because I was not well. I don't think she guessed to what extent depression had taken over my life. Did anyone? The others knew I was exhausted and feeling low. I kept saying to myself, 'I am horrible, I'm terrible – no wonder my family hates me.' When the demon thoughts were in my head, they were in charge and filled it, blocking communication with my long-time friend, the Lord, and I could no longer hear His voice.

I had always believed that it wasn't good to show I was feeling down. When I had to make a public appearance, I put on a happy face that felt as though it belonged to another person. At the same time that smiling face I wore was all too familiar. There had been so many times I had worn it in public – even though I was tired, troubled in my marriage, at the end of my tether with my mother, or stressed from work and staff disloyalty.

So how did I recover? I revisited the past and returned to Watson's Creek. I believe I had to return there to help heal myself. There were many years that I didn't go to the Creek. There wasn't anyone to visit after my grandparents and Uncle Les died. I became reacquainted with my cousin, Bert Skewes, who founded a Christian church group at Kootingal, just out of Tamworth. Bert brought me in touch with third and fourth Skewes cousins. Now, at last, I was part of an extended family. They accepted me with open arms and love. Bert invited me to be guest speaker at a service to be held in the old Watson's Creek Hall, the scene of those dances as a child. Now the corrugated iron was rusted and the dance floor somewhat warped.

I realised I had had a hard time facing my childhood because I had never confronted the past before. I had always pretended everything was all right. I had pretended my father was dead and didn't dwell on the unhappiness and loneliness of those days at Watson's Creek. I was shocked to think it took until this stage of my life to discover what happened to me as a little girl could almost break me. I would not have thought it possible. Maybe that's why I've had a very tender feeling toward my students. The name-calling and sadness of my childhood made me conscious of the potential sensitivities of my students and made me want to teach them to feel good about themselves.

Occasional visits to the business college helped in my recovery too. The end-of-year business college graduation came and went. The students were a delight and their parents said glowing things, which were like another 'get well' tonic. A light began to appear to lead me out of the pit into which I'd fallen. I was beginning to see a way out. Little by little, I could feel my prayers getting through and the gentleness of the Lord. Now when the demon thought whispered 'You must suffer', I was beginning to be able not to listen and to tell these thoughts to go away.

As much as I tried to fend off my depression alone, I needed the reassurance of my family. My grandchildren saved me: their sweetness and loving hugs. Ben was then nine. He had always spent time with me. He had been with me when I broke my leg at Sydney Central Railway Station and had stayed with me all that day, showing so much concern. Marc's children, Ben and three-year-old, Cameron, and Tim's sons Jack, seven, and Brody, four, came to visit. Their affection and cuddles were what I needed. Carel's son Chris, though 17, also hugged me and said 'I love you, Non.' Hearing them say this helped me. The love of little children is so sweet. I longed to hug my only grand-daughter Natalia June and soon-to-be-born grandson Leo in Florence. Christmas 2001 became the turning point. My family in Australia had gathered for Christmas lunch, including John, when Lisa phoned from Italy. I had not spoken to Lisa since my outburst in Florence. She was on the phone talking to John, who sensed there had been some tension between us. He urged me to speak to her. Tentatively, I took the phone and heard down the line, 'I love you, Mum.' Those words were like a spell to cast off my despair. The healing process began. It was as if I had been waiting for her forgiveness before I could forgive myself and like myself again. Lisa has never quizzed me over my actions in Florence. It was as though nothing had ever happened, and sadly reminded me of how my mother and I dealt with the backwash from emotional disturbances between us. Nevertheless, her words freed me to return her love and to tell my other children I loved them, and receive a loving response.

I used to think that by giving my children a privileged upbringing and raising them with all my love, I had ensured a lifetime of love, but I began to realise I had to keep working at my relationship with my children. Now, I tell my grandchildren and friends all the time that I love them. The love I receive back from them is the greatest joy. Their love is a blessing. Life would be empty without them. The students sense that I care for them too, and I think they respond. Having the love and respect of the students has been one of the reasons I've kept the school going. It's never been purely a business, but something that has nourished me. When I was growing up, at least in my small world, people were not as demonstrative emotionally. My grandparents seemed to love me, but never told me so. My mother was proud of me, but she didn't hug me or tell me she loved me either. I am grateful I learned to love my children unconditionally.

My depression turned into a period of personal and spiritual growth, so I have no regrets about the experience. Through this process, I faced up to issues in my marriage, and in my relationships with my children and mother. I learnt a lot about myself. I have been frightened to love in case I was rejected. I have had tough times, as we all do. Either they break us or make us stronger. As the saying goes, 'The hottest kiln produces the finest china.' Since confronting my past, I'm confident I won't feel down again. At least I know now that I'm resilient enough to keep smiling.

Epilogue: A new beginning

My business's courses, which are based on my personal beliefs, tackle what I perceive as the increasing decline in language, manners, etiquette, dress and behaviour. Today people seem less inclined to be the best, preferring to look as though they haven't made an effort. There is a trend that favours the lowest common denominator. People swear readily, flaunt body piercing, tattoos, and clothing that is either skimpy or sloppy, exposing a flabby midriff or trying to hide a bad figure. It's a world away from what I believe makes a person stand out in a crowd!

As an arbiter of Australian manners, fashion and style for more than half a century, I feel I have earned the right to have a view on current trends. Advertisers battle for our minds and freedom. People increasingly find their gods in celebrities, violence, sex and drugs. Fashion and young people follow these dubious role models. There is a fast-food mentality to sex: if you feel the urge, take it for instant gratification, and don't worry about the emotional damage. Pop songs, magazines, movies and television programs tell people that if they're not sexually active, there's something wrong. Maybe I'm old-fashioned, but I think there's more to life than sex. I believe in falling in love instead of lust and one-night stands. Not surprisingly, men respect women less. I don't believe women need to compete against men and undermine them in order to feel equal. We should compete as human beings, and respect and love one another.

If a parent and a school are unable to give 'tough-love' discipline, how is a child to learn self-discipline? A child can know right from wrong only if they are told. The world is becoming more like a jungle, but the animal kingdom has rules. No wonder young people are confused. I pray the world returns to dignity, self-respect, high moral values, and love not hate. Parents who enrol their sons and daughters in my courses are also alarmed by attitudes in today's society. Their appreciation and the friendships I have made with so many of them over the years have been more important than they would guess. Money has never been a dominating factor in my business life; providing quality education and training for students has provided greater rewards. I would rather take a good name to my grave than money.

I would like young people to believe, no matter what their circumstances, they can make it. Life is 10 per cent knock-backs and 90 per cent knowing how to handle them. It is important to get on and stay on the straight and narrow path to do well in life. I've found the straight road to be the surest and the quickest. Every diversion takes you off the track and it takes time and energy to return to the route again – and some don't make it back.

To help young people find their way, I decided that after fifty-two years in the business the school had to be rejuvenated, whilst still maintaining its values and high standards. I painted it in 'WOW' colours. The Business School became a college. I retained the Finishing Image classes at the request of parents and students. At the request of students, the uniform was kept, though I made it more relaxed and trendy. I have employed a male receptionist and encourage more young men to join the college. I make sure it is fun at the college, so that students get up on Monday mornings enthusiastic about the week ahead. My idea of discipline is to encourage, motivate and teach by example. Recently, a male student at my Business College, wrote: 'Miss Dally, thank you for all your support. You are my hero and saviour.' That is my reward.

Today, the Brisbane business incorporates Dally's Model Management with models working in various parts of the world. My Professional Model course includes all ages, from children to mature-age men and women for television commercials, photography and fashion shows. Personal Development, Corporate Training, Make-up Artistry and Retail Cosmetics are held on Saturdays, in school holidays and in the evenings. In Sydney, the focus is somewhat different. The Business Finishing College for young men and women is unique and graduates are the future movers and shakers in the corporate world. The June Dally-Watkins Education and Training School incorporates Personal Development, Corporate Success programs and Model Training on Saturdays and during school holidays. In the evenings the Business, Personal Assistant and Receptionist Update courses are held.

Running my own business is fulfilling and energising; and business is booming. Even so I have energy left to remain Ambassador-at-Large for Crossroads International. This is in part due to the fact that the teachers and staff share the management of the business with me. Trish Fraser, Colleen Fong and Margaret Whealy have remained after many years. My son Marc watches over the finances and the Brisbane business, whilst keeping his senior management job at one of the top twenty-five Australian companies.

I want to remain my own person. I don't want to be boxed exclusively into the role of grandmother or dependant mother. I am happy to be grandmother, as well as friend and confidante, to my six grandsons and one grand-daughter, when they want me. I find it offensive when senior people are treated as less intelligent and as though they should be shelved. We have gained from our experiences, made our mistakes and quite likely learned from them. My brain never stops; it is constantly coming up with new business ideas I would love to put into action. I run my business from my heart and, because of this, it can cause heartache, but I have dreams, enthusiasm and optimism – gifts my mother gave me – and with the love of my children and grandchildren, I have much to smile about in life.

INDEX

ABC 118
Abernathy, John 148
Aboriginal students 153
Aboriginal themed parade 159
Abram, Dr Geoff 187
Abram, Lois 187
accents 10–11
accessories 41–2
acting 80
Aeolian Islands 196
AGAPE 256
agencies, model *see* model agencies
Akubra 171
Albright, Sid 52, 113
alcohol 6, 7, 19–21, 56, 105, 125, 227
Alexander, Elliott 139
Americanisms 82
Andronicus brothers 153
animals 17–18, 23–4
Ann-Margret 139, 150
anorexia nervosa 79–80
Anthony, Ray 96
Arden, Elizabeth 92
Armidale 171
army students 154
Aruba 213

Ascot 80
Asia 155–65, 173, 175 *see also* place names, e.g. Hong Kong; Japan; Philippines
astrology 140, 167
Auckland 168–9
Australian Business Women's Network 3
Australian Democrats 185
Australian Department of Trade 155
Australian Fashion Awards 176
Australian Women's Weekly, The see Women's Weekly, The Australian
Aviano air base 250

'baby' models 229
Bacall, Lauren 98, 105
Bache–McLean, Jodie 230, 247
Balenciaga 100
Bali 123, 182
Balkans 237, 238
Balmain, Pierre 61
Bangkok 161
baptism 216, 222
Barrymore, Ethel 95
Bates, Frank 150
Bathurst 171

'Beauty and the Beast' 50
beauty quests
   franchises 177–8, 232–3
   judging 152, 161–2, 164, 171–3, 178, 185, 233
   model quests 176–8
   student winners 2, 82, 87, 149–50
Becky's Boutique 188
Begbie, David 235, 237–8, 240, 241, 243, 244
Begbie, Joshua 235
Begbie, Malcolm 234–6
Begbie, Sally 234–6, 237–9, 240, 241, 243, 244, 245
Beiger, Shirley 137–8
Bell Sisters 97
Bellevue Hill 116, 122, 131, 176, 183, 225
Bendemeer 13, 20, 22, 28
Bennett, June 63, 64, 67
Beretta, Gianmaria 196
Bettina 100
Bicentenary 140–2
Billingsley, Sherman 98
bisexuality 95
Bisley House 112
Bitola 238
Blades, Laraine 169–70
Blair, Roma 180
Blood Cord Bank 183
Boans 64, 114
boarding schools 125, 131–2
'Bob Hope Show, The' 97
Boer War 28
Bogart, Humphrey 105
Bondi Beach 46, 221
Bonynge, Richard 118
Booth, Josephine 164
Booth, Knox 164
born-again Christians 216, 219, 222, 223
Bosnia 238, 240, 255–7
bras 40, 41, 173
breast cancer 21, 50, 64
Brisbane 67–9, 151, 175, 188
British Commonwealth Pacific Airlines 90, 93

British handover of Hong Kong 219, 234–5
Brooker, John 111
Brooker, Liz 111
Brown, Ben 57–8
Brown, David 239
Brown, Robert 153
Bryant, Betty 106
Bryce, Bryan 163
Buckingham, Ashley 43
Budge, Donald 69
Bullmore, Gretel 61
Burke, Frank 171
Burns, Janet 189
bushrangers 7–8
Business Women's Hall of Fame 3
Buttrose, Charles (Jnr) 118–9
Buttrose, Charles (Snr) 118, 187
Buttrose, Clare 118
Buttrose, Ita 118, 119, 169
Buttrose, Margo 187
Byrne, Caroline 145–8

Cable, Muriel 33
Cagney, James 105
Cameron's 175
Campbell, Beth 63
Campbell, Naomi 227, 239
Canberra 171
cancer
   attitudes towards 6, 191
   fundraising 178
   photography 45
   sufferers 21, 50, 64, 105, 118, 191–2
   treatment 212
Cant, Di 151, 182–3
Capri, Isle of 104, 145
Cardin, Pierre 163
Carmagnola, Luce 155–6
Carmody, Jan 142, 143–5, 196
cars 60
Carter, Peggy 153
Casablancas, Johnny 176, 227
Castle Hill 57
catalogues, mail order 11, 12, 35
Cathay Pacific Airlines 155

Catholic Church 154
Catholicism 24, 110, 140, 220–1
Caulfield Cup 53, 186
Cebu Island 164
cerebral palsy 172
Chadwicks 175
Cham, Dr Bill 212–13
Chan, Ronnie 236
Chao, Cecil 213–14
Chapman, Ceil 92
Chappell, Greg 162
charity work 154, 170 *see also* Crossroads International; International Christian Women's Club; *Moj Bliznji*
Charles, Gordon 145, 175
Charles E. Blanks 39
charm schools 72, 98
Chaseling, Christine 171
Chater, Gordon 252
Chatswood 30
Chau, Sir Sik-Nin 155
Chequers 108
Chic Model Management 175
China Mail, The 157
Chipp, Don 185
choreography 159, 162, 215
Christian, Linda 97
Christian organisations 258 *see also* International Christian Women's Club; *Moj Bliznji*; Youth With a Mission
Christianity 24, 165, 175, 218–20
Chronicle 93
Clayton, Lucy 72
Cleland, Bob 47
Clemson, Pam 63, 64
Clifford, John 108–11, 113–14, 116, 118, 120–1, 122–3, 259
Clifford, Judy 113
Clifford, June *see* Dally-Watkins, June Marie
Clifford, Mel 232
Climpson, Roger 168
Clooney, Rosemary 97
Cocktails with Chic 107

Cohen, Maisy Bestle 168–9
Colbert, Claudette 101
Cole, Fred 143
Cole, Nat King 97, 108
Cole of California 143
Collins, John 152
colour photography 37, 47
Columbia Pictures 139
Compton, Dennis 68
Conover, Harry 72
Conrad Jupiters 206
Consolidated Press 86
cooking 51, 130, 132, 236
cooks 117
Cooksley, Joan 33
Cornwall 7, 144
cosmetic surgery 81
Coupland, Jenny 149
Cousens, Bill 34
Cousens, Peter 34
Crampton, Laura 236
Crawford, Joan 94, 98
cricket 22, 25, 26, 68, 180–1
Croatia 239–40, 241, 242, 247–51, 255–6
Crosby, Bing 101, 105
Crossroads International 102, 235–41, 244–5, 247–9, 255–6, 263
Cukor, George 95, 105
Cunningham, Loren 218
curaçao 170–1
Curacel 213
Currie, Eve 96
Currie, Gordon 95–6
curry 22
Curzon's 42, 43, 67–8

'Dad and Dave' 58
Daily Mirror 200
Daily Telegraph 48, 112
Dally Lashes 160
Dally-Watkins, Caroline Mary (née Skewes; also Kay, Carrie)
  alcohol consumption 56, 125
  appearance 11
  attitude to men 30, 31, 70, 110, 119

business nous 74–5
cancer 133, 174, 191–4
dates 15–16
depression 18, 56, 126, 127, 170
determination 38, 70
dreams 6, 12
emotional abuse 54, 55, 190, 220
gambling 53
manners 10–11
marriages
    Bill 118–19, 155
    David 28–30
memoirs 195, 197–9
modelling job 52
musical interests 9, 15, 118, 125–6
relationship with JDW 15, 50, 53–9, 70, 106, 110, 112–13, 121–2, 190, 198–9, 220, 260
relationship with mother 18, 255
sense of humour 55, 126
sewing 11, 53, 58, 108
single mother 5–7, 27
Dally-Watkins, David 28–30
Dally-Watkins, June Marie
    aunts
        Edith 21
        Elsie 7, 11, 20
        Emily 21
        Ethel 22–3
        Ida 18, 21
        Isabella 21
        Mercy 7–8, 22
        Pearl 21
        Thelma 20
    boyfriends 53–4, 57, 66–7, 68–71, 88, 99–100, 101, 102–4, 107, 108
    business ventures
        betrayals and competition 87–9, 173–7, 209
        Brisbane school 83, 151, 169, 180, 230, 247
        Business Finishing School 80, 231–2, 262–3
        corporate clients 154, 163–4, 168
        delegating 166–7

Femme salon 167, 169
Hong Kong school 180, 214–15, 218, 220, 222–3
Men's Executive course 80
model agencies
    Brisbane 169, 175, 182, 224, 230, 263
    Models Worldwide 211–12
    Sydney 83, 85, 119–20, 151, 167, 224–5
Model course 84
New Zealand school 168
Parramatta school 170
Perth school 152
regional NSW classes 171
School of Deportment, Sydney 73–80, 120, 180
Sydney satellite classes 170
Townsville school 169–70
Wollongong school 170
children 113, 116, 121, 124–34, 189, 193–4, 203, 205–6, 220–1, 257–8
    Carel
        advice to JDW 258
        birth 112–13, 136
        boyfriends 118–19, 212
        career 145–6, 177, 193–4, 209, 210–12, 215, 216, 228, 229, 233, 247
        childhood 117, 125–7, 138, 142, 201
        Italy 102, 134, 138–9, 195
        Switzerland 130–1
    Lisa
        birth 110, 117, 168, 173
        career 214–18, 220
        childhood 69, 188, 189
        Italy 102, 133–4, 193–4, 203
        meeting grandfather 205–7
        motherhood 196, 197
        relationship with JDW 254–5, 259–60
    Marc
        birth 168
        career 133, 178, 263
        childhood 127, 183, 188–9

Tim
    career 210
    childhood 119, 131–2, 142, 166, 189, 201
    meeting grandfather 205
children's partners
    Paolo 205, 214, 216–17, 238, 249, 255
    Trish 231
    Vicki 210
depression 253–5, 256, 257–60
dreams 12–13, 264
father *see* Monkton, Bob
friends 179–90 *see also* individuals by name, e.g. Elphick, Jeanette; McMahon, (Lady) Sonia
godchildren
    Jamie 159
    Jennifer 63
    Susie 183
grandchildren 258, 259, 260, 263–4
    Ben 259
    Brody 210, 259
    Cameron 259
    Christopher 140, 179, 185, 259
    Jack 210, 259
    Leo 102, 217, 238, 259
    Natalia 102, 197, 217, 235, 238, 254, 259
grandfather 7, 8, 9–10, 16–17, 255, 260
grandmother 8, 9, 11, 17–18, 255, 260
great-grandparents 7–8
growing up 4–35
    adoption 29
    illegitimacy 5–6, 109, 205
    schooling 25, 28, 31, 32
    teenage flirting 33–4
marriage 108–11 *see also* Clifford, John
marriage proposals 64, 71, 99, 104
memoirs 196–7
modelling days 35–74
    awards 1, 72
    catalogue work 36–7, 39
    department store parades 38, 42–4, 55–6, 57, 67, 74, 204
    first modelling job 36–7
    magazine & newspaper work 39–40, 47, 52, 67
    manufacturer's parades 42
    one-woman fashion show 90–1
    other jobs 36, 39, 58
    overseas collections 61–3
    television 93–4, 168
moon gazing 13, 182, 196
mother *see* Dally-Watkins, Caroline Mary
siblings
    half-siblings 201–2, 203, 204–5
    step-siblings 29–30
travel 120, 122
    in Australia 58, 64, 66, 67, 170, 201
    Balkans 237–43, 247–51, 255–7
    Bangkok 161
    Hawaii 90–2, 127, 128, 142–3
    Hollywood 94–8, 104–6, 143–4
    Hong Kong
        business 218, 222–3
        Crossroads International 235–6
        department stores 162–3
        good times 186, 188, 205
        handover 234–5
        lectures 170
        parades 155–7, 159–61
        spiritual rebirth 218–22
    Italy 101–2, 104, 145, 176, 195–7, 203, 251–3, 254–5
    Japan 128
    London 99–100, 128, 144, 161, 254
    Melbourne 58
    Moscow 243–5
    New York 98–9, 104, 176
    Paris 100–1, 144, 163, 253
    Philippines 157–9, 161, 163–5, 170, 181–2, 188
    Rome 101–2, 144, 176
    San Francisco 93–4, 127
    Seoul 161
    Singapore 145, 161
uncles
    'Blue' 20–1

Bob 22
  Jack 21
  Jim 21
  Len 21–2
  Les 9, 20, 23–4, 258
  Oswald 21, 110
  Sid 19, 32
  Will 21
Dallyence 178, 212–13
Daly, Maureen 196
dances 4–5, 12, 65, 108, 196
Dandenongs 185
Darling Point 187
Darlinghurst 108
Darwin 163, 188
Dauth, Geoff 89
David Jones 43, 55, 98, 152, 168, 201
Davis, Sammy (Jnr) 143
Davison, Kirsten 150, 233
de Chazal, Richard 171
Deamer, Tom 85–7
debutantes 171, 172
decision-making 222–3
deep-sleep therapy 126
Delaney, Delvene 150
Democrats 185
department stores
  Boans 64, 114
  boom time 83
  catalogues 12
  Curzon's 42, 43, 67–8
  David Jones 43, 55, 98, 152, 168, 201
  Farmer's 12, 36, 38, 42, 47, 57
  Grace Brothers 12, 150, 168, 219
  Hong Kong 162–3
  Mark Foy's 44
  Myer's 12, 58, 112
  Neiman Marcus 74, 97, 152
  parades 38, 42–4, 64, 67, 74, 201
  Philippines 161
  Tamworth 33
  Waltons 168
depression 151 *see also* Dally-Watkins, June Marie, depression; Dally-Watkins, Caroline Mary, depression

Depression, Great 12
Dereta, Stevo 240, 241–2, 257
Derek, Jenny Annette 233
didgeridoo 159
diet 62, 79–80
Dietrich, Marlene 14, 32, 153
Dinnigan, Collette 230
Dior, Christian 61–3, 64
Dirranbandi 171
discipline 262, 263
Dockie *see* Melville, Dr Bob
Don Pedro Theatre 157
Donaldson, Judy 162
Done, Judy 150
Done, Ken 150
Doomben races 108
Douglas, Lord Sholto 66
Dovey, Bill 66
Doyle, Kerry 221
Dragon Air 236–7
drama 80
dress 78, 81
dressers 42
driving 60
drugs 227–8, 239, 261
Du Pont parades 64
Duchess of Kent 237
Duchess of Windsor 11
Duckett, Lyndon 58
Ducksberry, April 176
Duffie, Patricia 155–6
Duncan, Paula 150
Dunkerley, Dorothy 112
Dupain, Max 45
Duval, Maureen 149
Dymocks building 112, 167, 170, 224

East-Meets-West parades 161–2
eastern suburbs 49, 106, 115, 120, 142, 145
Eastman, Yvonne 86, 136
eating disorders 79–80
Eaton, Ron 67
Edgewater Hotel 91, 93
Edwards, Katy 151
Elite 176, 227

Elizabeth Bay 192
Elle 230, 239
Elphick, Frank 138
Elphick, Jeanette 112, 138–42, 143, 151
Elphick, Neta 138
emphysema 139–40
English 82
etiquette 76, 82, 86
European tours 193, 233, 247
Evangelista, Linda 60
exercise 61–2, 79, 80, 180
eyelashes *see* false eyelashes
eyeliner 106

Face of the 80s 177, 178, 213, 232
facelifts 81
Fagan, Bill 64
Fahey, Joan 67
Fairfax, Lady (Mary) 142
Falkiner, George 66
false eyelashes 40, 119, 160
Farmer's 12, 36, 38, 42, 47, 57
Fashion 67
Fashion Model 211
'Fashions on the Field' 80, 112
Faulkenmire, Ken 34
feminism 43–4, 172–3, 212
Ferris, Jill 83
Fifty Years of Catwalk 183
Filicudi 196–7, 236
Findlay, Narelle 63
Fiorelli 111
Firman, Mickey 50
Firman, Pat 50, 152
first names 75
Fleming, Jim 153
Flemington 185
Florence 216–17, 235, 249, 254–5
Folkes, Fairy 46
Fong, Colleen 223, 263
Fonseca, Jose 176
Fontana sisters 103
Fonteyn, Dame Margot 100
Ford, Eileen 11, 153, 175–7, 225, 226, 228

Ford, Jerry 175–7, 225, 226
Ford, Lacy 177
Ford Models 176–7, 211, 225, 227
Ford, Tennessee Ernie 96
Foster, Richard 171
Fraser, Dorn 46, 50, 63, 64, 103, 254
Fraser, Malcolm 185
Fraser, Trish (née Sasse) 166, 263
French boutiques 61
Fuga 165, 181–2
Fuller, Jill Ellen 153, 163
furs 122, 128, 156, 172
Fuzine 242, 246, 247–8, 249–50

Gable, Clark 32
Gainford, Judy 189
Galom, Mr 21–2
Gap, The 146–7
Gardner, Ava 98, 103
Garland, Judy 95
Garson, Greer 106
Gee, Ingrid 153, 164
'General Hospital' 139
Giant's Den Mountain 8
Gibran, Kahlil 104
ginger beer 23
Girdler, Neville 34
Girl Guides 31
Girling, Betty 42, 67
Givenchy 193
Glassop, Patricia 161
Gleneagles 65
gloves 43, 62, 171
Gold Coast 179, 180, 184, 185, 201, 203, 204, 206
Gold Coast Bulletin, The 204, 208
Goldberg, Jose 89
Gomez, Maita 161–2
Gonzalez, Pancho 69
'Good Morning Sydney' 149
Goodwin, Reverend 119
Gordon, Ruth 99
Gordon Charles 145, 175
Grace Brothers 12, 150, 168, 219
graduations 85, 166, 170, 171, 184, 233, 259

Graham, Marg 34
'Graham Kennedy Show, The' 204
Grand United Building 85–7
Grant, Cary 95, 105
Gray, Colleen 105
Great Depression 12
Gregory, Diana 152
Griffith, Arthur 137–8
Griffith, Joe 63
grooming 76
Grzonkowski, Ingrid *see* Gee, Ingrid
Gstaad 130–1
Gulgong 171

Haddon Rig 66
hairpieces 40, 160
hairstyles 11, 62
Hammond, Elaine 168
Handley, Ian 34
handover of Hong Kong 219, 234–5
Hanlon, Peter 142, 145
Hannaford, John 247, 251
Harewood, Earl of 88
Harfield, Michael 220–1
Harlow, Jean 32
Hartnell 99
Harvey Norman 189, 248
Hatfield, Marcia 89
hats 62, 110
Hawaii 90–2, 127, 128, 142–3
Hawkesbury River 46, 111
Hayles, John 144, 160, 178, 188, 213
Hayman Island 67
Hayworth, Rita 100, 180
Hearder, John 45, 111
height of models 36, 84
Heinz, Sir Bernard 118
Henderson, Jane 234
Henie, Sonja 26
Hepburn, Audrey 102, 103
Hepburn, Katharine 99, 100, 104–5
Hermana Mayor 165
Herzegovina 240, 255–7
Heston, Charlton 143
Hickey, (Lady) Barbara 66, 178

Hickey, (Sir) Justin 66
Hickey, Noel 45
Hill, Sinclair 153
Hilton Hotel 160, 161, 163, 172, 213
Hollywood 94–8, 104–6, 139, 143–4, 188
homosexuality 94–5
Hong Kong
 Crossroads International 235–6
 department stores 162–3
 deportment school 213–16, 218, 222–3
 good times for JDW 186, 188, 205
 handover 234–5
 lectures 170
 parades 155–7, 159–61
 spirituality 218–22
Hope, Bob 105, 138–9, 143, 150
Hope, Delores 105, 139, 143
Hope, Ray 64
Hope Centre 242, 249
Hordern, Mary 61, 142
Hordern Brothers 155
Hotel Bonavia 239–40
housekeepers 112, 115–16, 117, 142
Howarth, Amy 12
Howarth, Joan 51
Howarth, Rosie 51
Hoy, Valmai 63, 64
Hufnagl, Ursula 175
Hunt, Colette (née Raynes) 180–2, 212, 213, 220, 234, 236
Hunt, Max 182, 236
Hunt, Nicholas 182
Hunt, Pascale 182, 236
Hutchence, Kell 107, 160–1
Hutchence, Michael 107, 161
Hutchinson, Lesley 159
Hyatt Hotels 163, 182

Identity Studios 45
Ilisonovic, Srecko 241, 243, 249, 250
Inche, Gûl 130–1
Incley Salon 58
Institut Montesano 130–1
International Christian Women's Club 243, 244

Iredale, Ron 48
Islam 165
Isle of Capri *see* Capri, Isle of
Isogawa, Akira 230
Italy 101–2, 104

Jackson, Marjorie 150
James, Bill 118–19, 155
James Bond Quest 178
Jantzen 45–6
Japan 128, 157, 233
Japanese bombing of Sydney harbour 31
Johnson, Andrea 74
Johnson, Reg 45–6
Jolo 165
Jones, Alan 187
Jones, June 68
Jones, Lorraine 111
Jones, Olga 68, 185
Jones, Stan 68, 185
Jones, Ted 111
Jones, Wendy 68
Joseph, Una 33
Joyce, Leighton 256
Joye, Col 153
judging quests 152, 161–2, 164, 171–3, 178, 185, 233
Jughead the Ostrich 97
June Dally-Watkins: Manners for Moderns 171

Kahanamuku, Duke 142
Kamahl, Rani 151
Kangaroo 51–2
Kanin, Garson 99
Karitane nurses 116–17
Katies 219
Keir, Steve 171
Kelly, Coralie 63–4
Kelly, Grace 103
Kelly, Orry 94–5, 96–7, 188
Kempsey 171
Kensington 35
Kent, Duchess of 237
Keyte, Len 54

Khan, Aga 100
Khan, Prince Ali (IV) 100
Kincoppal-Rose Bay Convent 115, 125, 130, 133
Kings Cross 29, 50–1, 52, 58, 142, 167
Kistle, Maureen 149
Knight, Lorraine 155–6
Konrads, John 153
Koo, Daniel 162
Kootingal 258
Kowloon 159–60, 163, 222
Kresonja, Ivon 256
Kresonja, Karmelo 256
Kroger, Michael 186

La Rue 97
Laidlaw, Aub 47
Lansbury, Angela 188
Lantau Island 235
Laughton, Charles 97
Lawson, Leonard 136–7
Le Guay, Laurie 47
Ledger, Bob 64–5
Lee, Adam 147, 148
Lee, John 45
Lee, Sandra 45
Leighton, Ray 47
Leilani 185–6
Leling, Lily 156
lend-lease model scheme 92, 93
Lennon's Hotel 68
lesbianism 101, 228, 253
Leser, Barbara 123
Leser, Bernard 123
Lewis, Jerry 143
Liberal Party 133, 185, 186
Life Centre International 241–2
Lightning Ridge 183
L'il Abner 144
Lilley, Dr Alan 45
Lim, Sonny (Jnr) 165, 181–2
Lindsay, Judy 156
lipstick 40, 160
Little, Arthur 107, 111
Little, Jeannie 151

Little, Thelma 107
Littlewood, Clare 196
Lloyd, Keith 151
Loew, Arthur 106, 144
Loew, Marcus 144
Loftberg, Em 31
Lollobrigida, Gina 143
Lombard, Carole 14
London 64, 72, 99–100, 128, 132, 133, 144, 161, 176, 226, 254
Long, Lionel 80
Longley, Eric 46
Look of the Year 176
Los Angeles 127 see also Hollywood
Louden, Barry 45
Lucignano 203
Lucky, Bud (Jnr) 104
Lufthansa Airlines 248–9
Luke, Monte 45
Lumley, Caroline 149
Luzon 165, 181

Macau 157
Macedonia 237, 238
McBurney, Judy 80
McDermott, Vivien 173–4, 175, 177
Macdonald River 22
Macdougall, Jim 112
Macfarlane, Colin 142–3
McIllree, Eric 151
McLeod, Bobby 153
McLeod, Jack 153
McLeod, Janette 150, 162
McLeod, Natalie 153
McMahon, (Sir) Bill 133, 177, 183–4, 185
McMahon, Debbie 184
McMahon, Julian 184
McMahon, Melinda 184
McMahon, (Lady) Sonia 116, 177–8, 183–4, 194, 213, 216
Macpherson, Elle 231, 239
McRae, Ian 186
McSweeney, Angela Belle 80
McSweeney, Molly 80

McSweeney, Tony 80
magazines 11–12, 111, 206 see also Fashion; Vogue; Woman's Day; Women's Weekly
mail order catalogues see catalogues, mail order
make-up 36, 39, 40, 49, 77, 78–9, 160, 228, 229
Malacañan Palace 164
Malaysia 183
Mallett, June 63, 67
Mandarin Hotel 159
Manila 157–9, 161, 163–5, 182, 235
Manila Hotel 158
Mannequin of the Year 176
manners 10, 76
Manners for Moderns 171
Marcos, Ferdinand 164, 182
Marcos, Imelda 164, 182
Marcus, Stanley 97
Mardi Gras 253
Margetic, Ruth 247
'Marjorie Trimball Show, The' 93–4, 97
Mark Foy's 44
Markson, Max 213
Marling, Helga 110
Marr, Marguerite 67
marriage 17, 29, 64–6, 109
Marshall, Herbert 95
Mary & Jane 92
mascara 40
Mason, James 106
massages 161
Massey, June 67, 99
mateship 120
'Mavis Brampton Show' 252
medical care 245
medical photography 45
meditation 180, 219
Meehan, Helen see Newham, Helen
Melbourne 58–9, 61, 186
Melbourne Cup 53, 112, 185–6
Melville, Dr Bob 22, 187, 188–94
Melville, Douglas 188–9
Melville, Fiona 189

Melville, Judy 189, 190
Menzies, Dame Patti 156
Menzies, Sir Robert 156
merienda 161
Methodism 7, 24, 29
MGM 94, 105–6, 143, 144
Mia Mia 182
Middleditch, Susan 67
Milan 138, 176, 193, 195, 226, 239, 251–2, 253
Milford, Diana 166
Milland, Ray 95
Miller, Harry 162
Miller, Keith 68
Milosevic 250
Mingay, John 107
Minogue, Dannii 184
Miracle in Mostar 257
miracles 223
Miramar Hotel 156, 248
Miss Asia Pacific 177–8, 232
Miss Australia 2, 39, 82, 87, 149–50, 172, 189, 221
Miss Australian Surf 142–5
Miss Hilton 161
Miss International 2, 150, 232–3
Miss International Australia 232
Miss Kangaroo 51–2
Miss New South Wales 87, 149
Miss Pacific 64
Miss Roselands 162
Miss Showgirl 172, 196
Miss Teen International 2, 150, 162
Miss Teen Time 151
Miss Universe 177–8, 215, 232
Miss University 172
Miss World 2, 150
Miss Young Liberal 185
Miss Young Teen 232
Mitchell, Frank 90, 91, 93, 94, 96
Moccora, Carmel 197
Moccora, Joe 197
model agencies
    before they existed 44–5
    Brisbane 224, 230

    competition 174–7, 227
    Hawaii 92
    Milan 211
    Models Worldwide 211–12
    overseas clients 120
    responsibilities 225–6
    ruthlessness 227
    Sydney 83, 224
model exchanges 92
Model of the Year 1, 72, 152, 156, 176
modelling
    equipment 40–1, 63
    past vs present 225–31
    suitability 84
Models Hawaii 92
Models One 176
Models Worldwide 211–12
Moj Bliznji 240–3, 249–50
Monaco 177
Monkton, Bob 6, 26–7, 55–6, 200–8
Monroe, Marilyn 96, 105, 144, 188
Monte-Cumming, Ana Donna 151
Monte-Cumming, Daisy 151
Monte-Cumming, Roanne 151
moon landing 170
Moore, David 99
Moore, Peter 148
Morgan, Squire 37
Morris, Arthur 68–9
Morrison, Peter 189
Mortimer, Alan 171
Mortimer, Shirley 171
Moscow 243–5
Moses, Sir Charles 118
Mosman 31
Moss, Kate 227, 239
Mostar 255, 256–7
Mount Isa 171
Mousoley's 36, 37
movies 32–3, 57
Mr Australian Surf 142–3
Mulder, Karen 227
multiple sclerosis 52
'Murder She Wrote' 188
Murphy, Cameron 153

Murphy, Justice Lionel 153
Muslims 165
Myer, Rod 59
Myer, Sir Norman 58
Myer's 12, 58, 112

nail polish 77, 78
naïvety 44–5, 227–9
names 75, 76
nannies 116–17, 201
Nathan, Trent 162
Neiman Marcus 74, 97, 152
Neretva Valley 256
Nesbitt, John 85
New England *see* place names in region, e.g. Tamworth; Watson's Creek
New York 72, 87, 98–9, 104, 176, 226
New Zealand 168–9
Newham, Greg 183
Newham, Helen (née Meehan) 57, 90, 110, 111, 140, 141, 142, 145, 183, 194, 204, 220, 248
Newham, Mike 145
Newham, Nigel 183
Newham, Susie 183
Newington, Jean 151, 152–3
newspapers
   advertisements 52
   articles on JDW 1, 45, 47, 54–5, 74, 110–11, 112, 114, 157, 204, 208
   articles on Kay Dally-Watkins 54–5, 119, 200
   competitions 155
   page three girls 48
Nicholas, Hilton 66
Niven, David 131
Nixon, Richard 158
Norman, Ian 189
Norman, Karen 189
Norman, Shirley 189
North, Billie 151, 175
North, Loretta 2
nun students 154
Nureyev, Rudolph 153
nurses 116–17, 142

Nutt, Ernie 47

Oberon, Merle 94, 95
O'Hara, Maureen 51
O'Keefe, Johnny 153
Olsson, Ann-Margret *see* Ann-Margret
Onassis, Christina 130
Opatija Riviera 251
Orange 171
Order of Australia 2
O'Skea, Bob 131, 158
Ossendryver, Leo 180

Packer, Clyde 153
Packer, (Sir) Frank 61, 86–7
Packer, Gretel 142
Paddy's Market 163
pageants, beauty *see* beauty quests
Pamela's Model Management 174
Paradise Sportswear 92
Paramount Studios 105, 144
Parco de Principe 226
Paris 100–1, 144, 163, 194, 226, 253
Pat Woodley School of Deportment 87
Paul, John 107
'Paul Hogan Show' 150
Payne, John 105
Peace Centre 240–1, 243
Peacock, Andrew 133, 185
Peacock, Anne 186
Peacock, Susan 185–6 *see also* Renouf, Lady Susan; Sangster, Susan
Peak, The 159, 215
Peck, Gregory 102–4, 106, 107, 249
Pelevina, Elena 244–5
Pembroke 144
perfume 77, 78
Perth 62, 64
Peters, Alison 169
Philippine Airlines (PAL) 157, 161, 163–4, 235–6
Philippines 157–9, 161, 163–5, 170, 181, 188
Phillips, Janet 166, 181
Phillips, Jill 243–4

photographers 44–8, 228–9 *see also*
  individual photographers, e.g.
  Dupain, Max; Shmith, Athol
photography 35, 37, 44, 45
Piazzi, Giorgio 211
Pickwick Club 65, 107
picture theatres 33
Pierre Cardin 163
Plater, Geoff 51
Platform 175
playboys 22, 66, 135, 161–2, 226–7, 249
Plummer, Penny 150
police students 154
political correctness 172, 187
Poole, Wendy 163
Port Moresby 163
Porter, Cole 95
posture 10, 76–7, 81
Poulsen's photographic studio 83
Power, Tyrone 97
Powers, John Robert 72, 98
prepubescent models 229
presentation 76, 81
Price, David 67
Price-Jones, Anne 47
Prince Albert of Monaco 113
Prince's 65
Princess Caroline of Monaco 113
Prophet, The 104
public speaking 5, 80, 201, 236, 247
punctuality 16
Purcell, Gervaise 45

Qantas 90, 163
Quest of Quests 150, 172
quests, beauty *see* beauty quests
Quirindi 188, 190
Quisenberry, Dr Walter 127

Radford, Glen 66
Radford, Jack 66–7
radio
  Alan Jones 187
  appearances by JDW 180
  cricket broadcasts 25, 180–1

Currie, Gordon 96
'Dad and Dave' 58
2KY 167, 180
Radon, Babs 169
Rafferty, Chips 52, 106, 138
Raffles Hotel 145
Raft, George 97
Ramsay, Ray 25
Randwick 80, 186
Ranelagh Estate 51
Ransom, Meta 151
rapes 136–7, 227
RAQ Australian Fashion Design
  Awards 182
'rat pack' 143
Raynes, Colette *see* Hunt, Colette
receptionists 231, 232, 262
Redfern, Mary 117, 201
Regio Calabria 196
religion 24–5, 32, 110, 220 *see also*
  Catholicism; Christianity; Islam;
  Methodism
Rennie, Michael 99
Renouf, Lady Susan 67, 178, 186, 216 *see also* Peacock, Susan; Sangster, Susan
Renouf, Sir Frank 186
Revlon 98, 210
Ricardo Gay Model Management 239
Richardson, Graham 148
Richardson, Lyall 180
Ridd, June 34
Ridley, Maria 149
Rijeka 238–40, 250
Rivkin, René 146, 148
Roberts, Marie 112, 151, 152
Robinson, Eric 133, 184–5
Robinson, Narelle 184–5
Robinson, Robbie 67
Rochford, Brian 162
Rocky River 7–8
Rogers, Brad 172
Rogers, Hazel 151
Rogers, John 152
Roman Holiday 102
Romano's 54, 64, 65

Romanoff's 95
Rome 101–2, 133, 176, 226, 228, 249
Ronchi, Lou-Anne 178
Rooney, Mickey 96
Roosevelt 65
Rose, Nola 63, 64, 99
Rose Bay 220–1
Roselands 162
Royal Ascot 80
Royal Hawaiian Hotel 91–2
Royal Randwick 80, 186
Rushcutters Bay 49, 52, 108
Russo, Renee 176
Rustans 161

Safargy, Michele 112, 151, 152
St Joseph's College 131–2
St Margaret's Maternity Hospital 116, 117, 170
St Mark's Cathedral 119
St Mary Magdalene Church 220–1
St Mary's Cathedral 110
'Sale of the Century' 150
San Francisco 93–4, 127
Sanders, George 97
Sangster, Robert 186
Sangster, Susan 186–7 *see also* Peacock, Susan; Renouf, Lady Susan
Sasse, Patricia *see* Fraser, Trish
Saxby, Kerry 150–1
Scacchi, Greta 211
Scalata 102
Scamp 46–7
scarves 40
Schiffer, Claudia 239
Sebel Townhouse 201–2
Secen, Teo 241
self-image 79–80
Seoul 161
sexuality 65–6, 94–5, 101, 261–2
Shaw, Victoria 139 *see also* Elphick, Jeanette
Shearer, Norma 94
shearing 9–10
shock value 230–1

Short, Wendy 170
Shui Hing 162
Shand, Alex 138
Shmith, Athol 88
Shmith, Clive 88
shoes 41
Simpson, Wallis 11
Sinatra, Frank 153
Singapore 161
Singleton, John 156
'Sixty Minutes' 140
Skelton, Pamela 174
Skewes, Bert 23, 258
Skewes, Caroline Mary (or Carrie) *see* Dally-Watkins, Caroline Mary
Skewes, June Marie 2 *see also* Dally-Watkins, June
skin-care 78, 178, 212–13
SKYWAYS 187
sleep 78
smiling 81
Smith, Roger 139
Smith, Sue 163
smoking 14–15, 65, 118, 131, 139–40
Solomons, Bertie 34–5
Solomons, Jan 34–5
Some Like It Hot 144, 188
Sorrento 104
Spastic Centre 172
speaking 76, 77, 80, 81–2
Spellson's 138
Spies, Ian 152, 194
Spies, Marie (née Roberts) 112, 151, 152, 194
Spring, Miriam 166
Springvale 4, 8–10, 12, 14–15, 19, 20, 23
Stafford, Trish 166
Stari Most Bridge 256–7
Stephens, Lois 63, 64
Stephenson, Jan 150
Stewart, Jimmy 97, 215, 221
Stirling, Bill 180–1
Stirling, Jan 105
Stone, Sharon 211
Stork Club 98–9

Strike Force Irondale 148
Strine 10, 144
stylists 42
suicide 146–7, 151
Sun Herald 148
Sunday Herald Magazine 45
Sunday Mirror 119
Sunday Telegraph 47, 155
Supermodel of the World 177
supermodels 45, 60, 84, 227, 229, 239
Surfers Paradise 201, 203
surnames 75
Sutherland, Joan 118
swimming 25, 34, 57, 66, 181
swimwear 42, 45–7, 143, 144, 162
Switzerland 128, 210, 226
Sydney 29, 35
   French boutiques 61
   JDW moved there 29
   returning after WWII 35
   sophisticated 13
Sydney Morning Herald 114
Sydney Ski Club 66

tai chi 180
Tai Tai 159
Tamarama Beach 46
Tamworth 19, 21, 28, 32–5, 171, 220
Taylor, Rod 144, 153
Tchou, Larry 163
'Teenage Mailbag' 168
Telegraph 48, 112
television shows featuring JDW
   'The Bob Hope Show' 97
   'The Marjorie Trimball Show' 93–4, 97
   'Mavis Brampton Show' 252
   'Sixty Minutes' 140
   'Teenage Mailbag' 168
   'This Is Your Life' 11–12, 29–30, 35, 140, 150
tennis 9, 12, 22, 33, 57, 67, 69, 108
Terrey Hills rapes 136–7
Thau, Benny 106
'This Is Your Life' 11–12, 29–30, 35, 140, 150

Thomas, Prudence 63
Thredbo 67
Thunderbolt, Captain 7–8
Tierney, Gene 98
Tingha 8
Tingwell, Bud 51
Toda, Benny 158, 164–5
tote bag for models 40–1, 63
tours of Europe *see* European tours
Townsville 151, 169–70
Tracey, Jay 169
Tracy, Spencer 99–100, 104–5
Trans-Australia Airlines (TAA) 67, 112
Treloars 33
Trenet, Charles 43
Truth 1
tuberculosis 155, 157
Tuckwell, Bambi 88
Turner, Ben 46–7
Tuscany 203
Tutsitala Club 48
Twentieth Century Fox 51–2, 113
2KY 167, 180

umbrellas 42–3
unconditional love 221, 260
uniforms 232, 262
United Nations 102
Universal Studios 188

Valentino 193
Van Otterloo, Carola 187
Van Otterloo, William 187
Vaseline 40
Venuti, Maria 151
Verstak, Tania 149–50, 233
virginity 65–6
Vogue 86, 123, 211
von Alderstein, Hans Heinrich Vladmir Sergie Krull 86
von Alderstein, Marion 86
Vyner, Margaret 12

Wadsworth, Elizabeth 189
Wadsworth, Mark 189

Wagstaff 190
waistlines 61–2
Wakefield, Shirley 204
Wakeley, Janice 151
Wakes 12
Wall, Mrs Jerry 97
Waltons 168
'Waltzing Matilda' 157
Ward, Arthur 145
Ward, Fred 7–8
wardrobe 78, 81, 182
Warlow, Celie 13–14, 28
Warlow, Ossie 13, 28
wars *see* Boer War; World War I; World War II
waterskiing 46
Watkins Place 169
Watson's Bay 140, 146
Watson's Creek
   childhood home of JDW 4–5, 8–11, 12, 13, 253, 255, 258–9
   Public School 21, 25
   visits by JDW 1, 24, 49, 60–1, 72, 258
Wayne, John 95, 188
Wayne, Pilar 188
Wee Waa 171
Weedon, Eileen 90–1, 93
weight 79–80
Wesley, John 7
Western Mail 114
Whealy, Margaret 263
Wheels 60
Wherrit, Lois 153
White Rose Orchestra Beauty Queen 171
Whiteley, Arkie 105
Whitlam, Margaret 66
Whittle, Tom 63
wigs 160
Williams, Keith 178
Williams, Peggy 144
Williams, Thea 178

Willoughby 29, 31
Windsor, Duchess of 11
Wing-on 162–3
Wolfenden, Val 140, 141, 248
Wollongong 170, 193
Woman's Day 11, 39
Women's Weekly, The Australian 12, 26, 39–40, 47, 61, 169
Wood, Gordon 146, 147–8
Wood, Helen 149
Woodley, Pat 87–8, 142, 149
Woods, Keith 151
Woolrych, Geoff 111
Woolrych, Sheila 111
Woollahra 111, 187, 192
working mothers 109, 114–5, 199
World War I 28
World War II
   effect on rental property 50
   end 35
   fundraising 16, 39, 61
   growth after 83
   internments 69, 180
   Japanese submarines 31–2
   parachutes 46
   regional reserve 30
   veterans 51, 63
Wyler, William 102

Yamba 22
yoga 80, 180
Young, Norma 219
Young Liberals 133, 185
Younger Garments 107
Youth With a Mission 142, 215–16, 218–19, 221–2
Yves St Laurent 193

Zagreb 255–6
Zampatti, Carla 162
zippers 42, 62